D0207817

A MILITARY HISTORY OF BRITAIN

A MILITARY HISTORY OF BRITAIN

From 1775 to the Present

Jeremy Black

PRAEGER SECURITY INTERNATIONAL
Westport, Connecticut • London

Library of Congress Cataloging-in-Publication Data

Black, Jeremy.
  A military history of Britain : from 1775 to the present / Jeremy Black.
p. cm.
  Includes bibliographical references (p.   ) and index.
  ISBN 0–275–99039–7 (alk. paper)
1. Great Britain—History, Military. 2. Great Britain—History, Naval. 3. Great Britain—
Foreign relations. I. Title.
DA65.B53 2006
335.00941—dc22   2006022876

British Library Cataloguing in Publication Data is available.

Copyright © 2006 by Jeremy Black

Library of Congress Catalog Card Number: 2006022876
ISBN: 0–275–99039–7

First published in 2006

Praeger Security International, 88 Post Road West, Westport, CT 06881
An imprint of Greenwood Publishing Group, Inc.
www.praeger.com

Printed in the United States of America

∞™

The paper used in this book complies with the
Permanent Paper Standard issued by the National
Information Standards Organization (Z39.48–1984).

10 9 8 7 6 5 4 3 2 1

Contents

Preface

This is an account of military structures and cultures, and relevant socio-political contexts; as well as of conflicts. Military history is defined to include sea and air capability and warfare, as well as their land counterparts. With such a range, there are inevitably questions of emphasis. Some of the decisions taken about what to include and what to exclude may surprise readers, but the intention is to challenge conventional assumptions and to offer illuminating new perspectives. Furthermore, writing in the early-twenty-first century, it is clear that some of the views advanced during the Cold War years concerning what this subject should focus on, and how it might best be approached, deserve reexamining. Writing in February 2006, when more British troops are being deployed in Afghanistan, a policy that would have seemed incredible thirty years ago, it is sensible to be cautious about comments on inherent and/or inevitable strategic interests and military roles. Due to the book's appearance in an American series, particular attention is devoted to military relations with the United States, as well as comparisons with American military developments, and the book is organized in three parts:

Part I. Britain as Imperial Parent, 1775
Part II. Britain as Imperial Rival, 1775–1904
Part III. Britain as Imperial Partner, 1904–

This classification does not exclude other themes and roles in these periods, but it provides a way to shape the story.

It is a great pleasure to record the hospitality of many Americans during recent visits. While working on this book, I had the opportunity to lecture at Hawaii Pacific and Yale Universities, the Naval War College, and Radley College. I am most grateful to Richard Harding and Stephen Manning for their comments on an earlier draft, and John Blair, Mark Fissel, Bob Higham, Jeffrey Meriwether, Nigel Saul, Gary Sheffield, and David Trim for those on particular sections. It is a great pleasure to dedicate this book to Blake Goldring, a good companion and a most generous host.

Abbreviations

BL. Add.	London, British Library, Additional Manuscripts
CAB.	Cabinet Office papers
CO.	Colonial Office papers
L.H.	London, King's College, Liddell Hart Centre for Military Archives
MM.	Montgomery-Massingberd
NA.	London, The National Archives (formerly Public Record Office)
WO.	War Office papers

Part I: Imperial Parent, 1775

CHAPTER 1

Origins

There is no one way to discuss the military history of Britain. As with other states, there are the contrasts that derive from deciding whether to address primarily the history of state, or country, or people. There is also the related tension between the long-term "structural" factors of environment and the medium- or short-term emphasis on the role of conjunctures in the shaping of goals and priorities. In the case of Britain, the former leads to an emphasis on island status and maritime destiny, a navalist interpretation that generally sees Britain as able, thanks to naval strength, to turn its back to Continental Europe, and as looking out instead across the oceans. This can then lead to discussion of the comparatively minor role of land warfare in British military history and the relatively modest part of related social-political practices, especially conscription. In place of a stress on structural factors, however, an emphasis on the role of conjunctures will lead to an underlining of the extent to which Britain has been linked politically to the Continent, and the consequences that had for military tasking. This reflects an important aspect of military history as a whole, namely, the extent to which developments are driven by tasks and their resultant consequences for priorities in military procurement, structure, and doctrine.

It is easiest to write military history in terms of environmental determinism. That, however, is a misleading approach because it underplays the role of politics in shaping the response to environmental and other factors; although politics itself was affected by both conflict and the distribution of force within society. One key feature in the political history of the country was the failure, until the campaigns of Oliver Cromwell in 1648–1651, of successive attempts to unite Britain (modern England, Wales, and Scotland), and indeed the British Isles (Britain and Ireland).

Prior to the arrival of the Romans, Britain was occupied by a number of independent tribes. Little is known of their history, but successive changes in material culture affected the ability to fight. For example, in the Mesolithic period (c. 8,300 B.C. to c. 6,000 B.C.), the number of hunter-gatherers increased. They were equipped with microlithic flints, mounted in wood or bone hafts, which provided effective tools for use, for example, as knives or as arrowheads. From *c.* 2,300 B.C., in the Bronze Age, bronze supplemented not only copper but also hard stone and flint. It has been suggested that it was a more bellicose age. There is increased evidence of fortifications, in the shape of hill forts, and weapons, and it has been argued that society was dominated by warriors. From *c.* 700 B.C., the smelting and forging of iron arrived. Iron made better weapons, particularly when carbon was added to make steel. Whatever the level of conflict, there was no one state nor federation of states.

Britain was the sole island attacked by Rome outside the far less tidal waters of the Mediterranean, and Julius Caesar's invasions in 55 and 54 B.C. therefore were bold steps. He claimed that they were necessary to end support for resistance to his conquest of Gaul (France). However, it was largely personal prestige and the dictates of politics in Rome that led to his expeditions, as they also did for the following expedition, that of the Emperor Claudius in A.D. 43. Caesar needed to show that the invasions were necessary for him to remain in control of the army, and he also wished to win glory.

In 55 B.C., Caesar did not move from his precarious bridgehead in Kent. The Romans were victorious in hard fighting, but the damage done to their ships by equinoctial gales and the scale of the resistance led Caesar to come to terms with the local tribes. The following year, however, in a reminder of the apparently inexorable persistence of a major state, Caesar led a larger invasion force. Landing in Kent, Caesar won a victory near Canterbury, defeating the tribal leader, Cassivellaunus, and crossed the Thames, seizing his capital, Wheathampstead. A settlement was then reached in which hostages and tribute were promised by the local rulers, before Caesar withdrew. The Romans had benefited from their opponents' naval weakness, which meant that they could not contest the passage of the English Channel, and from their own fighting advantage once landed. The disciplined Roman infantry, with its body armor, javelins, and short swords, was more effective than that of the British, who had little body armor and lacked effective missile power. British chariots were vulnerable to Roman archers and their hill forts to siegecraft. Furthermore, as a demonstration of the problems posed by universal military service when in conflict with regulars, the British farmer-soldiers could not afford to be soldiers all the time, and their farming also made them vulnerable to Roman devastation.

Due to rebellion in Gaul, civil war, and the higher priority of the German frontier, Caesar's expedition was not followed up until 43 A.D. when about 40,000 troops invaded. After an unopposed landing, probably in Kent, the Romans defeated a confederation of forces in three battles, two of which were caused by contested crossings of the rivers Medway and Thames. Claudius then arrived, with the first elephants seen in Britain, and received the surrender of Colchester. After he decided to make Britannia a Roman province, southern England was rapidly overrun. Prefiguring British imperialism in India, Malaya, and Africa in the nineteenth century, some rulers accepted client status, but there was also much fighting, with hill forts such as Maiden Castle outside modern Dorchester being stormed. This fortress, which belonged to the tribe of the Durotriges, survives as a striking manifestation of the task the Romans faced. The serried banks of the hill fort were calculated to break up an attacking charge. The innermost bank would have carried a palisade.

Caratacus, the leader of the Catuvellauni tribe, continued resistance from Wales, but was defeated in 50–51. In 60, a strong rebellion was launched when the Iceni tribe of East Anglia, enraged by vicious and corrupt Roman mismanagement and expropriation, and led by Queen Boudica, rebelled, storming the major Roman settlements: Colchester, London, and St. Albans, and slaughtering their inhabitants with great cruelty. However, as with the Indian Mutiny against English rule in 1857, there was no united response, in large part because there was no basis for political unity. For example, Cogidubnus, the client ruler of the Atrebates of Surrey, Sussex, and Hampshire, remained loyal to the Romans. The lack of a united response provided the key political context for decisive action by the regular forces, who moved rapidly, defeating Boudica's army. She died, probably by suicide. The Iceni and their allies were then "pacified" with typical Roman brutality. The pace of Roman advance resumed in 71 with the subjugation of the Brigantes of northern England (71–73/74) and of Wales (73/74–76).

However, Highland Scotland was never conquered. Agricola, Roman Governor from 77 to 83, completed the conquest of Wales and northern England, and invaded Scotland, winning a notable victory at Mons Graupius, but only the Scottish lowlands were conquered. As a reminder of the difficulty of judging the environmental factor, in explaining developments it is possible to stress the difficulty of the highland terrain in the Roman failure, but also the quality of the defense. Although Agricola considered its conquest, Ireland was not attacked by the Romans, and, indeed, it was probably a task beyond Roman capacity.

Thereafter, the main theme in the military history of Britain under the Romans was defensive. The competing demands of the vulnerable Danube frontier meant a reduction in the considerable military effort devoted to Britain. By the early years of the second century, the Romans had abandoned their occupation of southern and central Scotland. Instead, they constructed Hadrian's Wall, a 70-mile long fortified stone wall (with supporting forts such as Housesteads), built from about 122 by the Emperor Hadrian across Britain at its narrowest from Tyne to Solway. Designed to mark a frontier, this was not the end of Roman attempts to move north, but none proved more than short-term, and the wall came to have a defensive function, stopping the Picts from raiding south. Hadrian's successor, Antonious Pius, had ordered a fresh advance north. Eastern Scotland was occupied as far north as the river Tay, and a wall of turf on a stone base was built from the Firth of Forth to the Clyde in about 140. That line was held until about 163 or later, when Hadrian's Wall again became the frontier. The Emperor Septimus Severus advanced into Scotland in 209–210, but, thereafter the frontier stabilized on the Tyne-Solway line.

Similarly, the ten forts of the Saxon Shore built from the 270s onward from Brancaster, Norfolk to Portchester, Hampshire, were intended to limit attacks on the east and south coasts of England by seaborne raiders from Germany. These forts, most of which had bastion towers, were designed to protect harbors and estuaries. The construction of town defenses from the third century also indicated an attitude of growing defensiveness in the face of outside attack. Challenges from outside included Picts from Scotland, Scots from Ireland, and Saxons from north Germany. Their attacks became serious in the 350s, while a successful invasion in 367 led to widespread devastation. Some additions to Britain's defenses followed on the restoration of order.

Roman Britain was also weakened by the repeated inability of the Roman Empire to devise a consistently accepted system of imperial succession, and the willingness of military units to support their commanders in bids for power, although such bids were not continual. In the 400s, when Gaul was invaded by "barbarians," a cutoff Britain backed its own emperor, Constantine III, who took a significant part of the military forces to Gaul. They did not return. The disillusioned Romano-Britons expelled his administrators, and appealed to the true emperor, Honorius, for the restoration of legitimate rule, but he, hard-pressed in Italy, by Alaric, the Visigothic leader, who captured Rome in 410, could do no more than tell them to look to their own defense. This, the formal end of imperial government in 409, was the close of the Roman Empire in Britain.

The invaders who overthrew Roman Britain in the fifth and sixth centuries, particularly the Angles and Saxons, conquered England (though not Wales): England was divided into a number of kingdoms, particularly, but not only, eventually the Anglian kingdoms of Northumbria (north of England), and Mercia (Midlands), and the Saxon kingdom of Wessex (western England). The scarcity of sources makes the nature of the conquest uncertain. As elsewhere in Western Europe, "barbarian" mercenaries were initially hired, and probably came to demand power for themselves, although it is unclear how far there were large-scale migrations into England. The same is true of the movement of Scots from Ireland into Pict-dominated Scotland.

In any event, late- and post-Roman society in England and Wales was increasingly militarized and able to mount long-lasting resistance. In about 500, the resistance achieved a major victory, possibly under a warrior called Artorius (Arthur) at Mons Badonicus. However, the economy of Roman Britain collapsed after the formal end of imperial government, it was no longer possible to call for assistance from the Continent, and post-Roman Britain was divided into warring kingdoms. Most of lowland England had been conquered by the "barbarians" by 600. Furthermore, links between the surviving British communities were broken. Strathclyde, Wales, and Dumnonia (Cornwall, Devon, and West Somerset) were thus separated, at least by land: as a result of the Saxon victory at Dyrham (*c*. 577), Gloucestershire was taken, while a victory by the Northumbrians near Chester in 615 led to the conquest of Cheshire. Furthermore, the British kingdoms of Elmet, centered on Leeds, and Rheged, around the Solway estuary, were absorbed by Northumbria in the late sixth and seventh centuries, Dorset by Wessex in the same period, and Herefordshire by the Magonsaete (who were brought under the control of Mercia) in the mid-seventh century. Devon was absorbed by Wessex in the late seventh and eighth centuries. However, Cornwall was only conquered by Wessex in 838, and the kingdoms in Wales were not conquered, although pressure from the English shaped the extent of Wales. Offa, king of Mercia, in about 784–796, created a ditched rampart, known as Offa's Dyke, that was at once a boundary and a defensive line. The Welsh border on its full length was a composite and Offa's Dyke was only the central portion, along the Powys border.

Expansion helped to tip the balance between the Anglo-Saxon kingdoms, leading to a fall in the importance of the once leading kingdoms of Kent and East Anglia. Northumbria became the most powerful state for much of the seventh century, but defeat by Mercia (678) and the Picts of modern Scotland (685) ended its hegemony, and Mercia became the leading kingdom, until, in turn, defeated by Egbert of Wessex at Ellendum (near Wroughton) in 825. In Scotland, it is unclear how far violence was involved in the development of the kingdom of Alba in the ninth century, but it represented a fusion of Scots and Picts.

The Vikings from Scandinavia launched a wave of attacks on Scotland, Ireland, and Wales as well as Anglo-Saxon England from the late eighth century, overturning the existing order across most of the British Isles, but without creating a unitary Viking state, although kingdoms emerged based on York, Dublin, and the East Midlands. From the 830s, Viking pressure increased markedly. East Anglia was overrun in 865, Yorkshire in 866–867, and Mercia in 874. Having been nearly crushed in 871, Alfred, king of Wessex, stopped the Viking conquest of southern England in 878, defeating them at Edington, and his victorious successors, Edward the

Elder (r. 899–924) and Athelstan (r. 924–939), were able, as a result of campaigns in the early tenth century, particularly victory over the Scots, Strathclyde Britons, and Norse from Ireland at Brunanburh (937), eventually to claim kingship of the English and a tentative overlordship of Britain. The system of military recruitment and organization devised by Alfred, including that of burhs (fortified positions) and the creation of a large navy, rested on public authority, and all freemen were in theory obliged to serve in the fyrd or army; although the role of lords, their retinues, and landholding was also important, and there was also a tradition, from the 990s onward, of using taxation to pay for trained mercenaries in royal service. The debate about the "nation in arms" as opposed to a high status warrior army is long and complex. The core of armies raised on a shire base probably came from the landholding class.[1] As a comparable process, the kingdom based in central and southern Scotland expanded, overrunning the Britons of Strathclyde in the early tenth century and the Angles of Lothian later that century, the latter a success cemented by victory at Carham in 1018.

Fresh invasions of England in the eleventh century, first by the Danes, under Sweyn and his son, Cnut, who ruled England from 1016 to 1035, and then, in 1066, by the Normans, led, however, twice to the overthrow of the Old English monarchy and, instead, in each occasion, to England being joined to a wider realm. The Norman victory at Hastings on 14 October 1066 was crucial to the fate of England. It arose as a result of a conflict over the succession to the childless Edward the Confessor (r. 1042–1066). His relative William, Duke of Normandy, competed with Edward's brother-in-law, Earl Harold of Wessex, while Harald Hardrada, king of Norway also advanced a claim. In what became a year of three kings (like 1483 and 1936), Harold became king with the support of the bulk of the English aristocracy and having been designated by Edward. However, William and Harald both prepared to invade. In response to William's preparations, Harold deployed his forces on the south coast, but William did not invade first. Instead, Harald did so, close to York, defeating the local forces on 20 September at Fulford Gate. Harold then rapidly marched north, surprising, defeating, and killing Harald at Stamford Bridge on 24 September.

Four days later, however, William landed on the south coast. Harold rapidly marched south and the two clashed at Hastings. This was a hard-fought battle between two effective systems, and its outcome was far from certain. Eventually, the outnumbered English defensive shield-wall, well deployed on a ridge, was disrupted by attacks designed to exploit real or feigned retreats by the Normans, and, at last, the English position was broken. The Normans had crucial advantages in archers and cavalry. Harold's death was key both in helping what became the final Norman assault and in ensuring the outcome of the battle. Without clear leadership, England fell, as William rapidly exploited his victory and seized the throne, becoming William I, and going down in history as William the Conqueror. He then rapidly and brutally suppressed native risings in 1067–1069, 1075, and 1080, particularly with a brutal "harrying" of the north in 1069–1070. As so often in British military history, control of domestic opposition was a key task.

The Normans introduced a system, some elements of which had Old English precedents, spanning landowning, military service, and politics —feudalism, with land granted to vassals in return to military service. Norman lords were obliged to provide a number of knights (as likely to fight on foot as on horseback) for service roughly proportionate to the size of the estate, an obligation that was usually discharged by enfeoffing the required number with lands of their own in return for service. However, the *familia Regis*, the king's own military household, was a permanent and professional military body that was therefore more important than the feudal host. The obligation of all freemen to provide military service continued, but it was of only limited importance, essentially for local defense, as in the Battle of the Standard, when a Scottish invasion of northern England was defeated in 1138. Nevertheless, the tradition of rural and urban militias, important in later centuries, thus had early origins. In 1181, Henry II underlined the general responsibility for military duty by specifying military equipment, which was to reflect social rank. This, however, could not serve as the basis for projecting power abroad, which was a key requirement of the kings as they struggled to maintain their territorial interests in France.

The new order in England was also entrenched with the construction of numerous castles, though the principle of private defended residences is known from both documentary and archaeological evidence in the late Saxon period, some built by Norman and French protégés of Edward the Confessor. Castles were very different to the characteristic feature of Anglo-Saxon fortification, the burh or fortified town. Early Norman castles in England and Wales were generally motte and bailey, earth and timber constructions, thrown up in a hurry (although still requiring many man-days to construct) and able to give protection against local discontent. Not all early Norman castles in England and Wales, however, were built of timber and earthwork: Exeter, London, and others had also early stone phases. Timber-built forms were often of either motte and bailey or ringwork (enclosure) form, both of which had a long currency to the thirteenth century. Cost and the shortage of skilled masons affected the attraction of construction in stone. Castle design, whether of timber, stone, or both, was intended to promote a powerful symbol of the new authority over native society, as well as of the powers of the new landholding families in relation to each other. William I and his successors also maintained castles in the shire towns (as well as in London) as part of their framework of royal government. Domestic control was a key feature in British military history, and security against internal rivals was just as important as defense against external threat. Surviving examples of stone castles provide ample illustrations of how they literally towered over and commanded the surrounding countryside. Stone was not vulnerable to fire, but stone castles were expensive to construct, as well as posing different problems for attack. These difficulties were not only tactical, but also organizational as it was difficult to provide supplies for besieging forces.[2] At the same time, alongside their defensive purpose, castles had a key function as fortified residences, the importance of which is easily overlooked.

Although in 1072, William I led an army north and forced Malcolm III of Scotland to do homage for Lothian (southeastern Scotland), Scotland remained independent. There was a process of Normanization north of the border, but this reflected the immigration of Norman nobles sponsored by the Scottish kings, and not the piecemeal Norman conquest seen in Wales from the late eleventh to the late thirteenth century. Instead, in Scotland, the Norman military machine of knights and castles served as the basis for an extension of royal authority.

The kings of England in the Middle Ages used ships to transport and to reinforce blockades. Land conflict, however, was crucial in civil wars, in the warfare within the British Isles that led to the conquest of Wales, but not Scotland, and in the wars in what became France, where new territorial interests accompanied the Angevin kings who ruled from 1154. These wars reflected the long-term attempt to sustain a state that spanned the Channel. Although the Duchy of Normandy was lost to the French in 1204, the rulers of England, from the Norman Conquest until the fall of Calais to French forces in 1558, continually held part of the Continent.

The conquest of Wales was a lengthy process, which suggests that that of Scotland would have been even more difficult. The Welsh benefited not only from their terrain, much of which offered little advantage to the feudal cavalry of the Normans, but also from the military skills and determination honed by conflict within their own ranks. The numerous Norman castles provided refuge from Welsh attack but could be easily bypassed, and fortress construction did not really stabilize Norman control. Instead, anticipating the adaptation to circumstances later seen in British wars of imperial conquest, the Normans had to rely on light forces of their own to pursue Welsh raiders. Lightly armed cavalrymen, linked to castles, offered one remedy, and the employment of Welsh troops was also important. The fighting was not all one way: the Welsh were able to regain the initiative, as in 1094, again during the English Civil War in Stephen's reign (1135–1154), in the 1190s, and also in the mid-thirteenth century. The Anglo-Norman achievement was heavily dependent on the caliber and commitment of the monarch, with Henry I, Henry II, and Edward I being the key figures. Division among the Welsh was crucial. It sustained a culture in which physical prowess and military leadership were important, but helped provide the kings of England with allies. In 1277, when Edward I invaded Wales with a massive force, he did so with considerable Welsh support (more Welshmen fought for Edward than against him), and Llywelyn, Prince of Wales felt obliged to accept Edward's terms and do homage. This success was anchored with a major program of fortification. A large-scale rising in 1282–1283 was defeated and Llywelyn was killed in a skirmish in 1282. In 1283, his brother Dafydd was captured and Edward overran all of Gwynedd (northwest Wales), the core of independent Wales. There was little fighting in the form of battles, but Edward was able to grind the Welsh down by continuing his campaign, or at least staying in Wales, right through the winter of 1282–1283, and did much the same in 1294–1295 when there was a fresh rebellion.

As later with transoceanic imperialism, gains were consolidated both by local alliances and by fortifications. The major new fortresses built for Edward I by James of St. George—especially Caernarfon, Conwy, Harlech, and Beaumaris—were all coastal castles that could be supplied by sea. The construction of these massive stone-built works was a formidable undertaking, costing at least £93,000 and using thousands of conscripted English workers. More generally, this reflected not only the strength of the English monarchy in the sense of its being able to finance major projects, but also its administrative sophistication. This had increased greatly during the reign of Henry III (1216–1272), a period of frequent conflict in which the military bureaucracy had developed considerably. This was shown for example in the administrative resources that made it possible to construct, transport, and store the royal artillery.[3]

In the thirteenth century, native Welsh rulers had built castles, such as Dolbadarn and Castell y Bere, but now castle-building was to be under English control only. Revolts in 1287 and, more seriously, 1294–1295, encouraged Edward to press on with his program of fortification. Edward also ordered that undergrowth within 200 feet of main roads be removed in order to lessen the risk of ambush. There were to be other revolts in 1316 and, far more seriously, 1400–1408. The latter, under Owain Glyn Dŵr (Owen Glendower), saw the extensive use of guerrilla tactics and devastation, but these could not challenge the English castle garrisons effectively. Heavily outnumbered, Glyn Dŵr prudently avoided many occasions and his military career was not conventionally heroic. More significantly, he was leading his followers toward a dead end: English power was such that it was only possible during periods of English civil conflict, such as the Percy rising of 1403, for Welsh opponents to make much headway. At other times, the weight of English resources told.

The situation was very different elsewhere. In repeated conflicts in Scotland, Ireland, and France, the English found that they could win major victories, archers, more particularly longbowmen, being the key element at the expense of the Scots at Falkirk (1298) and Halidon Hill (1333), and at that of the French at Crécy (1346), Poitiers (1356), and Agincourt (1415). In each case, the English were also well commanded, although, as more generally in the period, battle accounts are frequently contradictory, which makes it difficult to supply precise accounts, let alone reasons for victory. The propensity of the French to launch ill-considered and poorly executed attacks was as important as the defensive capability of the English (not least the superiority of their archers), in the latter's victories. This compensated for the relatively modest size of the English forces. Edward III landed with 14,000 troops in 1346, and Henry V with 11,000–12,000 in 1415.[4]

Triumph in battle, however, could only achieve so much. Sieges, such as that of Calais after Crécy, proved formidable problems, and, in response, English forces ravaged the countryside in an effort to break the French will. More generally, it proved impossible to translate victory into a permanent settlement, although, on occasion, the kings of England gained a powerful position, for example in Scotland after Edward I's victory at Dunbar in 1296. English success rested as much, however, on division among the Scots, particularly between the Bruces and the Balliols/ Comyns, and exploiting this required political skill. Edward II (1307–1327) lacked both this and military ability, and the less intense pace of English military pressure helped Bruce to consolidate his position in Scotland and to defeat his Scottish rivals. He also turned on the English. In 1314, Edinburgh fell to Bruce and the garrison in Stirling promised to surrender if not relieved. Poorly led by Edward, the English relieving-force was defeated at Bannockburn on 23–24 June by the Scots, well-led pikemen on well-chosen ground routing poorly commanded cavalry. The English handled their archers very badly. The Scots pressed on to attack northern England and, in 1328, by the Treaty of Northampton-Edinburgh, Scottish independence was recognized. The fate of Scotland was also greatly affected by English commitments in France, particularly in the 1290s and the 1330s.

The political aspect to conflict interacted with a military dimension that reflected developments in weaponry. If, in the 1430s, the loss of the support of the Duke of Burgundy (by the Treaty of Arras of 1436, he allied with Charles VII of France) was crucial to the course of the war in France, in 1449–1451 the rapid fall of English-held Normandy and Gascony owed much to the impressive train of French artillery. It helped bring the speedy fall of fortified positions, as well as victory in battle over English archers at Formigny in 1450.[5]

Sustained conflict also had a major role in the development of the English constitution. War could not pay for itself, not least because the government relied on paid troops, rather than a feudal host, and the frequent need to raise taxation to pay for warfare led to Parliament becoming more important. Conflict also led to an enhancement of military capability, so that, by 1300, logistics was carefully organized with a sophisticated system for collecting foodstuffs, establishing victualing bases, and a system for planning requirements.[6]

Alongside war with foreign rulers came repeated civil conflicts. These reflected not only the issues in dispute, particularly quarrels over the royal succession, or between the king and the leading nobles, but also the extent to which the Crown did not monopolize the means of violence. Many nobles were loyal, but not all; the stakes in the struggle for access to power were great, and this helped to exacerbate disputes. From the outset, the succession created problems. Employing partible inheritance (division among heirs), rather than male primogeniture (succession by the eldest male child), William I (r. 1066–1087) left Normandy to his eldest son, Robert, who was in rebellion when William died, and England to the second, William II (r. 1087–1100). However, such division was unwelcome, not only in the ruling family, but also to nobles with estates on both sides of the Channel, and this led to conflict both then and after William II died in 1100. It took the defeat and imprisonment of Robert in 1106 by William I's third son, Henry I (r. 1100–1135), to solve the problem. Henry's one legitimate son, however, predeceased him. Henry turned to his daughter, Matilda, as his successor, but, when he died in 1135, the throne was seized by Stephen, son of Henry's sister Adela. Stephen failed to maintain control in England and Matilda invaded, touching off a lengthy civil war. This appeared near to an end in 1141, when Matilda captured Stephen at the Battle of Lincoln, but she alienated opinion in the capital, London, was defeated at Winchester by Stephen's wife, also Matilda, and exchanged Stephen for her captured half-brother. The war continued. Civil war was accompanied by the collapse of government authority. Prominent nobles, such as John the Marshal in Hampshire and Wiltshire, used the conflict to pursue their own interests and strengthen their local power, and many castles were built. In 1138, for example, Stephen's influential brother, Henry, Bishop of Winchester, is reported to have begun six castles.

Towns also had a need for walls, and their security was an ongoing issue from the late Saxon period to the later Middle Ages. In England, urban defenses generally represented loyalty to the kings, rather than independent ambition. Walls were often important emblems of urban status.[7]

Nevertheless, the readiness with which power flowed back to the crown once Matilda's son, Henry II (r. 1154–1189), came to the throne, as a result of the peace settlement of 1153, illustrated the desire of most nobles for peace and stability. His eldest son, Richard I (r. 1189–1199), spent most of his life campaigning on the Third Crusade and in France. The latter's brother, John (r. 1199–1216), was an unpopular king, whose lack of prestige was summed up in the epithet "softsword." Nothing would have raised his standing more than an ability to win battles. However, defeat by France in 1203–1204 led to the loss of Normandy, and repeated failure at the hands of France encouraged John's opponents among the nobility to rebel. In 1215, John was forced to accept the restrictions on royal powers enshrined in the charter later called Magna Carta. Civil war, however, soon resumed, and was affected by French intervention. Once ended by royal victory, political problems and issues concerning control of castles led to castle sieges by the government of John's son, the young Henry III (r. 1216–1272), notably at Bedford. Later, renewed failure in France and misgovernment led to another rebellion against Henry III in 1264. Defeated at Lewes where Henry was captured, the royal forces regained control after victory by his eldest son, the future Edward I, at Evesham the following year. Defeat, this time in Scotland, and misgovernment, led to fresh civil war under Henry's grandson, Edward II (r. 1307–1327). Edward was able to defeat his cousin, Thomas, Earl of Lancaster, at Boroughbridge, in 1322, but he was overthrown in 1326, and then killed. In turn, his wife and her lover were overthrown by his son, Edward III. This Edward's grandson, Richard II, suppressed the Peasants' Revolt in 1381, and aristocratic opposition, at the Battle of Radcot Bridge in 1387, but was overthrown in 1399 by his cousin, who became Henry IV.

In his turn, Henry (r. 1399–1413) faced opposition from the Percys, a mighty magnate family who wielded great power in the north of England and who had helped Henry depose Richard II. Henry defeated and killed the Percy heir, "Hotspur," Sir Henry Percy, at the Battle of Shrewsbury in 1403, but Hotspur's father, the 1st Earl of Northumberland, rebelled again in 1405 and 1408, before being defeated and killed on Bramham Moor in 1408. In 1405, Glyn Dŵr agreed with the Percys to depose Henry IV and divide England, the former's share to include England west of the Severn. The French promised assistance to Glyn Dŵr, and a French expeditionary force arrived in 1405. With French help, Glyn Dŵr advanced as far as Worcester, but then withdrew. The French faltered in the face of English naval power, while Henry IV's vigorous son, Prince "Hal," later Henry V, began to inflict serious defeats on Glyn Dŵr. This warfare overshadowed the first Lancastrian reign, but, looked at differently, it represented the consolidation of a new dynasty.

The dynamics of domestic political and military power changed with the spread of so-called "Bastard Feudalism," in which lords rewarded their followers and retained their services with an annual payment of money, rather than with land, although this concept of feudalism generally has been criticized by scholars, particularly with the recognition of the role of mercenaries in earlier centuries. At the same time, this form of professionalism was organized in terms of clientage within a society dominated by powerful nobles, whose willingness to raise troops was crucial to the ability of rulers to field armies.[8] The form of patronage and clientage described as "Bastard Feudalism" was not necessarily a cause of civil conflict, but, in the event of a breakdown in relations between monarch and nobles, or in the ranks of the latter, it made it easier for the nobles to mobilize and sustain their strength.

Defeat by France in the 1440s and early 1450s led to a crucial loss of royal prestige under the unimpressive Henry VI, and was followed by crisis in England, the Wars of the Roses, which also owed much to the war in France in the shape of battle-hardened veterans and nobles accustomed to military life. This was the lengthiest period of civil conflict in English history: 1455–1464, 1469–1471, and 1483–1487, a dispute over the succession that reflected and triggered wider political problems. One of the battles, Towton on 29 March 1461, was the largest and bloodiest battle ever fought in England: up to 60,000 men on both sides were probably involved. A revival of fortified features in the houses of the elite testified to concern about safety,[9] although there were few sieges in the Wars of the Roses: it was a conflict of battles, which were the centerpiece in short campaigns. The War of the Roses also provided the context for the working out of rivalries between the nobility in the regions (for example, Devon), as had also been the case in the civil war in Stephen's reign.

In the end, the crisis was settled by force, with the victories of Henry Tudor, Henry VII, at Bosworth (1485) over Richard III and at Stoke (1487) over the Yorkist pretender Lambert Simnel.[10] As with Hastings in 1066, and the Glorious Revolution in 1688–1689, military campaigning settled the fate of the country. The death of Richard at Bosworth on 22 August, in a battle in which betrayals played a key part, gravely weakened the Yorkist cause, and also reflected the extent to which leaders played a direct role in combat. Richard was killed when his attempt to overcome Henry and his bodyguard fell. Henry's standard bearer was killed by Richard. Henry VII's success provided the basis for a strengthening of royal authority which ensured that the military power of the state could be enhanced. The private armed forces of nobles were limited. Although he invaded France in 1492, Henry was also careful not to get involved in lengthy hostilities abroad.

In Scotland, there was also disorder followed by revival, although the armies involved in civil conflict were smaller than in England. Scotland faced not only dynastic conflict with two rival factions within the royal family competing for control from 1384, but also the issue of control over extensive peripheral regions to an extent far greater than in England.

The latter had been a major theme in the late twelfth and thirteenth centuries, with William the Lion (1165–1214) seeking to increase his authority in Galloway and also, in 1187 at the Battle of the Muir of Mamgarvy, defeating a rebellion in Moray, Alexander II (1214–1249) extending royal control in Argyll and Caithness, and Alexander III (1249–1286) extending power over the Western Isles. However, some powerful magnates, such as the Earls of Douglas in the Borders, had increased their possessions and power during the wars of independence against England and this restricted royal independence. James I (1406–1437) reimposed royal control in the Highlands, executing recalcitrant chiefs, but, in 1429 and 1431, he had to campaign against the Lord of the Isles. James II crushed the main branch of the Douglases in 1452–1455, James III gained Orkney and the Shetlands in 1472 and Ross in 1476, and in 1493 James IV destroyed the position of the Lord of the Isles and extended his authority to the Hebrides. James V established his power with expeditions to the Borders in 1530 and the Western Isles in 1540. Alongside this process, there was often bitter division. James I was murdered in his bedchamber in an attempted coup in 1437, while James III faced serious aristocratic opposition and in 1488, unable to muster sufficient support, he was killed shortly after his defeat at Sauchieburn at the hands of rebels who took over the government, only themselves to face rebellion in 1489. As in England after the Wars of the Roses, however, there was a consolidation of royal authority under James IV (r. 1488–1513).

Medieval themes were to be repeated in the sixteenth century. Military efforts, particularly under the male rulers of England, Henry VII (r. 1485–1507), Henry VIII (r. 1507–1547), and Edward VI (r. 1547–1553), focused on attempts to conquer Scotland and to make gains from France on the Continent. Battles were won, particularly Flodden (1513) and Pinkie (1547) against the Scots, but it proved impossible to consolidate gains either in Scotland or on the Continent. At Flodden (9 September 1513), the English had few cannon, but fire from those they had led the Scots to attack. The Scottish pikemen were unable to develop momentum in attack, and the more mobile English billmen defeated them. The Scottish center was further pressed as other English troops, victorious over the Scottish right, attacked it in the rear. James IV, much of the nobility, and at least 5,000—and possibly as many as 10,000—of his subjects were killed. English casualties were far fewer, although still substantial.[11] Flodden and Pinkie suggested that the Scots were not in a position to challenge the English field army; although after Flodden the Scottish military establishment developed in a similar fashion to other Western European armies, and Highland tactics were influenced by Continental precedents. However, the Scots' diverse forces lacked the ability to act as a coherent unit, and some individual sections, especially the Highlanders, were disinclined to accept the discipline of remaining on the defensive under fire.

The Scots also had less firepower than the English: in addition to their long-standing inability to match English archery, the Scots lacked the resources, expertise, and experience to match them in gunpowder weaponry.

Yet these disadvantages did not mean that Scotland was ripe for conquest. The English faced serious problems in locating and sustaining suitable allies in the complex mix of Scottish politics, and there were also significant military difficulties, not least major logistical problems. England was far stronger than Scotland in population and financial resources, and had the English been able to maintain and support a permanent military presence in lowland Scotland, then the Scottish kingdom would have been gravely weakened. However, as Scotland did not yield the funds for its occupation, the impossibly high cost of maintaining enough garrisons would have fallen upon England. The center of English power was far to the south, and in sixteenth-century Scotland it was challenged by French intervention which greatly affected the political and military equations of advantage.[12] Scotland was not to be conquered by England until 1650–1652, when France was distracted by civil conflict and another civil war.

Conflict with France also revealed operational and strategic deficiencies in English war making, although with the added complexity of a reliance on alliance partners who followed their own goals. This proved a particular problem for Henry VIII's invasion of France in 1513. That campaign saw a minor victory at the Battle of the Spurs, so named because of the speed with which the French fled from Henry's cavalry: the French were exposed to archery when their advance was checked, and this led them to fall back, eventually in disorder. In 1513, Henry's forces also captured Thérouanne and Tournai. The strength of the English artillery was revealed, but so also were serious problems in supply which was largely dependent on *ad hoc* arrangements. Recruitment, in turn, was heavily dependent on aristocratic social control and command, which was not the best means to secure professionalism, although, given governmental administrative capability, there was no viable alternative. The invasion of France a decade later revealed similar problems.[13]

Wars and, in particular, the cost of paying troops, left the English government dependent on parliamentary taxation, and therefore shifted the balance of political power at the national level. There was also a shift between center and regions, with local uprisings suppressed by professional troops, for example in Norfolk and southwest England in 1549, Kent in 1553, and northeast England in 1569. Militarily, the untrained, amateur forces raised in the rebellions were no match for the troops the government could deploy. Like American Natives fighting early colonists in the first half of the seventeenth century, the rebels tended to lack cavalry, firearms, and cannon; and such forces could not readily challenge the government if it had firm leadership and the support of an important portion of the social elite. The latter looked to the Crown and abandoned the earlier tendency to resist unwelcome policies by violence. Internally, England was largely demilitarized. The shift from castle keep to stately home was symptomatic of an apparently more peaceful society and a product of the heavy costs of castle-building. Town walls and castles fell into ruin. In 1597, a survey found that Melbourne Castle was being used as a pound for trespassing cattle, and it was demolished for stone in the 1610s. John Speed described Northampton Castle in 1610, "gaping chinks do daily threaten the downfall of her walls." When James I visited Warkworth Castle in 1617, he found sheep and goats in most of the rooms. In Wales, many castles were abandoned, and fell into disrepair and ruin, while others were enhanced not with fortifications but with comfortable and splendid internal "spaces," particularly long galleries, as at Raglan, Powis, and Carew. In contrast, Edward I's castle Beaumaris was described as "utterly decayed" in 1609, while a 1627 survey of its fellow, Conwy, revealed that it was in a poor state. Military training and a coterie of armed followers became less important to landowners.

In contrast, there was a need to protect the country against foreign foes in a situation of international competition made more volatile by the consequences of the (Protestant) Reformation, which divided England (and Scotland) from France, Spain, and the bulk of the Irish population. For example, a chain of defenses was constructed during the 1540s to defend southern England in the event of a French invasion; as another was to be constructed in the 1800s and (against the German forces in France) in the early 1940s. There was, however, no invasion: England was really protected by the Channel, growing naval power, and greater French interest in the Low Countries (modern Belgium and Netherlands) and Italy. International competition also drove a development of the army that was qualitative as well as quantitative. Siege artillery was improved, such that at the siege of Boulogne in 1544, over 250 pieces of heavy ordnance were deployed, including mortars firing exploding cast iron balls. The English infantry long focused on archery, and English archers and billmen proved very effective against the Scots at Flodden in 1513, and against the French at St. Quentin in 1557. Henry VIII, however, also wanted troops trained in the use of firearms, and he addressed this by hiring continental mercenaries, a costly policy continued into the 1550s, that did not always produce reliable units.[14]

England under Elizabeth I (r. 1558–1603) sent expeditions to Scotland in 1560, France in 1562–1563 and, from 1585, the Netherlands, France, Spain, and Portugal,[15] conquered Ireland, and produced a navy able, in 1588, to resist and disrupt fatally the Spanish Armada, the fleet sent to cover an invasion of England in a misconceived plan that was flawed by the absence of the land-sea coordination it presumed for the invasion. This was to have been carried out by the Spanish Army of Flanders based in the Low Countries, a force that would have posed a serious challenge to the inexperienced trained bands (select militia forces) assembled to confront them. In fighting the Armada as it sailed along the English Channel, the English benefited from the degree to which their navy contained effective, purpose-built warships and was well commanded. Furthermore, superior sailing qualities proved very valuable tactically. The defeat of the Armada also underlined the advanced state of English gunnery, although the key element was a night attack on 7–8 August using fireships that disrupted the Spanish fleet off Calais, permitting the English, on 8 August, to inflict considerable damage in a running battle off Gravelines: the Spaniards lost four ships. A strong southwesterly wind, seen as a "Protestant wind" in the providentialist culture of the period, drove the Armada, which had no deepwater base in which to take shelter, into the North Sea. Rather than risking the Channel, the Armada returned home to Spain round Scotland and Ireland, losing 28 ships to unseasonably violent storms that drove vessels onto the rocky coasts.[16]

In contrast, although James IV of Scotland (r. 1488–1513) had built up a strong navy, the conflicts of the 1540s to 1560s, both with England and civil wars, had led to the disappearance of the Scottish fleet, and the country lacked the maritime strength to provide a substitute from privateers and other parts of the world of commerce. Instead, it was affected by civil conflict in which aristocratic rivalry interacted with religious tension. In 1560, the French Catholic Queen Regent was deposed by the English-backed Lords of the Congregation, a Protestant grouping; in 1567, the Catholic Mary Queen of Scots was forced to abdicate and, when she escaped the following year, she was defeated at Langside.

The English also developed a considerable expertise in maritime expeditionary warfare. The impressive capture of Cadiz in 1596, in which the amphibious task force fought its way into a defended anchorage under the guns of the city defenses, and carried out a successful opposed landing, followed by the storming of the city walls, was one of the most impressive operations of the day (and contrasted with the failure of the poorly planned expedition against Lisbon in 1589). While England could not match the military capability of Spain, Christian Europe's leading military power, the situation was far more encouraging than that of France, which was plunged in particularly bitter civil war from 1585 to 1598.

Furthermore, the Stuart age began in 1603 with the British question temporarily solved. James VI of Scotland became James I of England, producing a union of the crowns; while the surrender in 1603 of Hugh O'Neill, Earl of Tyrone, brought to an end the bitter Irish rising that had begun in 1595 and ensured that, for the first time, the English controlled the entire island. The conflict in Ireland provided evidence of the strength of the Irish combination of traditional Celtic tactical methods with modern firearms, but the Irish were pitted against a powerful state, with a more sophisticated military and logistical organization, and naval support.[17] However, muster rolls reveal that bowmen were still the mainstay of the late Elizabethan militia because the government was reluctant to face up to the cost implications of training and equipping musketeers.[18] The key battle in Ireland was Kinsale on 24 December 1601, in which O'Neill, unusually, lost the tactical initiative, allowing the English to attack while the Irish forces were unprepared. The Irish lost 1,200 men, but, more seriously, their pattern of victory was broken.[19]

In the early seventeenth century, tensions within England over policy interacted with the precarious nature of public finances to ensure that the military lacked a sound domestic basis for continuing military strength. This was accentuated by a lack of interest by James I (r. 1603–1625), who was far from being a warrior king. The consequences were seen in the unsuccessful wars with Spain (1624–1630) and France (1627–1629) in which the poorly prepared and inadequately supported military failed to win success: amphibious expeditions against Cadiz (1625) and La Rochelle (1627) were embarrassing failures. The resulting public discontent interacted with political disputes over the taxation without parliamentary consent that the government sought to support the wars.

The outbreak of the British civil wars with a rising in Scotland in 1638 reflected disagreements over Charles I's commitment to religious change, rather than any tension over war finance, but the resulting crisis revealed the multiple problems of the military. Charles responded to the rising, leading to the Bishops' Wars of 1639–1640, but he lacked the means to sustain the struggle. Charles made a poor choice of commanders, while inadequate finance wrecked logistics. The English army was poorly prepared and deployed, and it collapsed when attacked in 1640 by the large and professionally officered Scottish army, much of which had gained experience in Dutch and Swedish service.[20] The Scots successfully invaded northern England.

As with the wars with Spain and France in the 1620s, the Bishops' Wars weakened Charles, first by undermining his finances, and then because he was unsuccessful.[21] They also altered the relationship between Crown and Parliament in England. Threatened with bankruptcy as a result of the Scottish invasion, the king was forced to turn to Parliament. This chipped away at royal powers, until, in an atmosphere of mounting crisis, the need to raise an army to deal with a major Catholic rising in Ireland in November 1641 polarized the situation. Who was to control this army? Charles responded to the crisis by trying to seize hostile Parliamentarians on 4 January 1642, but he mishandled the attempt and, lacking the strength to overawe London, the center of opposition, he left the capital to raise support elsewhere in England.

Fighting in England between Royalists and Parliamentarians started in the summer of 1642. In the resulting First English Civil War (1642–1646), control over London was a key strategic issue, but there was also a series of local struggles. Indeed, it has been calculated that 47 percent of the soldiers who died in conflict in England died in skirmishes in which fewer than 250 died, while only 15 percent died in major battles. Military units had a strong sense of locality, many were reluctant to travel far from home, and the role of local garrisons and their search for supplies were crucial to the struggle in the regions. As with other civil wars, this conflict saw growing demands on the localities from both sides, as the cost of the conflict rose, and resources available in the early stages were used up. In order to try to achieve central control, reliable and experienced commanders replaced local gentlemen in positions of local power. Localism was eroded, just as neutralism had been ended when people were forced to commit to one of the sides. This led to a violent response in the shape of the Clubmen movement in which, in 1644–1645, local people sought to keep troops out, and, in particular, to limit the demands of garrisons. However, the Clubmen were dispersed by Parliamentary forces.[22]

The fate of local struggles was influenced, and, at times, determined by the campaigns of the main field armies. In the first major battle, Edgehill on 23 October 1642, Charles narrowly defeated the Earl of Essex, the uninspired general who commanded the main Parliamentary army, but he failed to follow up by driving decisively on London, and was checked at Turnham Green, to the west of the city, on 13 November. Charles failed to press home an advantage in what were difficult circumstances, and retreated to establish his headquarters at Oxford. His best chance of winning the war had passed.

In 1643, the Royalists overran most of western England, crushing the Parliamentarians at Stratton and Roundway Down, while Bristol, the major port on the west coast, fell to Royalist assault after a brief siege. However, the Royalist sieges of Gloucester and Hull were both unsuccessful, and the principal battle in the vital Thames Valley and surrounding area, the First Battle of Newbury (20 September), was inconclusive: the Royalist cavalry outfought their opponents, but their infantry was less successful. The Royalists had many successes in 1643, but their plan of concentrating their forces on Oxford and then advancing on London[23] failed, and, more generally, they could not challenge the Parliamentary heartland. The eleven mile-long defense system rapidly constructed for London—an earthen bank and ditch with a series of forts and batteries—was never tested in action, but was a testimony to the resources available for the Parliamentary cause.

The British dimension played the key role in 1644. The Scots entered northern England on the side of Parliament that January. Both were united by opposition to Charles and suspicious of his religious leanings.

Scots and Parliamentarians jointly besieged York, the major city in northern England. The Royalist attempt to relieve it led, on nearby Marston Moor on 2 July 1644, to one of the two decisive battles of the war. The victory of the Parliamentarian/Scots cavalry on the allied left was followed by their joining the assault on the Royalist infantry in the center. Without hope of relief after the Royalist defeat, York surrendered, and the north of England had been lost to Charles.

Experience and discipline were important in the development of what finally became the war-winning Parliamentarian force in England, the New Model Army, which was eventually commanded by Oliver Cromwell. This army defeated the Royalists in England and Wales, bringing the First Civil War to a close in 1646, and subsequently defeated English Royalists in the Second Civil War (1648), as well as the Scots, both in England and in Scotland, and the Irish, a success that had eluded English monarchs throughout history. The remaining Royalist bases in the Channel Isles, the Isles of Scilly, the Isle of Man, and the English colonies were all also captured. The fighting quality and command skills seen in the New Model's victories, such as Naseby (1645) over the Royalists, and Preston (1648), Dunbar (1650), and Worcester (1651) over the Scots, were crucial.

At Naseby (14 June 1645), the second decisive battle of the First Civil War, the Royalists were outnumbered by about 14,000 to 7,600, but the battle was decided by the superior discipline of the Parliamentary cavalry. Prince Rupert, the Royalist cavalry commander, swept the cavalry on the Parliamentary left from the field, but was unable to prevent his troops from dispersing to attack and lost the Parliamentary baggage train. Cromwell, on the right, defeated the Royalist cavalry opposite, and then retained sufficient control to turn on the veteran, but heavily outnumbered, Royalist infantry in the center. They were already heavily engaged, with the inaccuracy of individual muskets countered by the proximity of the opposing lines and their close-packed nature. The Royalist infantry had advanced and driven back the front line of the New Model's infantry, but the most experienced troops were deployed in the second line, and they held fast, stopping the Royalist infantry. It was this struggle that Cromwell swayed by attacking the flank and rear of the Royalist infantry, which succumbed with about 5,000 men taken prisoner. The leading Royalist field army, poorly commanded by Charles I, had been destroyed.

Naseby, like Dunbar, demonstrated the importance of cavalry for success. This underlined the issue of command skills, as some commanders, such as Cromwell, were far better at retaining control over their cavalry than others, most obviously Prince Rupert. The nature of attack victories such as these, in which shock played the key role, ensures that battles should not be seen primarily in terms of firefights, with the accompanying temptation to view military progress in terms of technological and tactical innovations designed to increase firepower. A general who stressed the attack, Cromwell was a vigorous leader who led from the front.[24]

The New Model also benefited from a strong infrastructure. Parliament was backed by the wealthiest parts of the country, London, the major ports, and the navy, and, although this did not make the result of the war inevitable, it helped finance and sustain the war effort. For example, when they invaded Ireland in 1649, Cromwell's forces were well supplied, enabling them to operate most of the year round. Well equipped with carts, wagons, and draft horses, they retained the initiative, and were also supported by the navy. Like Wellington later, Cromwell was convinced of the importance of logistics. The New Model's capability was also fully demonstrated to foreign eyes, when, at the Battle of the Dunes on 14 June 1658, English troops joined the French in defeating the outnumbered Spanish Army of Flanders, a key engagement. In the subsequent peace settlement, England gained Dunkirk, although Charles II sold it to France in 1661.

The New Model's equipment and tactics were essentially similar to those of their British opponents. The major difference was that the New Model was better disciplined and supported by a more effective infrastructure and supply system. Promotion was by merit, and Cromwell favored officers and men imbued with equal religious fervor to his own. The social practice of war also varied between the two sides in England. The Royalists essentially relied on traditional notions of honor, obligation, and loyalty to raise troops. Charles I headed the social hierarchy, and his armies reflected this. Royalists were concerned mostly to defend the established order in Church, State, and Society: the peers and gentry thought their position bound up with that of the king. Leadership for the Royalists was, in large part, a function of social position, although an increasing number of Royalist officers came from outside the social elite. Prominent landowners, such as the Catholic Henry, 5th Earl of Worcester, provided Charles with much support. Aristocrats, such as the Earls of Essex and Manchester and Lord Fairfax, played a major role in the Parliamentary leadership in the early stages, but far less subsequently. The contrast between Cromwell and the Royalist cavalry commander Prince Rupert was one of different attitudes toward responsibility, position, quality, and merit. In this respect, the New Model Army prefigured the Continental Army of the American War of Independence, the Republican Army of the French Revolution, and the Red Army in the Russian Civil War. In each case, the army served as the expression of the political thrust of the revolution, as well as providing its force.[25] Alongside these factors, it is necessary to note the role in battles of chance, not least at Naseby, as well as to emphasize the importance of the army's combat experience in securing success.

Having won the First Civil War in 1646, the victors fell out. Parliament, the army leadership, and the Scots clashed over Church government, negotiations with the captured Charles, and army pay arrears. Delegates appointed by regiments pressed Parliament for arrears, and in August 1647 the army occupied London. The Scots were appalled by the rising influence of radical Protestantism in England, and, in 1648, in the Second Civil War, the Scots invaded on behalf of Charles. In addition, there was a series of Royalist risings, particularly in Kent and South Wales. All, however, were speedily crushed, especially with Cromwell's victory over the overstretched and poorly coordinated invading Scots at Preston on 17 August. In contrast, when earlier allied with the Parliamentarians, the Scots had been able to campaign as far south as Hereford in 1645.

The army followed up its victory by purging Parliament in order to stop it negotiating with Charles (Pride's Purge, 6 December 1648), trying and executing Charles for treason against the people (30 January 1649), and declaring a republic. Thanks, in part, to religious zeal, the army had become a radical force and had not been intimidated about confronting their anointed king. The army leaders were determined to punish Charles as a "Man of Blood" who had killed the Lord's People. His execution made compromise with the Royalists highly unlikely, and entrenched the new ideological position of the new regime. Radicalism was taken even further by the Levellers, a group with much support in the army, but their mutiny in the army in May 1649 was crushed by Cromwell. In April 1653, he seized power itself from the Rump Parliament that had been left after Pride's Purge.

The social and ideological politics of the New Model, however, ensured that it was impossible to demobilize and return to what struck most of the population as normal governance. Instead, the military dominance of politics was only ended by the implosion of the revolutionary regime in 1659–1660, an implosion followed by the restoration of the Stuarts in the person of Charles I's eldest son, Charles II. This restoration led to a marked rundown in the size of the army. Thus, the creation of a "modern" military, in the shape of the New Model, did not lead to a lasting governmental (or military) development.

In contrast, there was far more continuity across the Restoration in the shape of naval power. The English navy became the largest in the world by 1650, and the earlier dependence on employing large merchantmen in war ended with the establishment of a substantial navy which, in 1653, employed almost 20,000 men. In 1652–1654, England fought the Dutch, Europe's leading commercial power, in what was to be the First Anglo-Dutch War. This was a conflict of fleet actions in European waters, fought with heavy guns, as well as of commerce raiding and colonial strikes, and the balance of advantage lay very much with England. There was no land conflict between the two sides in Europe. Attempts to preserve, or cut, trade links, crucial to the financial and military viability of the two powers, played a major role in the war. Both sides realized the advantage of having a large permanent navy and greatly increased their naval strength, with the building of new and larger ships. Looking ahead from the 1650s, it is possible to see naval fighting instructions and line tactics as instilling discipline and encouraging a new stage in organizational cohesion that permitted more effective firepower.[26]

However, the complex political legacy of the mid-century wars greatly affected attitudes toward the military. The cost of the naval buildup had not been popular, but it had, at least, been associated with national goals abroad, including the Western Design against Spain in 1655–1659: hopes of Caribbean gains that led to a failure to capture Hispaniola, but to the conquest of Jamaica. Crucially, the navy was not linked with domestic oppression.[27] The situation was very different with the army. In 1655, the unpopularity of the latter, as an autocratic and expropriatory force, was accentuated when, largely in response to a Royalist rising, authority in the localities was entrusted to major-generals, instructed to preserve security and to create a godly and efficient country. They took authority away from the traditional gentry families, and were unpopular, not only with Royalists, but also with many republicans.[28] As another attack on the established order, many castles were "slighted," in order to weaken their defenses. In Wales, for example, the demolition of Raglan's Great Tower was a potent symbol of the fall of aristocratic power. Other castles slighted included Abergavenny, Aberystwyth, Flint, Laugharne, Montgomery, Pembroke, Rhuddlan, and Ruthin.

Oliver Cromwell died on 3 September 1658, the anniversary of his victories at Dunbar and Worcester. Cromwell's successor as Protector, his ineffective son Richard, unable to command authority and, crucially, lacking the support of the army, was deposed the following May. The resulting political crisis saw the bitterly divided army opposed to Parliament, which sought to end military rule. The Restoration of monarchy in the person of Charles II in May 1660 was achieved by the threat of violence in the shape of the march into England of the Scotland garrison under George Monck. The restored Charles, anxious about the New Model, disbanded it and sought to create a new force under royal control. However, in a reaction against the use of force, the Restoration was followed by a rejection of the idea of a large standing (permanent) army. Due to anxieties both about what such a force could lead to, and about royal power, Charles, who had to rely on parliamentary taxation, was only allowed a small army. The 1,200 strong First Foot Guards, later known as the Grenadier Guards, were formed in November 1660.

During the reign of Charles II (1660–1685), foreign policy was closely related to domestic political divisions, and this ensured that military preparedness and intentions were highly contentious.[29] This was particularly so as a result of The Third Dutch War (1672–1674), which was correctly seen as an aspect of a plot involving Charles to improve the position of Catholics in England, if not to restore Catholicism. Opposition to Charles culminated with the crisis of the so-called Popish Plot in 1678 and then with the Exclusion Crisis of 1678–1681, a political crisis that Charles finally surmounted but at the price of leaving himself too financially weak to maintain an army of any size: he had to dispense with Parliament, and therefore with parliamentary taxation. At the end of the reign, the army was 9,000 men strong, with another 8,600 on the Irish establishment, a tiny combined force compared to the army of France.[30] The reign, however, saw an important overseas expansion in British power, in part as a result of the wars with the Dutch (1665–1667, 1672–1674), which led to a conquered New Amsterdam becoming New York. There was also expansion into areas inhabited by non-Europeans. Carolina was named after Charles II, while, in India, Charles's Portuguese wife brought Bombay (Mumbai) as a dowry in 1661. She also brought Tangier, which was fortified further under Charles, but the cost of the defense and pressure from Moorish attacks led to its evacuation in 1684.

Charles was succeeded by his Catholic brother, James II (and VII of Scotland), in 1685, but he was rapidly challenged in a rebellion by Charles's charismatic (and Protestant) bastard, James, Duke of Monmouth. Invading from the United Provinces (Netherlands), Monmouth recruited support in western England, but was defeated when he attempted a night attack on the recently advanced royal army on Sedgemoor. The advantage of surprise was lost and the poorly organized rebel army was defeated by its experienced opponents' superior firepower (6 July). In contrast, the militia had earlier been unsuccessful against Monmouth. This made the greater effectiveness of professional troops abundantly clear, which was a lesson clear to James's heart. The supporting rising in Scotland was also unsuccessful. Sedgemoor was to be the last significant battle on English soil, and, like the First Civil War, suggested that it would not be possible to defy governmental power successfully from the basis of a regional power nexus. Furthermore, the conflicts of 1638–1652 had revealed that, irrespective of their precise constitutional relationship, England, Ireland, and Scotland had become an interconnected unit in the geography of military power.

Like Cromwell, victory gave James a conviction of divine approval, and the rebellion led him to increase his army. In his speech opening the parliamentary session on 9 November 1685, James made it clear that he wanted both a substantial standing force and no limitation on his right to employ Catholic officers, declaring "there is nothing but a good force of well-disciplined troops in constant pay that can defend us from such as, either at home or abroad, are disposed to disturb us." Both houses of Parliament, however, were opposed to the policy, and particularly anxious over the appointment of Catholic officers who they saw as likely to support James in his autocratic and Catholicizing policies. Unprepared to accept criticism, James prorogued Parliament in November 1685, and it never met again in his reign. He pressed ahead with Catholicizing policies, and also built up the size of the army and increased the number of Catholic officers. James wanted the army to be a powerful, professional institution, answerable only to the king. Whereas Charles II's army had cost £283,000 in 1684, under James it cost £620,322 per annum. His policies, which included the quartering of units on towns judged factious, helped associate a strong army with unpopular policies and contributed greatly to the antimilitary ethos that was important to eighteenth-century British and American attitudes to the army, and that was to play a major role in the American response to imperial control.

Had James II consolidated his position, then a powerful military as the crucial prop of an autocratic monarchy, ruling without reference to any independent Parliament (in England/Wales, Scotland, or Ireland), might have been a long-term factor of significance. Instead, James was to be overthrown in 1688, in the last successful invasion of England, one mounted by his nephew and son-in-law, William III of Orange, the key figure in the Netherlands. Storms and bad weather prevented the fleet, in what was to be the most ignominious naval campaign in English naval history, from blocking the invasion. As a reminder of the key role of politics, division and discontent among the captains were also crucial. Disenchanted with James, some of the English captains were less than fervent in their hostility to William. Once landed, on 5 November, William was outnumbered by James, but indecision, ill-health, and desertion by a series of senior officers, including John Churchill, the future Duke of Marlborough, led James to abandon his army, rather than blocking William's advance on Salisbury Plain. This weakened the morale of his troops, which had already been hit by dissension and conspiracy among the officers. As the army retreated along the Thames Valley, it largely dissolved through desertion, before being disbanded on James's orders. William pressed on to seize London and James's regime collapsed without any battle being fought in England. The campaign that led to William becoming king indicated the degree to which political developments in Britain continued to depend finally on the role of force and the willingness to use it.[31]

William's success underlined the role of conjuncture mentioned at the start of the chapter. Had William failed, then James would have been able to remold the political system, using the force he controlled and ensuring that it was better funded. This would have matched comparable governmental developments on the Continent, and led to a British version of the system described as absolutism. Victory for James in 1688 would have cemented the reaction against Parliament in Charles II's last years (1681–1685). The military would clearly have served as a force for repression.

Abroad, James would probably have allied with Louis XIV of France, and this would have had important implications not only for European policy, but also for possible transoceanic goals. Instead, William declared war on Louis XIV in May 1689, launching a series of conflicts that closed with Napoleon's defeat at Waterloo in 1815. William's army served to ensure control over Ireland and Highland Scotland, but its role was very much subject to the relationship between Crown and nation mediated through ministers able to lead Parliament. There was nothing inevitable in that.

CHAPTER **2**

The Struggle for Mastery with France, 1689–1775

The eighteenth century was a key formative period for the British military, one in which its structures eventually became firmly rooted in a system of (domestically) peaceful politics and legal governance, rather than being, as they had been in the seventeenth century, a central means to control over England and by England over Britain. This experience had left a strong legacy of concern over the army, one that was strengthened by the extent to which large armies had been crucial to the apparently autocratic policies of Continental rulers, most obviously Louis XIV of France (r. 1643–1715). Indeed, the *Craftsman,* the leading London opposition newspaper, captured, in its issue of 13 July 1728, the opposition to a large army that was a major feature of the political culture:

> History does not afford us one instance of a people who have long continued free under the dominion of the sword...the very situation of our country, which is surrounded with rocks and seas, seems to point out to us our natural strength, and cuts off all pretence for a numerous, standing, land force.

The military tasking in this period was twofold—domestic and international—and each responded to key challenges to the British political system. Furthermore, these were linked. The domestic challenge was from the supporters of the Jacobite (named after Jacobus, the Latin for James) claimant to the throne: until 1701 James II (and VII of Scotland), and then his son, "James III and VIII," and grandsons, "Charles III" (Bonnie Prince Charlie) and "Henry IX." This claim became in the 1760s inconsequential and ridiculous, but, earlier, it was of considerable significance. The Jacobites enjoyed much support in Ireland and Scotland and a reasonable amount of backing in parts of England. This ensured that William III's success in England in 1688–1689 was followed by a British War of Succession in which the new order was established by force in Ireland and Scotland. Thereafter, it was necessary to respond to Jacobite risings, of which by far the most serious occurred in 1715–1716 and 1745–1746, as well as conspiracies, such as the Atterbury Plot of 1723. From the Jacobite perspective, the army was part of an oppressive occupation on behalf of foreign rulers, from 1714 the Hanoverian dynasty.

Furthermore, Jacobite plots received foreign support, most prominently from France, and this included invasion attempts in 1692, 1696, 1708, 1744, 1745–1746, and 1759, while there was a Spanish counterpart in 1719. French support for the Jacobites was a key element in a long struggle for mastery between the two powers. This involved conflict in 1689–1697, 1702–1713, 1743–1748 (war only declared in 1744), and 1754–1763 (war only declared in 1756), as well as peacetime concern, rivalry, and, even, confrontation. For much of the period from 1700, when Philip, Duke of Anjou, a grandson of Louis XIV, became Philip V of Spain, Spain was an ally of France.

These domestic and international challenges set the tasking for the military, but there were also important political parameters that in large part reflected the legacy from the seventeenth century. The most significant was a hostility to a large standing (permanent) army, and a determination to keep the military within the law. Indeed, Britain was unusual as a great power in that it lacked a large army. The Revolution Settlement that followed the "Glorious Revolution" of 1688–1689, ensured that parliamentary approval was necessary for the maintenance of a standing army (which was illegal without Parliament's approval granted annually in a Mutiny Act), and this helped to discourage ministries from seeking a large force. Including the Irish establishment, the peacetime army was only about 30,000 strong in the first half of the century, and 45,000 strong in the 1760s. Furthermore, rapid demobilizations at the end of the conflicts lessened the combat effectiveness of the army.

Conscription was unacceptable. Indeed, the very fact that many Continental states resorted to such a system established it as unacceptable, although there were impressments of the unemployed during some periods of wartime acute manpower shortage, such as the War of the Spanish Succession (1702–1713). In 1756, when the Seven Years' War (a struggle known in the United States as the French and Indian War) began, compulsory enlistment was made possible by an Act of Parliament, but this policy disappointed expectations. It proved difficult to raise sufficient men, their quality was low, and desertion was a major problem; and the system fell into disuse in 1758. Britain lacked a regulatory regime and social system akin to those of Prussia or Russia and, without them, it was difficult to make a success of conscription or to control desertion. The army remained a largely volunteer force, and, as such, was affected by the growth of the civilian economy, which increasingly provided attractive job opportunities. In 1780, when Britain was at war with France, Spain, Mysore, and the American rebels, and under great pressure, Charles Jenkinson, the Secretary at War, wrote to Lord Amherst, the

Commander-in-Chief, that he did not see how the strength of the army could be maintained, but he added,

> I am convinced that any plan of compulsion…is not only contrary to the nature of the government of this country, but would create riots and disturbances which might require more men for the purpose of preserving the peace, than would be obtained by the plan itself…besides that men who are procured in this way almost constantly desert, or at best make very indifferent soldiers.[1]

The last was to be the view of most commanders during subsequent British history: their preference was for volunteers, particularly who were seen as offering the possibility for a long-service, motivated regular force.

There was also no adequate permanent force of naval personnel. Naval efficiency was measured in the ability to create fighting teams for existing ships once mobilization was ordered. The permanent navy consisted of ships and officers, with relatively few sailors. The formation of a reserve of seamen was proposed without result: the Register Act of 1696, which provided for a voluntary register of seamen, proved unworkable and was repealed in 1710. Subsequent proposals for legislative action met resistance. Although the enlistment of volunteers was important, and, in mid-century, landsmen, nearly all of whom were volunteers, composed close to one-third of the navy's wartime strength, the navy continued to be dependent on impressments by the press gang. Although, by law, this method applied only to professional seamen, it was both abused and arbitrary.

More seriously, the system was only partially successful. On many occasions, naval preparations and operations were handicapped by a lack of sailors. Possibly, however, there was no better option, in the absence of any training structure for the navy, and given the difficulty of making recruitment attractive when length of service was until the end of the war. The government never seriously considered paying sailors more; unsurprisingly so, given the size of the navy, and in light of concern over naval expenditure. The Bourbon alternative—the French and Spanish registrations of potential sailors—was not obviously superior and led to evasion and a shortage of sailors. Moreover, political support for impressments ensured that the British navy had the manpower to sustain a fleet that included numerous ships of the line. Furthermore, although not without many difficulties, manpower in large measure kept up with the rise in the number of British warships. Numbers of sailors in the Seven Years' War rose from 62,000 in June 1757 to 82,000 in the later stages of the war.

The demand for naval manpower helped limit that available for the army, but the relationship between the two was closer still. The lack of a large army made the British Isles more vulnerable to invasion, and thus both increased the need for naval superiority and limited the options available for naval strategy. This vulnerability was apparent in each of Britain's wars with France.

The lack of a large standing army could be lessened by several means. For home defense, this focused on the use of militia and other volunteer forces. Aside from the wartime expansion of the regular army, there was also a reliance on forces raised within the imperial system: colonial militias in the New World, the large sepoy (Indian) army raised by the East India Company, and also the black auxiliaries used against escaped and rebellious slaves in Jamaica in the 1730s and 1760. The hiring of forces in Europe and further afield was also an option, as was reliance on the armies of allies.

Relatively small regular forces made it easier to keep the British army well trained and equipped, and thus to respond to changes in the methods of fighting. These were important because weaponry and the nature of land battle changed fundamentally at the start of this period. In the battles of the mid-seventeenth century, such as Naseby, the infantry had been divided between the musketeers, who provided firepower; and the pikemen whose long pikes offered defensive strength, protecting both them and the musketeers from cavalry and pike attack, and also provided the opportunity for advancing forward. The squares of pikemen helped structure battlefield formations, while the pike was the last of the major weapons that focused on stabbing or slashing, rather than firepower. It also underlined the traditional nature of much warfare, for the pike looked back to its most famous exemplar, the phalanxes of the Macedonian army under Alexander the Great in the 330s B.C.

This system was swept away in the 1690s, thanks to the invention of an effective bayonet, one of the most important and underrated innovations in military technology. Whereas, with the plug bayonets devised earlier in the seventeenth century that were inserted in the barrel of the musket, it had been necessary to remove the bayonet before firing the musket, the socket bayonet enabled firing with the bayonet in place. All infantrymen were thus armed with a weapon that combined firepower and steel. However, this did not greatly encourage attacks, because bayonet drills were, for a long time, based on pike drills, with the weapon held high and an emphasis on receiving advances. It was not until the 1750s that a new bayonet drill, with the weapon held waist-high, made it easier to mount attacks. As pikes were replaced by muskets equipped by socket bayonets, so matchlock muskets were replaced by flintlocks. All the new regiments raised from 1689 were equipped with flintlocks. The new Land Pattern Musket could be fired at least twice a minute and weighed one pound less than the matchlock previously used. The army was not to experience a comparable change in weaponry until the introduction of rifled guns in the nineteenth century.

As the French were reequipping in a similar fashion, the British, however, did not benefit from a capability gap with their major European opponent, although the enhanced weaponry was very useful for conflict overseas for example in North America, not least because tactical mobility and flexibility were increased. Instead, it was necessary for the greatly expanded army to outfight European opponents. This was done in Ireland in 1690–1691, with the Jacobites defeated at the Boyne (1690) and Aughrim (1691), and William's forces conquering the island. The Boyne campaign was key to the fate of Ireland. The French advice to their ally James II was to play a waiting game, rather than to risk battle. James was urged to burn Dublin, to destroy all the food and forage in William III's path, and to wait for a French fleet to interrupt his seaborne supply route, and for subsequent privation to demoralize and weaken him. James, however, understood the need to consider political as well as military contexts. Grasping Dublin's symbolic and strategic significance, and fearing that the logistical and political strains of delay would lead the French and Irish to waste away before his opponents, James therefore decided to fight, rather as George Washington chose in 1777 to try to block the British advance on Philadelphia, then the capital of the Revolution. James, however, was a poor commander, not least for failing to reconnoiter the battlefield, and he was outmaneuvered. The fighting was not militarily decisive, most of the defeated escaping, but James projected his abiding fear of envelopment onto William's maneuvers, and his nerve failed. The disintegration of the Franco-Irish army after the battle was based on a moral collapse stemming from James's flight. This also gave the Williamites a propaganda coup. They could present William as an exemplar of calm and heroic leadership, and James as a coward. Thus, the Boyne took on a lasting role in political theater.[2] In contrast, in the Low Countries (modern Belgium and Netherlands), although the British troops fought well, William was beaten at Steenkirk (1692) and Neerwinden (1693) by the French army, then well commanded, at the peak of its capability, and the largest force in Western Europe since the days of Imperial Rome.[3]

The next war, that of the Spanish Succession (1702–1713), in which Britain, Austria, and the Dutch fought France, marked a significant expansion in the military and international roles both of the British state and of the British army. In this war, Britain took a greater proportional role in the conflict with Louis XIV of France than she was to take in the French Revolutionary and Napoleonic Wars (1792–1815) and in World War Two after Germany attacked the Soviet Union in 1941. British land capability depended on naval strength: thanks to naval dominance, which was apparent from the Battle of Barfleur/La Hogue in 1692, and was underlined by the French focus on land operations, Britain was able to deploy and support land forces, both in nearby areas of Europe and more distantly. The bulk of the military commitment was made in the traditional nearby region of military activity, the Low Countries, but there was also important activity in Germany and Spain, while the navy dominated European waters. The French increasingly focused their maritime efforts on privateering, which hit British trade but had no strategic impact.[4]

The British response to France was organized by John Churchill, 1st Duke of Marlborough, who was Captain-General of the English forces in the Netherlands from 1701 until 1711. Despite the caution of his Dutch allies, he repeatedly gained the initiative from France, and displayed an effective boldness. The best example was the march to the Danube in 1704 in order to defeat a French-Bavarian attempt to knock Austria out of the war and thus destroy Britain's strategy, which centered on the use of an alliance system to resist French expansion; the same method employed against first Germany and then the Soviet Union in the twentieth century. The 1704 campaign, which culminated in a total victory at Blenheim, was the most decisive British military move in Europe until the twentieth century and, unlike the culminating Waterloo campaign against Napoleon in 1815, which was a response to the French invasion of Belgium, was a combination of the strategic and the tactical offensive. The advance was also a formidable logistical challenge: depots of supplies were established along the route, providing the troops with fresh boots as well as food.

Two years later, at Ramillies in the Low Countries, Marlborough again obtained a victory by the use of well-timed concentrated force: breaking the French center after it had been weakened in order to support action on the flanks, the method he had employed at Blenheim. At both, he showed the characteristic features of his generalship. Cool and composed under fire, brave to the point of rashness, Marlborough was a master of the shape and details of conflict. Keeping control of his own forces, and of the flow of the battle, he was able to move and commit his troops decisively at the most appropriate moment. Successful anew at Oudenaarde in the Low Countries in 1708, Marlborough, however, only won at Malplaquet (1709) with great difficulty, in part because his tactics had become stereotyped, allowing the French to prepare an effective response. The heavy casualties on both sides at Malplaquet indicated the results of a sustained exchange of fire between nearby lines of closely packed troops, and Marlborough's tactics were based on the acceptance of such losses. Nevertheless, in 1710–1711 he became more cautious and was unwilling to attack the French in good defensive positions.[5]

The war closed with France no longer dominant in Western Europe, and with the British Empire extended by the gain of Nova Scotia, Gibraltar, Minorca, Newfoundland, and Hudson Bay: the conquest of Nova Scotia reflected the important cooperation of regulars with American colonials. Under Marlborough, the army had reached a peak of success that it was not to repeat in Europe for another century The combat effectiveness of British units, especially the fire discipline and bayonet skill of the infantry, and the ability of the cavalry to mount successful charges relying on cold steel, owed much to their extensive experience of campaigning and battles in the 1690s and 1700s. These also played a vital role in training the officers and in accustomizing the troops to immediate maneuver and execution. This was the most battle-experienced British army since those of the Civil War, and the latter did not take part in battles that were as extensive, or sieges of positions that were as well fortified, as those that faced Marlborough's forces. The infantry, drawn up in three ranks, were organized into three firings, ensuring that continuous fire was maintained. British infantry fire was more effective than French fire, so that the pressure of battlefield conflict with the British was high; the same was true of artillery fire at sea. The inaccuracy of muskets was countered by the proximity of the opposing lines, and their close-packed nature. The cavalry was made to act like a shock force, charging fast, rather than as mounted infantry, relying on pistol firepower, and Marlbourgh used a massed cavalry charge at the climax of Blenheim, Ramillies, and Malplaquet. The artillery were well positioned on the field of battle, and were resited and moved forward to affect its development. Marlborough was also effective in siege craft, as shown in the successful, although very costly, siege of Lille, a major French fortified position, in 1709.

It is important, however, to note that the war also revealed deficiencies in the military system. Major-General John Richards recorded of the siege of Valencia in May 1705, "our mortars could not be worst served...slow ...they shot as ill as could be...the fuses were so ill made that...great many of them never burnt at all...length of time taking it has delayed us."[6]

Marlborough's battles were fought on a more extended front than those of the 1690s, let alone the 1650s, and thus placed a premium on mobility, planning, and the ability of commanders to respond rapidly to developments over a wide front and to integrate and influence what might otherwise have been in practice a number of separate conflicts. Marlborough was particularly good at this and anticipated Napoleon's skillful and determined generalship in this respect. He was also successful in coordinating the deployment and use of infantry, cavalry, and cannon, and in turning an army and system of operations developed for position warfare into a means to make war mobile; although the combination of fortifications and field armies made France a serious challenge and it was not possible to invade it to any great distance.

Had the British army maintained this proficiency, then the military and political history of Britain might well have been different. In particular, an ability to inflict defeat on the French in the Low Countries in the 1740s and 1790s would have transformed the wars of the period. It is also worth considering how far the War of American Independence (1775–1783) would have taken a different trajectory if a general of Marlborough's ability had been in charge. However, there was a marked reduction in the effectiveness of the army after the War of the Spanish Succession. Numbers were heavily cut at the end of the war, a habitual pattern in British military history reflecting the relative weakness of the military interest and a pattern that gives this history a start-stop character. Hostility on the part of the opposition to a large, or, in many cases, any army, combined with the desire of Sir Robert Walpole, first minister from 1720 to 1742, to cut government expenditure and therefore taxation, and his reluctance to become embroiled in European power politics. As a result, little was spent on the army. Far from training for battle, it was divided into small units,[7] and its command positions were generally deployed for political purposes in order to reward political allies; opponents lost their posts. Dedication and morale were not high among officers and soldiers. Instead, absenteeism, cronyism, and the pursuit of the financial benefits of command occupied the time of most officers, a reflection both of the extent to which the army shared in the values of society and of its institutional character.

Appointments to senior positions reflected family influence and royal and government favor. Thus, Sir Charles Hotham (1693–1758) received his first commission (appointment as an officer), when only 13, and was promoted to Lieutenant-Colonel in 1720 and Colonel in 1731 thanks to royal friendship. This was an important aspect of the emphasis on loyalty in appointment to positions of command, an emphasis that reflected the key role of the army as the support of government in the face of both a rival claim to the throne and a people willing to use force to protest against unwelcome policies. This role serves as a reminder that professionalism has to be understood within its political context, which was vital to the tasking of the military. Nevertheless, both George I (r. 1714–1727) and George II (r. 1727–1760), each of whom had experience of military service on the Continent, also supported the principle of long service as the main way to advancement, and did their best to counter the purchase of commissions. George II, who personally signed military commissions and was keen on competence, used his formidable memory for names to good effect in keeping oversight of the leading members of the officer class. The monarchs were far less interested in and knowledgeable about naval affairs.

Although the desire of both George I and George II to end corrupt financial practices, and, in particular, officers' pecuniary perquisites, was only partially successful, the traditional character of proprietary soldiering (officers owning their units) at troop and company level was fundamentally changed, to the detriment of the incidental income of captains. Regimental entrepreneurship, however, largely escaped, and colonels maintained their private financial position until the later nineteenth century. Indeed, until the 1750s, regiments were known by the names of their colonels.[8] This was not the best basis for an effective response to a larger French army that had recently gained success and combat efficiency in the War of the Polish Succession (1733–1735), a major European war in which Britain had stayed neutral. The British army was no longer at the cutting edge in tactical practice, let alone debate or innovation.

Its ability to act as a campaigning force was lessened by the separate and clashing number of administrative departments and officials, including the Board of Ordnance, the Paymaster General, the Secretary at War, and the Secretaries of State. Furthermore, problems could arise from civilian control. In 1782, the 3rd Duke of Richmond, Master General of the Ordnance, wrote to Major General Charles Grey about how to repel a possible French attack on the major naval base of Plymouth, noting,

> I am sure you can have no idea of the many real difficulties that exist and prevent one's doing business with that dispatch that could be wished. I have many delays to surmount in my own office, but depending also upon others, upon the Commander in Chief who has his hands completely full and then upon a numerous Cabinet which is not the more expeditious for consisting of eleven persons who have each their own business to attend to.[9]

Richmond captured the central feature of British military organization arising from the state's politics: the military answered to civilian control, and was expected to do so in war as well as in peace.

Despite these problems, officers who owed appointment and promotion in large part to social background and connections could still be effective commanders. This was true, for example, of John, Marquis of Granby (1721–1770), the eldest son of the Duke of Rutland, who became a colonel in 1745 and a Major-General in 1755. A brave and talented cavalry commander in Germany during the Seven Years' War, he became Major-General of the Ordnance in 1763–1770 and Commander-in-Chief in 1766–1770, but was less successful in these roles, in part because he allowed himself to be manipulated by the regimental agents and the assorted business of army politics. The work of the Ordnance was then taken on by the Honorable Henry Seymour Conway (1719–1795), the second son of a peer, who became a colonel in 1746 and a Major-General in 1756. Conway worked very hard at the Ordnance and mastered its administration. Another aristocrat, George, 4th Viscount Townshend (1724–1807), who had become a colonel in 1758 and a Major-General in 1761, was Master General of the Ordnance in 1772–1782 and in 1783. Appointments tended to reflect political factors. Seventeen of the 57 colonels in 1762 were MPs, and Conway, who had bitterly attacked the War of American Independence, became Commander-in-Chief in 1782 with the change in government and the decision to bring the war to a close.

In 1743, when conflict resumed with France, the army lacked both numbers and an effectiveness that could enable it to compensate for this inferiority. The mixed results of the wars of the 1740s demonstrated this. In 1741, during a conflict with Spain that had broken out in 1739 and was to continue until 1748, the War of Jenkins' Ear, the major amphibious operation launched against Cartagena on the coast of modern Colombia failed due to poor army-navy cooperation and the inability to mobilize sufficient resources.[10] Two years later, George II, in the last battle in which a British monarch commanded an army, defeated the French at Dettingen, near Mainz in Germany, in large part due to superior British musketry. However, political and military indecision, and serious differences of opinion, combined with the effects of poor weather and disease, and the absence of an adequate artillery train, to ensure that this victory could not be exploited. There was nothing to match the determination and unity of command that Marlborough had offered. The other battles on the Continent, Fontenoy (1745), Roucoux (1746), and Lawfeldt (1747), were French victories, reflecting the skillful generalship of Marshal Saxe, although the dogged fighting quality of the British troops helped to ensure orderly retreats.[11] The British lacked another Marlborough.

A more urgent challenge occurred in Britain in 1745–1746, when a Jacobite uprising in response to the arrival of James II and VII's grandson, Charles Edward Stuart (Bonnie Prince Charlie), led to a loss of control in most of Scotland, with the regulars losing the first battle at Prestonpans (21 September 1745): a Highland charge overcame defensive firepower in a battle in which the Jacobites successfully used the initiative. They then invaded England, outmaneuvering defending forces. The Jacobites were helped by the unfortified nature of most of the British Isles. The major British fortified positions were naval dockyards or overseas bases, such as Gibraltar and Fort St. Philip on Minorca. In contrast, there was no system of citadels protecting major domestic centers of government, especially in England. Not only did this ensure that the Jacobites did not have to fight their way through a series of positions, losing time and manpower as they did so, but it also meant that the British army lacked a network of bases that could provide shelter and replenish supplies. After Charles Edward captured poorly fortified Carlisle, he faced no fortified positions on his chosen route to London. The Jacobites only turned back at Derby in December 1745 due to disappointment about receiving limited English support, which contrasted with what Charles Edward had promised his Scottish troops. The Jacobite army was a newly created volunteer force, with nonbureaucratic supply and recruitment systems, and this necessarily affected its methods of operation, not least in matters of control and command, and logistics. Charles Edward had only limited control over his officers and men, and had to keep them going with promises.

The extent of new recruitment in England was important, not least as an indication of political support.

Retreating into Scotland, the Jacobite force avoided being cut off on the way back and checked their pursuers at Clifton. Once returned, it won another victory at Falkirk (17 January 1746), but this was followed by the government forces under George II's son, William, Duke of Cumberland, gaining the initiative, a key element in the successive closing down of Jacobite options. This led to the Jacobite defeat at Culloden (16 April 1746) at the hands of Cumberland's larger army. The circumstances were not suitable for a Highland charge, because the numbers enabled Cumberland to rely on defense in depth, and this helped make the firepower more effective. Furthermore, whereas at Prestonpans, Clifton, and Falkirk, the government cavalry had plunged, or been plunged, into the fray regardless, and the control of the engagement had passed to the Jacobites, at Culloden the cavalry was fed around the two flanks, ready to intervene when the favorable opportunity offered, and, for the first time, the action on the side of the government forces was initially left to the artillery. The discipline of the government infantry blunted what would otherwise have been sensible preliminary Jacobite lunges. The heavy casualties at Culloden marked the military end of Jacobitism. The remains of the Jacobite army would not have been able to mount an effective resistance as they lacked supplies. Guerrilla resistance was more of an option, but the Jacobites would have been penned in between Cumberland and those Highland clans that were hostile, while, without the presence of the fugitive Charles Edward, the resistance now lacked focus. The way was clear for Cumberland's repression of those clans that had supported the rising.[12]

The suppression of rebellion was not the sole domestic task for the army. Indeed, the army was the essential force used to check public disorder, and that in a society in which collective protests were common. However, the army's ability to respond was affected by the antimilitaristic nature of society, and by the army's dependence on an often hesitant civil magistrature for its authority in civil policy, which was to frame both American and British political culture. In the British Isles, lawlessness was often endemic and large in scale. Smuggling, wrecking, and cattle-rustling were serious threats to law and order. Warships were used against smugglers and pirates and helped stamp out the latter. Tax riots led to the use of the army, as in Glasgow in 1725 where nineteen rioters were killed. Food riots were also a major cause of disturbance. The absence of any equipment other than firearms and the lack of any training in nonviolent control, which was not part of the military culture of the period could lead to fatalities when the army acted. Such fatalities could outrage local opinion, as in 1736 when the Edinburgh town guard responded to disturbances after Andrew Wilson, a popular smuggler, was executed. Captain Porteous's troops fired on the crowd, causing fatalities, and he was tried, sentenced to death, reprieved, but lynched. The role of the army in the St. George's Fields Massacre in London in 1768 and in the Boston Massacre of 1770 also led to bitter responses. More generally, military support to the civil power did not endear the army to the populace, and contributed to the antimilitarism of this very patriotic age, a situation that was to continue in the first half of the nineteenth century.

The navy played a key role in the campaign against the Jacobites in 1745–1746, joining the weather in dissuading the French from invading in support of the Jacobites. The navy also covered the movement of troops back from the Low Countries in 1745 and the supply of advancing forces in eastern Scotland in 1746. Furthermore, two naval victories off Cape Finisterre in 1747 badly hit the French navy. They demonstrated that the French fleet could no longer escort major convoys bound for French colonies, and this destroyed the logic of the French imperial system. More generally, the war showed that the British navy was an effective fighting force and administrative body, and this was true not only in European, but, also, in transoceanic waters. In the war, transoceanic naval strength was joined to a developing imperial military capability when warships and New England militia in 1745 jointly captured Louisbourg, the major French fortified base on Cape Breton Island. The combination of forces from different areas was to be an important characteristic of British military power, helping give it a range, flexibility, and versatility lacking with other militaries. Countering disease was one goal of this versatility, as in 1741 when Britain was at war with Spain and Colonel John Stewart wrote from Jamaica,

> if ever Britain strikes any considerable stroke in this part of the world, the blow must come from the North American colonies not by bringing raw men from...[Britain], but by sending officers of experience and good corps to incorporate with and discipline the men to be raised there, these troops as the passage from thence is much shorter might be transported directly to any part of the Spanish West Indies and arrive there with the health and vigour necessary for action, whereas troops sent from home as our own experience has taught us, are by the length of the passage one half disabled with the scurvy and the other half laid up with diseases contracted by confinement and the feeding of salt provisions.[13]

Transoceanic naval capability was to be much in demand during the Seven Years' or French and Indian War, fighting in which broke out in 1754 as a result of competition over the Ohio Valley. British concern that French activity would exclude them from the interior of North America was responsible for clashes that escalated when domestic political pressures obliged the government to adopt a firm attitude, and led to the dispatch of regulars ordered to mount attacks. Fort Beauséjour, which threatened Nova Scotia, was captured in June 1755,[14] but a force under the inexperienced General Braddock was defeated on 9 July 1755 near Fort Duquesne by the outnumbered French and their Native allies, who made excellent use of tree cover. The unprepared column's response to the ambush was inadequate. Instead of attacking the ambushing troops, they held their ground, thus offering excellent targets.

War was formally declared in 1756, and, over the next seven years, British forces were to be engaged against the French in home waters, Germany, the Mediterranean, North America, the West Indies, West Africa, and India. The war started badly, with the French driving the British from Lake Ontario, and capturing the Mediterranean base of Minorca after a British fleet failed to press home a relief effort; while, in India, in an unrelated conflict, the Nawab of Bengal stormed the British base in Calcutta. Initial failures revealed inadequacies in the British military, for example with the garrison of Minorca, and improvements were not always easy to effect. Deficiencies threw considerable light on peacetime priorities and, in particular, on the extent to which the army was not at the cutting edge and to which defense depended on the navy and not on fortifications. Henry Conway reported from Dublin in 1756,

> among the places commonly spoke of as garrisons the greatest part are improperly termed so, such as Dublin, Cork, Limerick etc which not being in any state of defence are no otherwise to be considered as garrisons than as they want some troops to defend any stores, trade etc that are in them and to keep the Papists [Catholics] in awe, so that the only places which deserve to be thought of as garrisons to be held against an enemy are almost reduced to Charlesfort and Duncannon Fort now repairing.[15]

In 1757, the situation dramatically changed in eastern India with Robert Clive's striking victory over the far larger forces of the Nawab of Bengal at Plassey, but there was no comparable success in North America. Instead, poor weather and the presence of a French squadron ensured that the planned attack on Louisbourg, the French base on Cape Breton, was not mounted, while the French successfully besieged Fort William Henry at the head of Lake George. In Europe, an attack on the French port of Rochefort failed due to a combination of poor intelligence, inadequate cooperation between naval and army commanders, and indifferent and hesitant generalship.

In 1758, British commitments broadened out with troops sent to Germany, to help Britain's ally Frederick the Great of Prussia; while a massive three-pronged offensive was launched against New France (Canada), taking the initiative from the French. Separate expeditions attacked Louisbourg, Carillon (Ticonderoga), and Fort Duquesne, in an unprecedented effort at this distance for any world power. The advance on Carillon, of 6,400 British regulars and 9,000 American provincials, became a frontal assault, and was a costly failure. The successful attack on Louisbourg involved 13,000 troops and indicated the importance of army-navy co-operation in the amphibious deployment of striking power. That on Fort Duquesne, by an army of 7,000, mostly American provincials, indicated the value of experience. Braddock's mistakes were avoided and the French position was weakened when Pennsylvania authorities promised the Native Americans that they would not claim land west of the Appalachians.[16] The consequent shift of Native support obliged the French to give up the Ohio region. Viewed from Europe, this was still a two-sided conflict, whereas on the ground, the shifting support and fears of Native groups could be decisive.

In 1759, the British concentrated on the St. Lawrence valley where their naval power could be used most effectively. The navy convoyed a force of 8,600 troops under James Wolfe to near Quebec. Eventually, Wolfe moved his troops past the city, scaled the cliffs from the river, and, on 13 September, defeated the French outside the city. The French advanced in columns, but were hit by British volley fire, and then attacked with a bayonet charge. A participant recorded,

> About 9 o'clock the French army had drawn up under the walls of the town, and advanced towards us briskly and in good order. We stood to receive them; they began their fire at a distance, we reserved ours, and as they came nearer fired on them by divisions, this did execution and seemed to check them a little, however they still advanced pretty quick, we increased our fire without altering our position, and, when they were within less than an hundred yards, gave them a full fire, fixed our bayonets, and under cover of the smoke the whole line charged.[17]

Earlier that year, at Minden in Germany on 1 August, an Anglo-German army defeated the French thanks to the courage and fire discipline of the British infantry which defeated cavalry and infantry attacks.[18] Also, in what became the "year of victories," the navy inflicted two major victories on the French fleet. The French lost five warships near Lagos on the Portuguese coast on 18–19 August. An invasion attempt on Britain that November was thwarted by British blockaders, but the French fleet took refuge in Quiberon Bay, counting on its shoaly waters and strong swell to deter the British. The latter, however, launched a bold attack on 20 November. With topsails set, despite the ferocity of the wind, which was blowing at nearly 40 knots, his ships sailed into the confined space of the bay and forced a general action in which British seamanship and gunnery proved superior, leading to heavy French casualties.

The war continued to bring triumphs for Britain, although its result no longer appeared to be in the balance. In 1760, the fate of Canada was finally settled, with the three-pronged advance converging on Montreal where the French surrendered. This campaign was an impressive triumph of resources and planning, and indicated the accumulated skill of the

British army in North America.[19] In southern India, the French force was decisively defeated at Wandewash; Pondicherry, the major French base, surrendering to the British besiegers in 1761.

In 1762, the war broadened out, when Spain entered it on the side of France. This did not end operations against the latter, and, in the West Indies, the British captured Martinique, Grenada, St. Lucia, and St. Vincent. The major effort, however, was directed against Havana, the principal Spanish base in the West Indies and their leading naval facility in the New World. The siege force was badly affected by malaria and yellow fever, leading to a loss of valuable experience in the army, which was to weaken the subsequent response to the American Revolution; but the British finally stormed the key fortification and the city then surrendered. The Spaniards also had to cede Florida at the subsequent peace to regain Cuba. As with the Americans in 1898, the British also captured Manila. Another British force played a crucial role in thwarting the Spanish invasion of Britain's ally Portugal.

These expeditions displayed the strength of the British position at the close of the war. Naval superiority gave them the ability to choose where to direct efforts and permitted the application of strength to achieve a local superiority at a time of choosing at crucial points. The French Empire depended on the maintenance of its major bases, but, unless the French could threaten the British at sea, these bases could be isolated and attacked with overwhelming force. Fortifications could prolong the defense and force the British to resort to siege, but fortifications were only designed to last so long against an effective siege; indeed they were principally designed to force attackers to resort to a siege. The effectiveness of British sieges could be lessened by poor leadership, inadequate resources, especially manpower, and disease. Poor leadership and inadequate resources, nevertheless, were increasingly overcome as the British developed considerable and unmatched experience in amphibious operations. The creation of overseas naval bases, providing refitting and repair facilities, helped considerably.

This was important to sustaining naval strength, which was a difficult task, not least as a consequence of the natural decay of what were organic working parts. The longevity of most ships of the line was about twelve to seventeen years, longevity defined as the time between launch and the need for at least middling repair, although a complex combination of factors, beginning first with the cutting of the timber, its storage, the mode of construction, weather conditions, the service of the ship, and its care while in reserve, determined the longevity of a ship and the amount of repair that it was likely to need. In 1749, as a result of long war service, including damaging operations in the Caribbean, the battle fleet in good condition had been greatly reduced, and the dockyards could not cope with requirements for repair and replacement. This problem was overcome in the early 1750s, not least through using the private sector to build new ships. In the long-term improved infrastructure and better naval construction lessened the problems of cyclical decay.[20] Until the age of air power and space, fleets were the most complex and costly public artifacts of their societies.

Military success depended upon a systemic coordination: the ability to mount amphibious operations stemmed from a degree of naval superiority in home waters that both made invasion improbable and could permit the dispatch of fleets to distant waters. These fleets had to ensure superiority there, sufficient both to cover expeditions and to provide supporting firepower. Such an account may make the task seem both obvious and easy, but it was neither. It was necessary to make calculations about relative strengths in a context in which reliable information was scanty. Even if reliable intelligence about the strength and moves of opposing naval forces could be obtained, such intelligence could only move at the speed of the fastest ship. Strategy was also challenged by operational uncertainties, most obviously disease and weather.

More generally, both in Europe and further afield, the British faced the problems of being a maritime power using amphibious forces against Continental states. British options were far less in the face of powerful opponents whose coastal strength was supported by an extensive hinterland, the problem facing amphibious attacks on France, as well as consideration of action against Russia in 1719–1720 and 1791. This problem was also serious during the War of American Independence. Britain was fortunate during the Seven Years' War that the attacks on metropolitan France were subordinated to those on the more vulnerable French Empire. Nevertheless, despite British organizational success in lessening the deleterious impact of distance and the challenge of the oceans, the French Empire was not conquered rapidly, while Louisbourg, Ticonderoga, and Martinique only fell at the second attempt. An ability and willingness to sustain the war was part of the reason for British success, an ability that rested in part on the strong public finances that stemmed from Britain's central role in world trade, as well as from public confidence in government. However, as is always the case in warfare, systemic advantages had to be translated into operational achievements.

The same was true of the conquest of Bengal which was completed in 1765. This was attributed by contemporary Indian histories not to British military superiority, but to the factionalism and moral decline of the ruling India families of the region. The British certainly benefited from their ability to win local allies, but it was also necessary to sustain forces and to defeat opponents. Victories at Patna and Buxar in 1764 were crucial to British success.

There were also conflicts with Native forces in North America. Native military potential was considerable given their hunter-warrior training and their not inconsiderable numbers, particularly in the South, especially in comparison to the back country whites. The heavy losses inflicted on the Tuscarora in North Carolina in 1713 owed something to colonial artillery, but the army consisted of fewer than 100 whites: the support of over 700 Catawba, Cherokee, and Yamasee was crucial. Farther north, the Cherokee resisted regular and colonial forces successfully in 1759–1760. Governor William Bull of South Carolina reported in 1761 that Anglo-American prisoners released by the Cherokees claimed that

> their young men from their past observations express no very respectable opinion of our manner of fighting them, as, by our close order, we present a large object to their fire, and our platoons do little execution as the Indians are thinly scattered, and concealed behind bushes or trees; though they acknowledged our troops thereby show they are not afraid, and that our numbers would be formidable in open ground, where they will never give us an opportunity of engaging them.[21]

However, a shortage of ammunition, and British scorched-earth tactics, led the Cherokee to opt for peace. There was effective resistance to regular and colonial forces in Pontiac's War (1763–1764), with the Natives driving them from the Ohio Valley, although the capacity of the regulars and colonials to respond to Native successes and to mount fresh efforts was indicative of the manpower resources they enjoyed. Conflict with Natives tested both regulars and colonials and encouraged the development of experience with what was termed small war.[22] The politics of power, particularly the display of force, were also at a premium. This was captured by Captain William Cornwallis in his report to the Admiralty about a voyage to the vulnerable limits of the empire on the River Gambia in West Africa in 1775,

> Upon sending an officer up to James' Fort, I was informed by the commanding officer that the French had spirited the natives up against the English, and that he had been obliged to take a schooner of some force belonging to the traders into the service in order to supply himself with water. I thought the appearance of a man of war might be of service. I therefore went up the river in the *Pallas* to James' Fort, which I found in great distress for want of stores, and particularly gun-carriages, not having above three or four serviceable ones in the fort, and most of their guns rendered totally useless for want of them...I stayed in the river eight days, during which time we got the king of the country on board and showed him all the civility we could. He seemed very well pleased, so I hope all will go on well again.[23]

Cornwallis's mission reflected one aspect of British power, for fort and warship were protecting part of the British stake in trade from West Africa, which included the leading role in the slave trade, to the New World. Alongside a very different form of coercion, the use of impressments to obtain sailors, this scarcely suggests a benign account of British military power. However, naval strength also reflected a less authoritarian society than what lay behind the land-based military systems of Continental Europe. As also in the United Provinces (Netherlands), it was the creation of consensual practices and institutions within Britain that were important in producing the readiness to sustain naval power. Relatively open and participating societies have been seen as a precondition for naval efficiency, while, as part of the same relationship, armies can more easily hold down societies, by direct force or its threat, than navies can do.[24]

Part II: Imperial Rival, 1775–1904

CHAPTER **3**

Conflicts with America and France, 1775–1815

The bulwark of the nation, the wooden walls of Great Britain.
—George III of the navy, 1804[1]

The new and different challenges that were confronted in 1775–1815 posed problems for the ways in which the British waged war. A large-scale transoceanic revolution, the War of American Independence, was a new military challenge, as, from 1793, was the particular way in which the armies of Revolutionary France fought. In each case, the strategic questions and tactical problems facing British forces were matched by how best to define winnable goals and to bring the conflict to a close accordingly. It was here that failure was most obvious, but there is a tendency to focus on operations in the field as if they explain the entire failure. This is mistaken. Even had the run of British success continued in North America in 1776, there was still the serious problem of devising, negotiating, and sustaining a successful peace settlement. The experience of negotiating with Revolutionary and Napoleonic France indicated very similar problems.

While it is understandable that these wars dominate attention, it is important also to appreciate the range of warfare that Britain faced in this period, as that indicated the interacting nature of problems and capability that was important to the molding of development. This range also became characteristic of the British military and anticipated that of its American counterpart in the twentieth century. As a far from exhaustive list, British forces in 1775–1815 fought Native Americans in North America and St. Vincent, rebel slaves in the West Indies, a revolution in Ireland in 1798, a series of local powers in India, as well as opponents in Egypt, Sri Lanka (Ceylon), the Persian Gulf and the East Indies, and, in 1788, established the first European colony in Australia. In terms of the development of the British Empire, this was a key period of activity, as it also was for the military, especially with the creation of a large British-led and trained Indian army, able to act both in India and further afield.

This was a vital resource for British imperialism until India gained independence in 1947. At home, the army was used to suppress riots, most prominently the Gordon Riots of 1780, when anti-Catholic demonstrators rampaged through London. Eleven years later, troops were sent to Birmingham in response to the anti-Dissenter Priestley riots. The use of the army was also frequent at more commonplace levels of policing. Lieutenant Oliver wrote from Dublin in 1789,

> A very melancholy affair happened last Thursday. The mob were baiting a bull in one of the streets and were ordered by the sheriff to disperse but to no purpose, and he was obliged to send for a party from the Castle Guard which unfortunately were the 64th [Regiment]. They were very ill used by the mob, and the sheriff ordered them to fire over their heads, which they did, but, instead of alarming them [the mob], it had a very different effect. They swore they had only powder in their pieces and began pelting them with bricks and stones. The sheriff ordered a part of the party to fire which they did and killed four...we are now called the bloody 64th.[2]

To turn to North America in 1775–1783, the image is clear, and the message obvious. Across a sun-kissed meadow, dappled with shade, lines of British soldiers, resplendent in red, move slowly forward, while brave American Patriots crouch behind trees and stone walls ready to blast these idiots to pieces. Frequently repeated on page and screen, the image has one central message: one side, the American, represented the future in warfare, and one side, the American, was bound to prevail. Thus, the War of American Independence (1775–1783) is readily located in both political and military terms. In both, it apparently represents the triumph of modernity and the start of a new age: of democracy and popular warfare. Before these forces, the *ancien régime,* the old order, was bound to crumble and its troops, the British, were doomed to lose. Thus, the apparent political location of the struggle, in terms of the defining fight for freedom that supposedly ushered in the modern world, helps locate the conflict as the start of modern warfare, while considering the war in the latter light helps fix our understanding of the political dimension. Definition in terms of modernity also explains success, as most people adopt a teleological perspective (arguing that the course of developments was inevitable) and assume that the future is bound to prevail over the past.

In making the war an apparently foregone conclusion, this approach has several misleading consequences. First, it allows historians of the period to devote insufficient attention to the fighting and, instead, to focus on traditional (constitution-framing) and modish (gender, ethnicity, discourse, et al.) topics, neglecting the central point: no victory, no independence, no constitution, no newish society. Second, making British defeat inevitable gravely underrates the Patriot achievement in thwarting Britain. Third, any appearance of inevitability removes the sense of uncertainty in which contemporaries made choices. The war, instead, needs rethinking. It has to be understood as a formidable challenge for the Patriots. Britain in 1775 was the strongest empire in the world. Other states, especially, but not only, China, Russia, and Austria, had larger armies, but no other state had Britain's capacity for force projection. Britain not only had the largest navy in the world, but also a navy that had soundly beaten the second largest navy, that of France, as recently as 1759. In 1770, in a confrontation with Spain and her ally France over the Falkland Islands, it was the Bourbon powers that had backed down. Supporting its navy's capacity to operate at a distance, Britain had a network of overseas bases, especially around the North Atlantic. Halifax was a particularly important one, guarding the mouth of the St. Lawrence and enabling Britain to project its naval power down the Atlantic seaboard of North America.[3] There were also bases in the West Indies. The navy also rested on the best system of public finances in the world. The National Debt, guaranteed by Parliament, enjoyed international confidence to an extent unmatched among Britain's rivals, and the British could therefore borrow easily, and borrow large amounts. Indeed, in a marked contrast to the situation facing the Patriots, the War of Independence was to be waged without a serious financial crisis. In part, this reflected the buoyancy of government customs revenues, based as they were on Britain's central role in Europe's global trading system.

Rich, Britain was also politically stable. The ministry of Frederick, Lord North, the First Lord of the Treasury from 1770 to 1782, had just won the general election of 1774. Under the Septennial Act, it did not have to fight another election until 1781. In fact, perfectly legally, it was to hold the next election in 1780, and to win that. The parliamentary opposition criticized the war in America, but the government was in control of Parliament and this position was not lost until a collapse in parliamentary confidence after defeat at Yorktown led to North's resignation in March 1782. The war divided the political elite and some officers refused to serve, although there was no serious breakdown in discipline within the army. Naval politics proved more divisive, leading in 1779 to the unsuccessful court martial of Admiral Augustus Keppel, the commander of the Channel Fleet, who was a member of the opposition. He then resigned.

As far as North America was concerned, the British army had plenty of experience in fighting there as a result of conquering Canada from France in 1758–1760. Compared to Havana and Manila, which the British had captured from Spain in 1762, the eastern seaboard of North America was a relatively benign area for operations. In particular, the killer diseases of the Tropics were absent. It was also an area especially vulnerable to amphibious operations, in which the British were potent and skilled. In 1775, 75 percent of the population of the Thirteen Colonies lived within 75 miles of the coast, and this included most of the people who counted politically. Their vulnerability to sea power was accentuated by the weak state of roads and bridges, which led to an emphasis on coastal traffic, and because inland towns, such as Philadelphia and Albany, were also ports reachable up rivers. All the major towns could be reached by water, while the eastern seaboard of North America is bisected by waterways that help maritime penetration: round Charleston, farther north the Chesapeake, the Delaware, and Long Island Sound, and, countering any American invasion of Canada, the St. Lawrence. The last, for example, enabled a British squadron to relieve Quebec from American siege in May 1776 as soon as the ice melted.

Once ashore, the British did not have to face a new type of foe. Pressed by George Washington to adopt the form of a conventional European army, the Americans trained and deployed the Continental Army, which relied on the volley fire and linear formations with which the British were familiar. The major difference to conflict in Europe was that the general absence of cavalry from the battlefield ensured that troops fought in a more open order. Nor were there new weapons that might make a difference. One was tried and, had it worked, it would have changed the war, neutralizing British naval power; but, as yet, the submarine could not fulfil its potential: the dependence on human energy for movement, and on staying partially above the surface for oxygen, made it only an intimation of the submarine of the future. On land, the American rifle was very useful in sniping, but its slow rate of fire and inability to carry a bayonet gravely reduced its value as a battlefield weapon. Anyway, the British had riflemen.

The major role of the American militia, however, created a problem for the British. This was true both in operational terms, for example by restricting the range of the British supply-gatherers, and in the political context of the conflict, especially in harrying Loyalists. At the outset of the Revolution, militia units overcame royal governors, and defeated supporting Loyalists. In December 1775, the Earl of Dunmore, the last royal Governor of Virginia, was defeated by Virginia militia at Great Bridge, Josiah Martin, his North Carolina counterpart, following two months later at the battle of Moore's Creek Bridge. The British failure to crush the rebellion in 1775 gave the Americans time to organize themselves politically and militarily, to extend the rebellion greatly, and to weaken the Loyalists. These successes helped give the Americans strategic depth, lessening the importance of British operations first in New England and subsequently in the Middle Colonies: British victory in either would not ensure automatic compliance farther south. Furthermore, the militia could provide at least temporary reinforcements for the Continental Army. It helped to ensure that the British were outnumbered and thus limited their effectiveness as an occupation force.

Lastly, the political context was crucial. Had all the colonies in the Western Hemisphere rebelled, then the British would not have stood a chance, but the economically most crucial ones (the West Indian sugar islands, such as Jamaica and Barbados), and the strategically vital ones, those with the naval bases (Nova Scotia, Jamaica, and Antigua), did not rebel. As a result, the British had safe bases—to the north and the south of the Thirteen Colonies, from which to mount operations. When, in March 1776, General Sir William Howe withdrew from Boston, leaving the Patriots, whose artillery now dominated the harbor, victoriously in control of the Thirteen Colonies, he did not have to retreat to Britain. Instead, he sailed to Halifax and rebuilt his force, so that, that summer, the Empire could strike back, Howe landing on Staten Island at the start of the New York campaign. The eventually successful British defense of Canada against American attack in 1775–1776 ensured that, as with East Florida (modern Florida minus the Panhandle), there were also land frontiers across which the Patriots could be attacked. Burgoyne mishandled the invasion south from Canada in 1777, but the strategic challenge posed by British forces there would have been more apparent had Carleton in 1776 and Burgoyne in 1777 been more successful.

More serious from the American perspective were the Loyalists, for this was a civil conflict, the first major American civil war. Loyalists fought and died for their vision of America, just as Patriots did, and in some areas, especially Georgia, North Carolina, the eastern shore of the Chesapeake, and parts of New Jersey and New York, Loyalists were numerous. Furthermore, the boundaries between Patriots and noncommitted, and between noncommitted and Loyalists were porous, not fixed. Politically, the British had to move as many Americans as possible across these boundaries; and American strategy provided them with their opportunity. The American emphasis on position warfare in order to protect their major cities (New York in 1776, Philadelphia in 1777, and Charleston in 1780), or to capture those in British hands (Boston in 1775, Philadelphia in 1777, Newport in 1778, and Savannah in 1779), gave the British opportunities to defeat their opponents and thus to affect opinion within America.

In doing so, they were helped by the problems facing the Americans. To create and sustain an effective army was no easy task, and the Americans encountered many difficulties in doing both. Money and supplies were serious issues, and much of Washington's correspondence is an account of organization and improvisation under pressure. The antiauthoritarian character of the American Revolution, and the absence of national institutions, made it difficult to create a viable national military system for land —and, even more, sea—power. Initial enlistments for one year did not amount to a standing army. In early 1777, for example, Washington's army was badly affected by desertion, expiring enlistments, and supply problems. There were difficult negotiations over the militia, as seen in

Washington's letter to the Pennsylvania Council of Safety on 29 January, "If some mode is not adopted for obliging the officers of the militia to return the arms and accoutrements that are lent to them, we shall be in the greatest want of them when the regular regiments are raised." On 3 February, he wrote to Jeremiah Wadsworth, "The present unsettled state of the Commissary's department in this quarter, makes me fearful, that unless some measures are fallen upon to reconcile the jarring interests of these who act, or pretend to act, under the appointments of Colonel Trumbull, that the army will in a little while want supplies of every kind." These problems did not disappear. In 1780, Nathanael Greene resigned as Quartermaster General because of his anger with civilian politicians and what he saw as their responsibility for his failure to meet the logistical demands of the Continental Army. Such a clash looked ahead to later disputes between the American military and their civilian overseers.

The Americans also faced a central strategic dilemma. They could not defeat the British, other than in the limited (but important) sense of denying them victory in North America and hoping that this would lead them to abandon the struggle. As John Paul Jones showed, the Americans had privateers able to operate in British waters, but they lacked a fleet, let alone the amphibious capacity and strike force to take the war to the British Isles. Indeed they did not possess this during the subsequent War of 1812, and did not gain such a potential until the twentieth century. France and Spain, which entered the war as America's allies in 1778 and 1779, respectively, possessed such a capability. However, their joint invasion attempt on southern England in 1779 was, partly due to disease among the invasion fleet, as unsuccessful as others separately mounted during the century, and, without that, Britain could stay in the struggle. Moreover, although there was sympathy for the American cause in Britain, there was no movement of civil disobedience, and this sympathy anyway ebbed from 1778 when France entered the war as an ally of the Americans. The major outbreak of violence in Britain, the Gordon Riots in London in 1780, obliged the government to use troops to restore order, but these riots were directed against legislation favorable to Catholics, and not against the war.

The ability of Britain to stay in the struggle was a real problem for the Americans, as only a brief conflict had been envisaged in 1775. Instead, as they hoped, of a willingness to fight overawing George III, and forcing him to negotiate, the British, in 1776, sent a major army to defeat the Revolution. The struggle, in which at that stage Britain faced no other enemies, then became more sustained and bitter than had at first seemed likely, and, as later with the American Civil War (1861–1865), the political differences between the two sides were accentuated. Even worse, in 1778, the British displayed a determination to continue the struggle on land despite French intervention. This was against the advice of the British parliamentary opposition and despite the fact that the British now faced challenges in home waters, the Mediterranean, the West Indies, West Africa, and India, challenges that greatly expanded when the war widened to include Spain in 1779 and the Dutch in 1780.

Did any of this matter? After all, the British at one stage or another held all the major towns in North America, and they won a series of major battles, including Long Island (1776), Brandywine (1777), and Camden (1780). Yet, the Patriots were willing to continue fighting. In short, was there a basic strategic problem for both sides: that neither could knock out their opponent, however many battles they won? The war would have to end, as indeed it did, with a compromise peace. Even after Yorktown (1781), there was little assumption that the British defeat meant the end of the war:[4] the British still held on to New York City and Charleston. Indeed, the eventual peace settlement partitioned British North America, leading to the creation of what became Canada as much as what became the United States.

Whether this could have been changed by repeated British victory depended on how far Patriot resilience would have survived defeat. The willingness of Charleston to accept the consequences of British victory in South Carolina in 1780 was instructive, and poses a question mark against the bombastic claims of liberty or death made by some Patriots. On 5 June, over 200 of the more prominent citizens of Charleston congratulated the British commanders on the restoration of the political connection with the Crown. A loyal address came from Georgetown the following month, while several of the leading politicians of the state returned to Charleston to accept British rule. This appeared to be a vindication of the British policy of combining military force with a conciliatory stance, offering a new imperial relationship that granted most of the American demands made at the outbreak of the war. It is scarcely surprising that northern politicians, such as Ezekiel Cornell of Rhode Island, came to doubt the determination of their southern counterparts, and it is important to underline the extent to which British military operations were intended to improve the chances of successful negotiations.

More generally, the voluntaristic character of American military service was also a serious problem for the Patriots, and, in 1776, the British nearly succeeded in turning it against the rebels. As the British scored one victory after another in the New York campaign between August and December 1776, Washington's army all but disintegrated. Men laid down their arms and returned home. At the same time, covered by the British advance, Loyalists came forward in numbers in New Jersey. As a result, Washington's counterattack in the Trenton campaign, launched at the close of 1776, was a make-or-break operation. It was important for its results for both sides. Richard Henry Lee wrote to Washington on 27 February 1777,

> I really think that when the history of this winter's campaign comes to be understood, the world will wonder at its success on our part. With a force rather inferior to the enemy in point of numbers, and chiefly militia too, opposed to the best disciplined troops of Europe; to keep these latter pent up, harassed, and distressed. But more surprising still, to lessen their numbers some thousands by the sword and captivity!

Stemming the tide of success led the British to abandon much of New Jersey in early 1777, which had disastrous political and military consequences. The local Loyalists were hit hard, compromising future chances of winning Loyalist support in the Middle Colonies. Furthermore, militarily, the British advance on Philadelphia in 1777 was mounted, not rapidly by land from Trenton, but, instead, slowly, by sea, via the Chesapeake. Philadelphia did not fall to Howe until 26 September 1777.[5] By then Burgoyne's force that had marched south from Canada was very exposed in the Hudson Valley near Saratoga. It was to surrender on 17 October. A speedier victory near Philadelphia in 1777 would have put Howe in a better position to mount operations that would have made it harder for the Americans to concentrate against Burgoyne. This would also have given substance to the plan of cutting the Thirteen Colonies in half along the Hudson Valley, a move that would have dramatically reduced the articulation of American power and made it more a series of local forces, which the British could try to fight and/or negotiate with separately.

Victory at Trenton also revitalized resistance and permitted Congress to raise a new army, including many men who agreed to serve for three years, a luxury Washington had never enjoyed before. Yet it had been a gamble, a dangerous operation that was dependent on surprise and, anyway, partly miscarried. It is worth asking what if Washington had failed to achieve surprise, or if he had been no more successful at Trenton than he was to be at Germantown the following year, when he failed to defeat the British in a counterattack near Philadelphia, or if the Hessians in Trenton had driven him back to Pennsylvania and the British had continued to garrison New Jersey. Not only is it unclear that Congress would have been able to raise a new army for 1777, but also uncertain that the Americans, who were anyway to be defeated at Brandywine (11 September 1777), could have put up a better effort earlier in the year had it been in the aftermath of defeat in battle.

Late 1776 was not the only low ebb for the Americans. By 1780, they faced growing exhaustion and war-weariness. The absence of major engagements in the Middle Colonies in 1779 and 1780 did not indicate a disinclination to fight. However, the manpower situation in both armies was a testimony to the strains they were suffering from. The British had lost one army at Saratoga, and now had other pressing commitments, while the Americans were finding it increasingly difficult to sustain a major army. As a result, both sought new support: the British looked to the Loyalists, especially in the South, while the Americans sought to persuade the French to intervene in America, rather than fighting the British in the West Indies. The war therefore became a curious interplay of cautious moves and bold aspirations, as increasingly exhausted participants played for stakes that had been made higher as a consequence of the new factor of the intervention of French naval power, and in an atmosphere that the changing arithmetic of naval strength helped to make volatile for both sides.

Hyperinflation had wrecked the American economy, and the war indeed reduced median household wealth by more than 45 percent. Furthermore, the resources that existed were mismanaged. The limited creditworthiness of Congress, and the reluctance of the states to subordinate their priorities and resources to Congress, meant that the army had to live from hand to mouth. Much of the supplying of the Continental Army relied on the issue of largely worthless certificates. In January 1781, short of pay, food and clothes, and seeking discharge, both the Pennsylvania line and three New Jersey regiments were to mutiny. The Pennsylvania mutiny was to be ended only by concession, including the discharge of five-sixths of the men. This episode is a reminder of the precarious nature of the Revolution militarily, and the extent to which the situation did not improve as the Revolution continued. This provides an instructive perspective on the war: both sides faced serious difficulties and had major drawbacks. Militarily, this meant both that there was everything to play for, and that managing limitations was as important as grasping opportunities. Politically, these drawbacks also ensured not only that there was everything to play for, but also that whichever side was better able to respond to its weaknesses and persist was likely to win the struggle of will.

In 1780, this was still unclear, as it was a year of disappointment for Britain's opponents. Despite the anxieties expressed in 1778, French entry had not obliged the British to abandon New York, nor had it led to another attack on Canada, nor to the permanent postponing of operations in the South. Similarly, the British position had not collapsed outside America, and, by the beginning of 1781, Britain had lost few possessions outside North America. The French expeditionary force that arrived in Newport achieved nothing in 1780, while Washington was unable to shake British control of New York. His troops were increasingly demoralized. The British still controlled the sea, and, if their impact in the interior was limited, they revealed at Charleston and around the Chesapeake an ability to use their amphibious forces to considerable effect, taking the initiative, harrying their opponents, and disrupting the American economy. That year, the British strategy in the South was successful—at least until Patrick Ferguson's defeat at King's Mountain on 7 October.

In the Middle Colonies, General Sir Henry Clinton, who had succeeded Howe as Commander-in-Chief in 1778, had a plan for crushing Washington by advancing on his position in New Jersey, and forcing battle on the outnumbered Americans. Clinton planned to land two armies on the Jersey shore, each larger than Washington's, and to send them through the two passes of the Watchung Mountains. If Washington waited (and he did not have enough horses to move all of his artillery), he would have been overwhelmed at Morristown. If he attacked either invading force, Washington would have been outnumbered and on the offensive, conditions generally fatal for the Americans during the Revolutionary War. Had Clinton achieved that objective, he would have moved against the French when they landed that year in Rhode Island. The French would not have been able to withdraw into the interior. With Washington's army gone, Clinton would probably have captured West Point thanks to the treachery of Benjamin Arnold, and thus would have gained naval access to the entire Hudson Valley.

But he told nobody in New York about this plan, and, before he returned from Charleston, the Loyalists, who were convinced that the generally indecisive Clinton was incapable of bold action, had persuaded General Wilhelm von Knyphausen, the commander of the Hessian auxiliary forces, to land in New Jersey with a smaller force than Clinton had envisaged. By the time Clinton returned, there was no chance for surprise, and he pulled back to New York after the indecisive engagement at Springfield. This was the last major engagement north of Virginia and it was a major morale-boosting encounter for the Revolutionaries: a fighting withdrawal by the Americans in the face of large British forces was followed by the establishment of a stronger defensive position, and by a British retreat that led to the abandonment of New Jersey.

The close of 1780 saw the central themes of the 1781 campaign in America already clear: the need for Franco-American cooperation if a major blow was to be struck against the British; Cornwallis's problems in the South; the rising importance of the Chesapeake; and the crucial role of naval power. The contrasting results of the campaigns of 1780 and 1781 indicate, however, that these circumstances and problems made nothing inevitable.

Although Springfield, King's Mountain, and Banastre Tarleton's defeat at Cowpens on 17 January 1781 did not involve the main field armies, they ended the impression of Britain successfully gaining the initiative, tarnished the Southern strategy, and indicated that it had not had any significant consequences for the British in the Middle Colonies. Until early 1781, the odds of winning the war on the ground, at least in so far as battle was concerned, were not therefore too bad for Britain. After then, it was unclear that the British could have won in North America. A different balance of naval power and advantage would have led to a successful

British withdrawal from Yorktown in September or October 1781, but this would not have led to victory. Instead, having fought their way to impasse in the Middle Colonies and the South, the British would have had to evacuate Virginia. Flawed naval command decisions made that impossible, and led to the temporary and localized superiority the French enjoyed, with crucial results, in the Chesapeake that autumn. Although this superiority was neither the consequence, nor the cause, of a climatic battle in which one fleet destroyed the other, and there was no decisive shift in naval advantage against Britain, Cornwallis, besieged by American and French forces and under heavy artillery fire in his exposed position at Yorktown, was obliged to surrender on 19 October.

Nevertheless, more generally, for the British, paradoxically, the war was a defensive success, or, at least, achievement. Once France had come in, it was a global struggle in which Britain was alone. Aside from France, Spain, and the Dutch, Britain was also at war with India's two leading military powers: the Marathas from 1778 to 1782, and Mysore from 1780 to 1784. There were serious defeats and blows during the conflict, not only the loss of the Thirteen Colonies, but those of West Florida (the Florida Panhandle over to the Mississippi) to well-led Spanish forces (1779–1781), the Mediterranean island of Minorca to French and Spanish forces (1782), and the Caribbean islands of Dominica (1778), Grenada (1779), St. Vincent (1779), Tobago (1781), and Nevis, St. Kitts, and Montserrat (1782) to the French; as well as defeats in India at the hands of the Marathas at Wadgaon (1779), and by Mysore at Perumbakam in 1780 and near the Coleroon river (1782).

Yet, the bulk of the empire was held. The American attempt to gain Canada was defeated in 1776, the French and Spanish invasion attempt on Britain in 1779 was unsuccessful, Gibraltar withstood a long siege from 1779, and the British were able to hold their key positions in India against both the Marathas and Mysore, and to end up with peace treaties that left these powers with no gains at Britain's expense. Crucially, the French fleet was defeated by Admiral Rodney in the Caribbean off the Iles des Saintes south of Guadeloupe on 12 April 1782. Thereafter, the Bourbon fleets remained on the defensive in the Caribbean. Britain had failed in the Thirteen Colonies, but the crisis of the empire had been overcome. This was no mean achievement.

While true, it is important to probe the range of conflicts, in what, from 1778 to 1783, was a world war, for the light they throw on British military capabilities. The war had revealed the problems posed by the absence of a large enough army. During the conflict, there was a major expansion in the size of British land forces, and in the East India Company's forces in India, while German units were hired for service across the empire, from North America (where the Hessians were defeated at Trenton) to India. However, troops were spread thin, which ensured that casualty levels were a particular problem. Moreover, the limited forces at their disposal affected the strategic options, operational plans, and tactical moves of British generals. The initial stages of the war with France also highlighted serious issues of naval preparedness, although, by the end of the conflict, the British were outbuilding their Bourbon rivals. Furthermore, the need to confront a number of challenges around the world placed considerable burdens on the ability to control and allocate resources, and raised issues of strategic understanding and of the accurate assessment of threats. The nature of communications prevented the exercise of close control and made it difficult to respond to developments adequately. This accentuated problems in cooperation between army and navy. Poor operational decisions were indeed responsible for specific failures on land and sea, most obviously in the Yorktown campaign. However, only so much weight should be placed on poor British leadership. After all, the British did enjoy important successes, there had been many failures in command in conflicts that had eventually been successful for the British, including the Seven Years' War (which is a pointed reminder of the fine balance of advantage between success and failure) and poor leadership in the War of American Independence was not restricted to the British.

Instead, it is worth noting the formidable nature of the tasks facing British commanders. When there was rebellion in Scotland in 1745 and in Ireland in 1798, Britain was also at war with France, but, despite later mythmaking, both these rebellions were weak, not least due to limited support, while neither posed the military challenge of the rebellion in the Thirteen Colonies. Furthermore, from 1778, Britain lacked the initiative overall. There were individual advances, such as the invasion of first North Carolina and then Virginia in 1781, or the expedition the previous year against Fort San Juan in modern Nicaragua which was intended to push through to the Pacific but, instead, fell victim to yellow fever. However, on the whole, Britain's opponents were able to take the initiative in North America, the West Indies, and the Indian Ocean, and this caused major problems for British force availability.

Without naval dominance or the initiative, the British found that troops had to be spread out on defensive duties, and it was therefore difficult to take units from garrisons in order to assemble an expeditionary force, which was, for example, to be the pattern with attacks on French colonial positions during the Napoleonic War. Furthermore, as in 1940–1942, for example in Malta in the face of German and Italian threats, and in Malaya and Burma when attacked by the Japanese, losing the initiative exposed the weaknesses of British preparations. Being pushed onto the defensive did not necessarily lead to failure: Quebec and Gibraltar both defied attack during the War of American Independence; but on other occasions the situation was less favorable.

The war in India was separate but also linked in that the French sent troops to help Haidar Ali of Mysore, in a repetition of the strategy they followed in North America. In India, as in North America, the British confronted issues of space-force ratio that were very different to those of the Low Countries. British forces were expected to advance major distances, for example an advance of 785 miles from Bengal to Surat in 1778–1779, and faced serious problems with logistics. These were exacerbated by the major role of light cavalry in the forces of the Marathas and Mysore, which contributed powerfully to the asymmetric character of warfare for the British in India.[6] Thus, the maintenance and protection of its supplies became a major operational objective for British forces. In some respects, the role of opposing cavalry prefigured the difficulties British forces were to face from guerrillas in the wars of decolonization post-1945, although the major focus of their attack in the eighteenth century was logistical rather than political support.

At the same time, Britain's opponents in India had not only superior cavalry, but also an increased ability to emulate the infantry-artillery combinations of European armies. This was seen in January 1779 when a slow-moving British advance from Bombay on the Maratha capital, Pune, failed in the face not only of cavalry but also of effective artillery. Surrounded and bombarded, the British army, with its ammunition failing, signed a convention at Wadgaon that provided for the withdrawal of the army. At Perumbakan on 10 September 1780, the heavily outnumbered British force, drawn up in a defensive square, was fought down by repeated attacks by Mysore cavalry and infantry while under fire from artillery. The defeat at the Coleroon River on 18 February 1782 was a repetition, with the Mysore cavalry held off until the British ammunition ran out. These battles repay consideration, because all too often the emphasis on colonial warfare is on British successes. The battle always remembered when British operations in eighteenth-century India are discussed is Robert Clive's victory at Plassey in 1757. This indeed was a key success, but it is clear that there was no necessary reason for British success, and, moreover, that Indian leaders able to combine firepower and shock in attack stood a good chance, especially if their cavalry could also weaken British logistics.

The wider consequences of individual battles are also illuminating as they reveal a major strength of the British position, namely the extent to which an international trading system ensured that money could readily be made available to support operations. This reduced greatly the value of Indian cavalry for, whereas it could play a major role operationally by hitting British logistics, it could not wreck the British economic support system by ravaging the countryside. In 1781, money could be sent from Bengal to cope with the crisis in Madras created by the strength and advance of Mysore's force. The interdependence of the different parts of the British system was amply demonstrated.

This was a system presided over by the king, although he did not direct military affairs. For George III (r. 1760–1820), the *métier* of kingship indeed did not provide release, resolution, or glory in war. His male predecessors back to Charles I had led troops into battle, but, in this respect, George represented a major break in the practice of British kingship. As a young man, George followed his father, Frederick, Prince of Wales, in neither being trained for war, nor being given opportunities to serve, despite his firmly pressed request to do so in 1759, which was rejected by George II. George III, nevertheless, took an interest in military matters, as well as fulfilling his responsibilities. He was particularly active in controlling promotions, about the permutations of which he displayed considerable knowledge, and was extremely jealous of his authority in the army. From the early 1770s, George chose to have himself painted wearing military uniform, as in Benjamin West's *Portrait of His Majesty* (1779), while in June 1771, the Danish Secretary of Legation reported that it was almost superfluous to note that George reviewed troops twice or thrice weekly, as was his normal occupation each June. George's determination to increase the army's effectiveness involved not only reviews and the oversight of promotions, but also consideration of weaponry. In 1786, Sir William Fawcett, the Adjutant General, returned to George two guns the king had sent him, "the bayonet of that which is intended for the use of the Light Infantry having been made to fix, agreeably to your Majesty's directions."[7] George also visited the fleet in 1773, 1778, 1781, 1789, and 1794. On his visit to Plymouth in 1789, George visited the dockyard twice, going on board the *Royal Sovereign,* and inspecting the Victualing Office and the Gun House, and also "went on board the *Southampton* to see the sham fight."

In 1778, George associated himself with the war effort not only by visiting the naval dockyards at Chatham and Portsmouth, but also by visiting military encampments that reflected the fear of French invasion. These brought the king into contact with the militia, part of a voluntary stream on which the security of the country appeared to depend. The following year, a sense of national emergency led George to consider distributing pikes to "the country people."

An even greater crisis for British power arose when the French Revolutionary War broke out in 1792 and Britain joined the following year. Initially, the prime commitment was to operations in the Low Countries, but the French success in overrunning them in 1794–1795 forced the British army to range more widely in order to exert pressure on France, prefiguring the situation with Germany in 1940–1944. Furthermore, as with Germany in 1940, the French threatened the security of the British Isles, most clearly in 1798 when a French expeditionary force was landed in an unsuccessful attempt to repeat what had been achieved in the previous war in North America by backing revolution in Ireland. The Irish, however, lacked the discipline, experience of heavy fire, and training necessary for tactical success, although they displayed both determination and cohesion. The British also benefited from the failure of their opponents to concert their risings and also suffered from the divided nature of Irish political opinion. As in India, this was not the case of an imperial power suppressing a people, but, rather a more complex and nuanced set of religious, social, political, and economic relations that enabled the government to recruit a significant amount of support. Furthermore, as in 1745–1746 in Scotland, there was no effective cooperation between the French and the insurgents.

There was no comparable need to face rebellion in Britain, but the government's strategy for the war involved action against domestic radicalism, as well as a major attempt to encourage loyalism. Neither might appear to have a role in any account of military history, but this is mistaken, as the ratio between domestic opposition and loyalism was crucial to military capability. This was particularly true of raising volunteer support, which was seen as a key resource in the face of the threat of French invasion, and one that permitted the dispatch of more regular troops abroad. Indeed, local volunteers acted successfully against the small French force that invaded Wales in 1797. The 1,400 strong *Légion Noire* (named after their dark-brown coats, captured from the British and dyed), commanded by the American Colonel William Tate landed in Pembrokeshire. Once landed, the French seized food and alcohol, while the defending Fishguard Fencibles, only 190 strong, retreated. However, the defense was rallied by Lord Cawdor, the local aristocrat, who assembled a 600-strong force and advanced with determination. Intimidated by this advance and affected by a collapse of confidence, Tate surrendered on 24 February. Seeking to exploit social strains, the French had planned to win the support of the local poor and disaffected, and to press on to attack and burn Bristol. However, although the invasion force included two troops of grenadiers, much of it was composed of jail-sweepings and Tate was not up to the task.

More generally, large-scale volunteering ensured that the situation prefigured that with the Home Guard in World War Two, although, in the French Revolutionary War, there was felt to be a far more potent threat from domestic opposition, as indeed there was, particularly in Ireland. As a result, loyalist volunteers were seen as crucial in the defense against radicalism, and this was regarded as a central war goal.

British forces were not alone in the 1790s in falling victim to the tactics, numbers, and enthusiasm of the Revolutionary French. The armies of Britain's allies were also defeated in what was a general crisis of an entire politico-military system. In Parliament, in April 1797, an opposition spokesman, Richard Brinsley Sheridan, mocked governmental assurances about the ease with which the French would be destroyed, "I will not remind those gentlemen of their declaration so often made, that the French must fly before troops well disciplined and regularly paid. We have fatal experience of the folly of those declarations; we have seen soldiers frequently without pay, and without sufficient provisions, put to rout the best paid armies in Europe." Indeed, the tactics adopted by Britain in 1792 drew on those of Prussia, and were based on Colonel David Dundas's *Principles of Military Movements Chiefly Applied to Infantry, Illustrated by Manoeuvres of the Prussian Troops, and by an Outline of the British Campaigns in Germany* (1788), in short on the experience of Continental European warfare. This represented a deliberate rejection of the more flexible tactics used by the British in the War of American Independence and Dundas, who was to be Commander-in-Chief in 1809–1811, belonged to what was termed the "German," rather than the "American," school of officership. He placed the organized firepower of the close-order line at the center of military practice, claiming that such a line could resist cavalry in open country, but was much less concerned with light infantry, believing that interest in it had led to a decline in the close-order line. The British neglect of such troops, however, served them ill in the Low Countries in the 1790s when the French successfully combined columns and covering skirmishers. Traditional close-order linear formations were vulnerable to French soldiers in open order, and also to the impressive French artillery.

Furthermore, the army was weak because of the blows to morale suffered in the War of American Independence and due to the poorly handled disbandment of 1783. A low level of peacetime capability had been further manifested in an absence of large-scale maneuvers and of adequate training. This caused problems when Britain went to war in 1793 as, more generally, did the need to increase greatly and rapidly the size of the army and to introduce an effective command and planning structure. The peacetime military system was not up to the challenge of war, and there were no comparisons to the preparations made before entry into the two World Wars with Germany, in each of which it also proved necessary to expand the military rapidly.

Nevertheless, there had been improvements. Tactical conventions were standardized in 1792 and, in 1793, the Royal Horse Artillery was formed, an important enhancement of the army's mobility and of its battlefield firepower, although Lord Pelham, the Home Secretary, criticized the consequences of contracting out services in this case, "Our ill-judged economy in these matters makes us trust to contracts to supply horses which when called for are never fit for service, kept at grass or in straw yards for the sake of a little saving in their food, and unused to the collar, their shoulders soon gall, they will not draw."[8] The pace of reform, nevertheless, greatly accelerated during the war, as deficiencies were highlighted by failure. Much was due to the efforts of George III's second son, Frederick, Duke of York, who became Commander-in-Chief in 1795 and was a more effective administrator than he was a field commander: in the latter role, he was to be commemorated as the general who marched the troops up to the top of the hill, and then down again, a reference to his command of the unsuccessful invasion of Holland in 1799. In the face of defeat, the army needed to be revived, and York took particular care to raise the quality of the officers.

He could not abolish the practice of purchasing commissions (positions as officers), while, in 1801, Pelham pointed out that "regiments have been raised by persons having real or supposed influence in the counties they resided in; rank has been given as the price of recruits."[9] York, however, made the purchase of commissions less deleterious, both by raising the number of free ones and by establishing minimum periods of military service for promotion. However, he was unsuccessful in ending absentee-ism among officers. The appointment of a Military Secretary to the Commander-in-Chief was designed to encourage more regular proce-dures, especially with regard to appointment and promotions. York also encouraged schemes for military education, especially the plans of Lieutenant-Colonel John Le Marchant for a military college that would both train cadets and also staff officers. The former was opened in 1802 at Marlow, and developed into the Royal Military College at Sandhurst; the latter in 1799 at High Wycombe: it was the basis of what in 1858 was to be the Army Staff College. Le Marchant had already produced two important cavalry manuals.

York also addressed the conditions of the ordinary soldiers, including food, accommodation, medical care, and punishment regimes. The sol-diers were provided with greatcoats. He was a supporter of the standardi-zation of drill, and, in 1796, the Adjutant-General, Sir William Fawcett, published *Instructions and Regulations for the Formations and Movements of the Cavalry*. Consistency was a standard theme in York's policies and this helped to turn a collection of regiments into an army. It aided the transfer of troops and equipment, and improved operational flexibility. However, there was little improvement in some areas of training, such as bayonet training, where a system for the entire army was not introduced until 1857. Most British infantry continued to be armed with smooth-bore mus-kets, because rifled ones (rifles) were expensive and difficult to produce, required special ammunition, and, though more accurate, were much slower to load and fire than smooth-bores.

York was also a supporter of the cause of light infantry, one associated in particular with Sir John Moore, who, in 1803, was appointed com-mander of a new brigade at Shorncliffe Camp in Kent, which was designed to serve as the basis of a permanent light infantry force. Moore had been much impressed by the system of training and maneuvering light infantry developed by Major Kenneth Mackenzie the previous decade. Particular emphasis was placed upon marksmanship. Moore's force was to become the Light Brigade and, subsequently, the Light Division, but he was killed at the battle of Corunna in 1809 while managing, in the face of stronger French forces, the successful evacuation of a force he had led into Spain in a failed attempt to thwart the French conquest of the country. York was forced to resign in 1809 when a former mistress, Mary Anne Clarke, falsely accused him of selling promotions, but he was reappointed Commander-in-Chief in 1811, holding the post until he died in 1827.[10]

Alongside the development of the regulars, there was a major attempt to supplement strength by raising militia and Volunteer units. These underlined the need for the state to cooperate with local interests in obtaining resources, an aspect of the long-standing balance between the Crown and local interests. Militia colonels regarded their regiments as patronage fiefs, immensely valuable to them as county magnates and public men for both patronage and prestige. As a result, important changes in the militia laws had to be negotiated with the colonels, and even the practice of regular drafts into the army was carefully conducted to protect their interests. Military service by militia and the Volunteers was conditional. Nevertheless, the number of militia rose to over 100,000 in the mid-1790s, and Volunteer numbers were comparable.[11] George III's reviews of the Volunteers helped associate him with the war effort. He reviewed Volunteers in Hyde Park on his birthday in 1799 and 1800. There was also a process of building, with the construction, from 1792, of barracks to house the expanded forces (in place of the traditional reliance in England on billeting them in inns); as well as of fortifications to resist invasion. These included Martello Towers along the south coast (74 in Kent and Sussex) built from 1804, as well as the Berry Head fortifications built to the east of Brixham between 1794 and 1804.[12] In 1796, Dundas produced a memorandum outlining the total war envisaged if the French invaded:

> When an enemy lands, all the difficulties of civil government and the restraint of forms cease; every thing must give way to the supplying and strengthening the army, repelling the enemy...The strongest and most effectual measures are necessary...The great object must be constantly to harass, alarm and fire on an enemy, and to impede his progress till a sufficient force assembles to attack him...every inch of ground, every field may to a degree be disputed, even by inferior numbers...The country must be driven, and every thing useful within his reach destroyed without mercy.[13]

This anticipated Churchill's language in 1940 when German invasion threatened.

The army York was struggling to improve was sent on a series of operations on the Continent, as the British attempted to complement their, generally more successful, attacks on the colonies of France and her allies, by playing their part in coalitions against France by weakening its grip in Europe. Many operations (Holland, 1799; Ferrol; 1800; Spain, 1808–1809; Walcheren, 1809; Antwerp, 1814) were failures, although there were also valuable successes. A force landed in southern Italy in 1806 defeated an attacking French opponent at Maida thanks to superior firepower.[14] The following year, an expedition to Copenhagen led to the defeat of a Danish force, the capture of Copenhagen, and the enforced handing over of the Danish fleet, a key element in the process by which Britain thwarted the naval consequences of France's ability to extend its alliance system.

The key operation was the dispatch of troops to Portugal in 1808, which began Britain's participation in the Peninsular War, in which Portugal resisted French invasion while an uprising challenged Napoleon's attempt to place his brother on the throne of Spain. This gave Britain an opportunity to contest French power on land.[15] In a series of battles, in what proved a long and costly struggle, the British showed that they could repeatedly defeat the French in the open. The disciplined firepower of the British infantry played a major part in the Duke of Wellington's victories, of which the most important were Vimeiro (1808), Talavera (1809), Bussaco (1810), Salamanca (1812), and Vitoria (1813), although this firepower was not necessarily immobile, but, rather, often used as a prelude to a bayonet charge. Wellington ably executed a form of contracted fire-and-movement tactics, balancing the well-drilled line with the extensive use of light infantry, the conservatism of an emphasis on linear firepower formations with a greater role for maneuverability. Wellington never had more than 60,000 British troops under his personal command and was always heavily outnumbered in both cavalry and artillery, but his troops were among the best in the British army. Wellington was also a fine judge of terrain and adept at controlling a battle as it developed.

The French conversely suffered from sometimes indifferent command, as well as the frequent unwillingness of their generals to cooperate and Napoleon's inappropriate interference. The French also had inadequate battlefield tactics, relying on crude attacks in dense columns which provided easy tactics for the British, as at Vimeiro, Talavera, and Bussaco. Wellington was also very active in counterattacks, and the well-timed bayonet charge, launched when the French were disorganized by their approach march and by British fire, was as effective as the volley. Medical records on casualties, and other sources, suggest that the bayonet was essentially a psychological weapon in most Napoleonic engagements. Firepower caused more casualties and was therefore crucial to the decision of the battle. However, the bayonet charge permitted exploitation of the advantage. Such a charge, preceded by a volley, had become a standard British tactic from the late 1750s, used with effect in the War of American Independence, and, with his fine grasp of timing and eye for terrain, Wellington brought the system to a high pitch of effectiveness.[16] At Salamanca, Wellington rapidly and effectively switched from defense to attack, and the offensive was also key to British victories at Vitoria and Toulouse (1814). Casualties were often heavy: more than a quarter of the British force at Talavera and 40 percent of those at Albuera (1811).

The British also played a crucial role in Napoleon's final defeat at Waterloo on 18 June 1815. This found Wellington with 67,000 troops, 31,000 of them British, holding the route to Brussels against attacks by Napoleon's 74,000. Wellington was encouraged by a Prussian promise that four corps would be sent to his help. Neither Wellington nor Napoleon was fighting with armies that were as good as those they had commanded at the peak of their careers. Instead, the forces were in several respects scratch armies: many of the troops had seen little combat and many of the units had no experience of fighting together. This was a particular problem for Wellington: he was justifiably dubious about many of the Dutch and German units in his army. This unevenness helped encourage him to rely on a defensive deployment anchored on British units. Conversely, French intelligence and staff work were inadequate, Napoleon, who was ill, underestimated Wellington's generalship, and there was no effective coordination of French infantry, cavalry, and artillery. The British line was not weakened by prior engagement, and British firepower decisively defeated a number of separate and poorly coordinated French assaults. Yet, for all Napoleon's failings, the French were a formidable army, willing to take heavy casualties, and Wellington regarded Waterloo, in which he suffered over 15,000 casualties, as his hardest battle and described it as a "pounding match." Napoleon was frustrated by the overnight rain, which had left the clay soil soggy, and delayed (perhaps fatally) the start of the battle as the artillery were hauled into position. Flank attacks, which Napoleon neglected, or yet more frontal assaults, might have succeeded, but the arrival of Prussian support in the battle helped Wellington greatly in its later stages. After the battle, Wellington and the Prussians advanced into France. Napoleon surrendered to a British warship and was taken to the South Atlantic island of St. Helena, where he died in 1821, his imprisonment a consequence and sign of British power.

Britain had fought France for longer than any combatant, keeping the resistance to Napoleon alive in 1810–1812, but, in 1812–1814, it was Russian, Prussian, and Austrian forces that had defeated him and, in the subsequent peace settlement, Britain had to accept their expansionism as the price for containing France. Yet the British made an important contribution in the Peninsula and this distraction of French forces made an impact elsewhere in Europe. The British had found a way to use their limited military power to maximum effect, something that was not possible in the Low Countries. Alongside deficiencies, British fighting quality emerged repeatedly. It was evident from the campaigns of 1793–1794 and was demonstrated strikingly, before the Peninsula War, in the victories over the French in Egypt in 1801 and at Maida in 1806. Combat required a disciplined willingness to accept hazardous exposure. When troops approached the Egyptian coast in a landing contested by the French in 1801, "the enemy commenced their attack upon us with round shot and shell which as we approached nearer was changed into the hottest discharges imaginable of grape, canister and musquetry without our being able to make any return. In spite of this destructive opposition the boats still advanced," and, indeed, the landing was successful.[17] Victories in the Peninsular War and at Waterloo greatly improved the reputation of the British army and helped strengthen it in public approval. The dominant image of this war on land is of Waterloo, of lines and squares of infantry bravely fighting off larger numbers of attacking French. This was to be much celebrated in subsequent paintings.

The naval counterpart was Admiral Lord Horatio Nelson's victory at Trafalgar (1805), in which the French and Spaniards lost nineteen ships of the line and the British none. This was the last of a series of major naval victories (Glorious First of June over France, 1794; Cape St. Vincent over Spain, 1797; Camperdown over the Dutch, 1797; the Nile over France, 1798; Copenhagen over Denmark, 1801) in which command skills and fighting quality combined to deliver victory over France and her allies. Victories provided protection against invasion, served as the background for a successful defense of British trade, and enabled Britain to launch attacks on hostile colonies around the world, as well as to mount and sustain operations against the European Continent. The naval war protected and encouraged the British economy. Colonies captured included Martinique, St. Lucia, and Guadeloupe in 1794, Cape Town in 1795, Demerara and St. Lucia in 1796, Trinidad in 1797, Surinam in 1799, Gorée in 1800, Cape Town in 1806, Martinique in 1809, and Guadeloupe, Réunion, and Mauritius in 1810: some colonies were taken more than once because initial gains were handed back under the Peace of Amiens of 1802. Transoceanic operations faced serious logistical challenges, but the inroads of disease were more striking, with massive casualty figures for expeditions to the Caribbean. Colonel Gordon wrote in 1808 about the possibility of a campaign on the Caribbean coast of South America, "My fears on that subject are the climate, the climate, the climate!!,"[18] which was seen as responsible for heavy losses from disease.

Naval hegemony rested on a sophisticated and well-financed administrative structure, a large fleet drawing on the manpower resources of a substantial mercantile marine (although there were never enough sailors), and an ability to win engagements that reflected widely diffused qualities of seamanship and gunnery (the latter consistently better than that of the French), a skilled and determined corps of captains, and able leadership. This was true not only of command at sea, particularly with Nelson's innovative tactics and his ability to inspire his captains, his "band of brothers," but also of effective leadership of the navy as an institution. Resources permitted, and administrative systems supported, the maintenance both of the largest battlefleet in the world and of a crucially large number of smaller warships. Better leadership helped in avoiding a repetition of the very serious naval mutinies of 1797, initially a mass protest about conditions, particularly a failure to raise wages and the operation of the bounty system.

New naval facilities were developed, both in Britain and across the expanding empire. The 1,095-foot-long ropery opened at Portsmouth in 1776 may well have been the largest building in the world. Whereas the naval bakery built in Portsea in 1724 could turn out 34 cwt (hundredweight) of biscuits weekly, the new, larger factory opened in Gosport in 1828, with mass production equipment, was capable of producing 10,000 naval biscuits daily.[19] Signaling at sea, crucial to tactical effectiveness, communications, and coordinated action, improved from the 1780s, and a quick and flexible numerical system of signals was developed. Thanks to her naval resources, which rested on her maritime and industrial strength, Britain was able to turn tactical triumphs to strategic advantage. As on land, mobility, firepower, and determination were crucial in battle, although at sea these were always most readily applied in the offensive. Successive victories, particularly Trafalgar, which was correctly presented as a heroic triumph,[20] conditioned British and foreign expectations about naval power, a vital resource to Britain's military status. Naval strength was the distinctive aspect of British military power, and this was to remain the case for over a century.

Strengths and limitations were relatively apparent in the War of 1812–1815 with the United States. This tends to be remembered in the United States in terms of the successful defiance of British forces at Fort McHenry outside Baltimore in 1814, the inspiration of Francis Scott Key's poem *The Star Spangled Banner,* and also outside New Orleans in 1815. The capture of three British frigates in 1812 is also recalled. Alongside these failures, it is important to note the resilience of the British military system. Despite fighting Napoleon, the British were able to hold off successive American attacks on Canada in 1812–1813. Canadian resolve was a key element as the British had few regular troops there. Thanks to Napoleon's abdication in 1814 (he seized power anew in 1815), the British then had enough regular troops to take the war to the Americans. An expedition was sent to the Chesapeake in 1814, and troops were landed that defeated the Americans at Bladensburg and captured Washington: the public buildings were destroyed in retaliation for American destructiveness in Canada. The effective blockade of the eastern seaboard of the United States was an important factor in encouraging war-weariness in the United States.

The war, however, ended with a powerful impression of British military failure due to the defeat outside New Orleans on 8 January 1815. The delay in mounting the attack surrendered the initiative brought by amphibious operations and ensured that the Americans under Andrew Jackson had time to prepare their defenses. American artillery and musket fire blunted a British attack on prepared positions, with 2,000 casualties, compared to 71 among the Americans. The British attacked in a tightly packed formation on a narrow front, providing a good target for defensive fire. The assault was led by inexperienced regiments that had not fought under Wellington. Instead of pressing home the attack, they halted, losing impetus and the initiative, and increasing their vulnerability to American fire.

This was not the sole British failure in transoceanic expeditions. In 1806, Colonel John Hely-Hutchinson, who had served in Egypt in 1801, claimed that the country could easily be conquered, "a corps of 4 or 5000 infantry, 7 or 800 cavalry with a proportion of artillery will be sufficient to accomplish this object...This operation would certainly be only a march."[21] In fact, an expedition to Egypt in 1807, designed to thwart the possibility of French intervention, that reflected growing British sensitivity about possible opponents on routes to India, ended in failure. Having taken the port of Alexandria with ease, the British marched overland to attack Rosetta, only for the troops to take heavy casualties from snipers in the narrow streets of the town and to retreat. A subsequent advance on Rosetta ended in failure in the face of larger Egyptian forces.

The same year, an attack on Spanish-ruled Buenos Aires met strong resistance in the barricaded streets and failed with heavy casualties, leading to a humiliating surrender. Looking ahead to more recent difficulties, the problems of staging attacks in towns was amply demonstrated at both Buenos Aires and Rosetta. Street fighting rewarded detailed knowledge of the terrain, rather than general firepower, and also placed a premium on small-unit effectiveness for which the training of the parade ground and the linear tactics of the battleground were little preparation.

The British were more successful in India, defeating Tipu, Sultan of Mysore, in 1799, the Marathas in 1803–1806, the Kingdom of Kandy in Sri Lanka in 1815, and the Gurkhas of Nepal in 1815–1816. Key episodes included the storming of the Mysore capital of Seringapatam in 1799 and Wellington's victories at Assaye (1803) and Argaon/Argaum (1803), in which British bayonet charges played a decisive role. Casualties accounted for over a quarter of the British force at Assaye. Aside from British units, the British relied on Indian manpower. The first Indian troops raised by the East India Company appear to have been two companies of Rajputs enlisted at Bombay in 1684. The mostly native army of the

British East India Company rose from 18,200 strong in 1763 to 154,000 in 1805. Britain had come to dominate the market for Indian military manpower, but this was an active relationship in which the British molded the situation. In Bengal in the 1800s, for example, an effective force of cavalry supported by light artillery was created, greatly enhancing mobility, while a company of skirmishers was added to each regiment of sepoy infantry. This reflected both responsiveness to developments in Europe, and a degree of hybridization between British and Indian military practice. India proved a base for expeditions sent to Egypt, Ceylon (Sri Lanka), the Persian Gulf (1809), Mauritius (captured from France in 1810), and the East Indies, where Batavia (Djakarta), the leading Dutch position, was taken in 1811. Both in India and more widely in the region, Britain benefited from the inability of potential opponents to cooperate. Thus, in 1815–1816, the Marathas and Sikhs failed to support the Gurkhas. The Marathas themselves were very divided.

Methodical, planned, and disciplined and relatively orderly military and administrative structures were important to British success, as was the crucial ability to buy military service. The systematic application of power ensured that the British army in India was not one that, like most forces there, dispersed in order to forage and ravage, or a force that had to be held together by booty and that thus dedicated itself to a strategy of pillage. Furthermore, the British succeeded in combining firepower with a reasonable degree of mobility.[22]

Similar processes of co-option to those seen in India occurred elsewhere. Ireland was transformed from a conquered territory into a military resource: large numbers of Irishmen volunteered for service in the army and by 1830 there were more Irish than English soldiers in the army. The terms of service were very different for blacks in the West Indies, but they were a valuable support in the conflict with the French in the Caribbean.[23] Already, in 1741, Etienne de Silhouette, a French agent in Britain, in a letter intercepted by the British, had reacted with alarm to the news that the British were arming blacks in order to use them against Spanish-ruled Cuba. He felt this might be very dangerous for all American-Europeans, but argued that the British were too obsessed by their goals to consider the wider implications.[24] Concern about the implications for the West Indies, specifically the views of local whites, had led to little support for arming blacks during the War of American Independence; but in the 1790s, in response to the French arming blacks in the West Indies, the British did the same. During the War of 1812, the British willingness to receive and arm escaped slaves aroused American anger.[25] In Europe, subsidy treaties brought in support from allies compensating for the relatively small size of the regular army forces available for service in Europe.[26]

The military challenges faced by the British and allied forces were a product of international rivalry and of hostility within the empire leading to rebellion. There was no real sense that the armed forces and military system were under pressure from technological improvements by potential and actual rivals, let alone any equivalent to the ratchet-like competitive emulation in developments in steamships, armor plating, steel artillery, rifles, and machine guns that was to be seen in the last three quarters of the nineteenth century. Neither the first working submarine in the 1770s, nor balloons and rockets in the 1790s posed comparable challenges. None was sufficiently accurate, nor available in large enough quantities, to undermine conventional means of waging war. Indeed, in comparison with the following century, the process of military change was essentially static. Instead, the challenge was to understand methods of warfare in particular environments.

Alongside resources and responsiveness, ambitious, determined, and skillful leadership was also crucial. At Assaye, Wellington had one horse shot from under him and another piked. His coolness under fire was impressive, but so also was his ability to respond immediately, boldly, and flexibly to a confusing battle that did not conform to any plan. The soldiers' fighting quality was also important, not least a willingness to take heavy casualties. In 1807, the Bengal army of the East India Company was rebuffed when it tried to storm the fortress of Kamonah:

> Out of 300 of the 17th Regiment which headed the storm, 145 are either killed or wounded. No men could behave more nobly than both Europeans and sepoys, but no courage, no bravery could surmount the obstacles thrown in their way. The ditch was filled with bags of powder covered over with straw. The enemy awaited until our men had advanced within shot point blank. They then opened a most tremendous fire. Our men coolly advanced to the breach. Immediately the enemy set fire to the straw...as fast as our men mounted [ladders], they were either shot or scorched with powder bags thrown on them.[27]

During the remainder of the nineteenth century, other European powers would try to create empires comparable to that of the British in India. None would succeed. The British had gained an unassailable position in the imperial stakes.

CHAPTER 4

Imperial Ascendancy, 1815–1871

By 1815, Britain was the strongest power on the shores of both the Atlantic and the Indian Ocean, as well as on the oceans themselves. The defeat of France had been crucial to this achievement, but success in a holding war against American attacks on Canada, and repeated victories in India, were also vital. The British war effort had benefited greatly from a burgeoning economy and a robust oceanic trading system. The strength of public finances was also important. Thanks largely to the introduction of income tax from 1799, tax revenues had risen from £18.8 million in 1793 to £77.9 million in 1815. Sustained conflict had also had an impact on military structures. The rise of the War Office, under the Secretary at War, from 1783, especially under the energetic Henry, 3rd Viscount Palmerston, Secretary from 1809 to 1828 (Prime Minister, 1855–1858 and 1859–1865),[1] had provided a larger and more effective bureaucracy for the conduct of overseas operations. This process of administrative reform was taken further from 1806 with the appearance of the first of a number of reports by the newly established Commission of Military Enquiry.

Given the successes, resilience, and range of British military activity in the first fifteen years of the century, its development over the following half-century was somewhat paradoxical. On the one hand, Britain remained by far the strongest naval power, able to see off challenges from other states and arising from new technology; while, thanks, in part, to a series of successful wars, she maintained her position as the leading trans-oceanic empire. On the other hand, there were also spectacular setbacks, particularly in Afghanistan and, to a far lesser extent, Russia, which contributed to an impression of complacent, if not atrophied, military structures presided over by mediocrities, anticipating the criticisms that were to be made about the generals of World War One (1914–1918). In part, there was no paradox, because a lack of serious challenge to Britain's position ensured that it was possible to have both leading status and weak structures. Nevertheless, the latter underlined the conditional character of Britain's relative power, a relative power which emerges clearly in a history of the international relations and military operations of the period.

Compared to other European forces, for example those of Austria and France, the most striking feature of British military history in this period was the relatively limited extent to which it was deployed for internal political and policing purposes involving serious violence; although such internal goals did have an impact on the military. For example, domestic factors, specifically the search for a prestigious image to dissuade opposition, have been seen as encouraging the use of nonutilitarian uniforms and other practices.[2] Support for economic transformation and social order when either was seriously threatened were key internal tasks. The Luddite riots of 1812 against new industrial technology had led to the deployment of over 12,000 troops to deal with popular unrest, and troops continued thereafter to be used against economic and other discontent. The "Plug Plot Riots" of 1842 in Scotland, Yorkshire, and elsewhere brought soldiers into conflict with demonstrators protesting about wage cuts and unemployment; their name came from the removal of plugs from boilers to depressurize them and prevent machinery being driven. In Manchester, the Grenadier Guards marched through the streets with fixed bayonets. In 1844, troops were used against striking coal miners in St. Helens and Wigan. However, the creation of uniformed police forces, under the Metropolitan Police Act of 1829 (for London) and the County Police Act of 1839, lessened the routine need for such deployment.

Troops were also used against political radicalism, defeating the Merthyr Rising in Wales in 1831. In 1839, a Chartist (radical) rising of over 5,000 men, many of them coal miners, that sought to seize Newport, South Wales, as part of a revolutionary uprising, was stopped when a small group of soldiers opened fire and the rioters dispersed.

Yet, the unwillingness of the Chartists, the leading radicals of the late 1830s and 1840s, to resort to violence ensured that demands on the military for civil policing were limited, and there was no parallel to the Year of Revolutions on the Continent in 1848. On 10 April 1848, a Chartist mass meeting in London saw the deployment of over 8,000 troops and army pensioners (as well as the 4,000 members of the Metropolitan Police and the enrolling of 85,000 special constables), but there was no fighting. The same was true that June when 5,000 troops were deployed.

If the political system rarely had to use force to protect itself from outside pressure, the tensions within this system were also contained without a radicalization of the two sides. Pressure for reform in the late 1820s and 1830s led to the repeal of the Test and Corporation Acts which maintained the Anglican ascendancy (1828), and the passage of the Roman Catholic Relief Act (1829) and the First Reform Act (1832). Ultimately, first George IV (r. 1820–1830) and then William IV (r. 1830–1837) responded to such pressure with concessions. They refused to support the "ultras," those opposed to change, as their brother, Ernest, Duke of Cumberland, would have done. This refusal lanced the boil of reformist pressure, ensuring that the pro-reform riots in Nottingham and Bristol in 1831 did not become part of a large-scale challenge to the establishment. In turn, this limited the role of the army, and also ensured that it was not seen as a key support of political reaction, as in so many other states. Troops had been deployed in response to the riots. In 1831, hussars (regulars) and yeomanry restored order in Derby, but, in Nottingham, the situation got out of control. The jurisdictional situation was important to Colonel Thackwell of the 15th Hussars, who ordered his troops to support the constables only in the presence of a magistrate, specifically a town magistrate when in Nottingham and a county one outside its boundaries. Legal concerns and initial delays ensured that the riots in Nottingham were more serious than might otherwise have been the case. Outside Nottingham, the yeomanry deployed in defense of Wollaton Hall were equipped by the owner, Lord Middleton, with several pieces of cannon.[3]

As with George Washington in the United States, the role of Arthur, Duke of Wellington, was crucial in managing the relationship between force and politics, the military and civil contention, and in ensuring that the resort to the army was limited. Master-General of the Ordnance, the body responsible for the engineers and artillery, from 1819 to 1827, and the army's Commander-in-Chief from 1827 to 1828 and then again from 1842 to 1852, Wellington was the key figure, not only as a symbol, whose reputation was carefully defended,[4] but also in practical control, particularly through patronage. The Peninsular War in which he had made his name was pushed to the fore in the culture of print, with works such as William Napier's *History of the War in the Peninsula* (1828–1840) and James Wyld's *Maps and Plans, Showing the Principal Movements, Battles and Sieges, in which the British Army Was Engaged during the War from 1808 to 1814 in the Spanish Peninsula* (1840). Napier was also involved in controversy about Sir John Moore's campaign, publishing *Observations Illustrating Sir John Moore's Campaign* (1832) in response to criticism expressed by another veteran, Moyle Sherer, in his *Popular Recollections of the Peninsula* (1823). Sherer also published a commercially successful *Life of Wellington* (1830–1832), while Napier defended his brother's campaigning in India in *The Conquest of Scinde* (1844–1846) and the *History of Sir Charles Napier's Administration of Scinde and Campaign in the Cutchee Hills* (1851). George Gleig, who became Chaplain of Chelsea Hospital in 1834 and was Chaplain-General from 1844 to 1875, published *Waterloo* (1847), *Sale's Brigade in Afghanistan* (1847), and biographies of Clive (1848) and Wellington (1862). He also published his account of Peninsular service in *The Subaltern* (1825), just as Captain James MacCarthy's *Recollections of the Storming of the Castle of Badajos* appeared in 1836, and the *Recollections of Rifleman*

Harris in 1848. Such works testified to widespread and sympathetic public interest in the military.

Wellington's protégés dominated the army, a process encouraged by the considerable age of the commanders. Fitzroy, 1st Lord Raglan, the youngest son of the Duke of Beaufort, who had fought hard in the war with Napoleon, losing an arm at Waterloo, was Military Secretary at the Horse Guards, the headquarters of the army, from 1827 to 1852, before being appointed Master-General of the Ordnance. Wellington was also the head of the Tories, serving as Prime Minister (the sole professional soldier to do so) in 1828–1830 and 1834, and as leader of the opposition in the House of Lords in 1835–1841. In this role, Wellington crucially was willing to accept Catholic emancipation, and to keep his opposition to parliamentary reform peaceful. This contributed greatly to the legacy of the British military as a force that did not take a key role in politics.

Wellington's legacy, particularly his attitude to reform, which was dominated by his concern with tradition and financial restraint, however, was less happy as far as the continued effectiveness of the military was concerned. This was to be made abundantly clear when the Crimean War of 1854–1856 with Russia exposed serious deficiencies in logistics, medical care, and command structures, all combining to ensure that the troops served in conditions of diseased squalor in what was clearly a major failing of the duty of care of government and military hierarchy to those who were expected to risk death. The fault was more particularly that of a protracted peacetime financial retrenchment, most pronounced in the mid-1830s, although the tendency of late has been to suggest that earlier criticism of an unwillingness to seek improvement went too far; and, instead, that there were important reform impulses in the 1840s and early 1850s, beginning with the commission appointed in 1837 thanks to an initiative by the Secretary at War, Lord Howick.[5] Furthermore, Russia was a difficult target. Nevertheless, the Crimean War was to reveal a failure of preparation for power projection into a difficult environment. There were particular deficiencies in logistics and transport, both aspects of a more general administrative weakness. The troops sent to the Crimea in 1854 lacked sufficient tents and wagons. More generally, the Crimean War demonstrated a lack of preparedness for war with a major European opponent. The army was certainly relatively modest in size prior to that conflict. It strength was cut to 87,993 by 1838 and in 1846 it was still only 116,434 strong: of the infantry that year, 44,980 were based in Britain, 23,000 in India, and 32,620 in the rest of the empire.[6]

Prior to the Crimean War, the army had focused on non-European opponents. The last of the Maratha wars, in 1817–1818, led to major acquisitions of territory and brought to an end the challenge posed by one of the most dynamic elements in Indian society. This was largely a mopping-up operation intended to complete the expansion of 1803–1805 which had been brought to a stop by concern about costs. Victories at Kirkee, Sitabaldi, Mahidpur, Koregaon, and Satara reflected the extent to which the British were proficient in Indian warmaking and also the high tempo of conflict. Battles were hard fought. At Mahidpur (21 December 1817), the infantry under Brigadier-General Sir John Malcolm advanced under heavy fire from the Maratha artillery, a force that repeatedly showed its quality in the early nineteenth century. The Maratha infantry mostly retreated, but the gunners continued to fire until bayoneted beside their cannon, a reminder that bravery was not only displayed by British troops. The British infantry advance was supported by a cavalry attack before which the Marathas retreated. At a far smaller scale, Aboriginal opposition in Australia in the early nineteenth century was overcome, with the army being particularly active in Tasmania.[7]

The pace of activity was maintained in the 1820s. The aggressive, expansionist kingdom of Burma, keen to consolidate its frontiers, stirred up the fears of the East India Company. In response, the amphibious range of British power ensured that it was possible to hit at the center of Burmese power and to avoid fighting only in the jungles of the frontier zone. Although the British did not appreciate the difficulties of fighting in Burma, and failed to make sufficient logistical preparations, an amphibious force captured Rangoon in 1824, fresh amphibious attacks were launched in 1824–1825, and, in 1825–1826, the British advanced up the river Irrawady to Mandalay. This was a much contested advance, but the British were victorious. They benefited from the effective use of their river fleet and from the disciplined firepower of the infantry. Britain was ceded Assam, Arakan, and the coast of Tenasserim in the subsequent peace.[8]

The war saw the value of the new technology of steam power. The 60-horsepower engine of the steamer *Diana* allowed her to operate on the swiftly flowing Irrawady, towing sailing ships and destroying Burmese war boats. Technologies overlap and in 1827, at Navarino Bay, in the last great battle of the Age of Fighting Sail, an Anglo-French-Russian fleet under British command destroyed a Turkish-Egyptian opponent. Western fatalities were far lower than those of their adversaries: 177 to about 17,000. Another reminder of imperial military responsibilities was provided by the Demerara insurrection in British Guiana (now Guyana) in 1823. Dealing with risings in imperial possessions was a major responsibility of imperial garrisons, looking toward the traumatic Indian Mutiny of 1857–1858. Aside from in Demerara, there were slave rebellions on Barbados in 1816 and on Jamaica in 1831–1832.[9] Racism and violence remained an issue after the end of slavery, as seen with the harsh suppression of the Morant Bay uprising in Jamaica in 1865: the introduction of martial law by the Governor, Edward Eyre, was followed by the use of court-martials and the burning down of homes.

In the 1830s, British activity focused on India, consolidating their position in regions in which they were already dominant, as well as expanding their power into new areas. Mysore was gained in 1831, and Karachi fell to amphibious attack in 1839. That year, in what was a major extension of British commitment and capability, the first war with an East Asian power began. The Opium War of 1839–1842 arose from the Chinese attempt to enforce their prohibition on the import of opium, the profits from which were important to the economy of British India, while the seizure of opium held by British merchants and their expulsion from Canton led to pressure within Britain for a response. The demand for compensation was taken up by force. British amphibious forces seized key coastal positions, and China ceded Hong Kong by the Treaty of Nanjing of 1842. Also in 1839, Aden was annexed, for the first time by a European power, giving Britain a key position where the Red Sea met the Indian Ocean.

In the 1840s, conflict again focused on India, where there was major expansion to the northwest, although also major difficulties. In Afghanistan, where policy was motivated by a desire to contain Russian expansion, support for an unpopular client ruler was initially successful, and, in 1839, the major towns of Kandahar, Ghazni, and Kabul were easily captured. In 1841, however, a general revolt was mishandled. When the poorly led British force retreated from Kabul toward India in January 1842, it was delayed by snow and destroyed in the mountain passes by Ghilzai tribesmen. Major-General William Elphinstone, who commanded the retreat, had fought with great credit at Waterloo, but by 1842 he was elderly and infirm, as well as poorly prepared. A British force, the "Army of Retribution," reoccupied (and sacked) Kabul that autumn in a punitive campaign, but it was then deemed prudent to withdraw swiftly.[10] The failure to establish garrison control on the Indian model, was followed, however, by a successful policy of containment, with the diplomatic isolation of Afghanistan and the strengthening of the Indian border, and not by an Afghan invasion of northern India comparable to that in the 1750s.

In contrast, farther south, victories over the Baluchis at Miani, Umarkot, and Mirpur Khas in 1843—smaller infantry forces, supported by cavalry and horse artillery, successfully attacking opposing lines—led to the conquest of Sind by Sir Charles Napier. That year, Gwalior also was overrun, with battles at Maharajpur and Gwalior. To the northwest of British India, the British also fought the Sikhs of the Punjab in two hard-fought struggles.[11] The Sikhs had a large army, many of whose officers were trained in European drill and tactics, it was armed with effective firearms and cannon, and it fought bravely. In the First Sikh War (1845–1846), British victories at Mudki (1845), Firozshah (1845), and Sobraon (1846) owed much to infantry actions with the bayonet. Thomas Pierce recorded, we were now within 300 yards of the enemy's batteries which were dealing forth grape and canister without mercy. All of a sudden, they were observed to waver under our severe cannonading, and the line giving a wild hurrah, rushed forward, drove them from their guns, which we spiked, pursued them onwards as fast as we were able. They rallied, formed square, the 16th Lancers were ordered to charge.[12]

In the Second Sikh War (1848–1849), the Sikh army was weaker. The key victories were Chillianwala and Gujrat, both in 1849. A British participant recorded of the Sikh artillery in the former, "The havoc they committed was fearful...and every bush you passed out rushed a Sikh and tried to cut you down. Of course we never thought of looking into every bush we passed and thus they go in our rear."[13] Once conquered and annexed, the Punjab was to become a major center for recruitment into the British army.

Elsewhere, naval and amphibious action against Mehmet Ali of Egypt in 1840—the blockade of Alexandria, the occupation of Beirut, and the bombardment and capture of Acre—blocked Egypt's northward advance in Syria and Egypt. In South Africa, the British expanded inland from Cape Colony, annexing Natal in 1845 and British Kaffraria in 1847.

The major conflicts in the 1850s occurred with Russia and in India. Begun between Russia and the Turks in 1853, the Crimean War widened when Britain and France came to the support of the latter in March 1854 in order to prevent Russia from dominating the Black Sea and the Balkans (in each of which the Turks were under considerable pressure), and thus apparently threatening the overland route to India. Despite French suggestions of a march on Moscow, this was to be no 1812: the Allies lacked the land resources of Napoleon, not least because both Austria and Prussia were neutral; but, conversely, were far more powerful at sea. The war focused on naval and amphibious action, with a major naval deployment in the Baltic, matched by a full-scale expedition to the Black Sea. Initially designed to protect Constantinople (Istanbul) and help the Turks against the Russian advance into the Balkans, this force was left without a clear mission when, under Austrian pressure, the Russians withdrew. As a result, attention fixed on another goal that had been mentioned, but for which planning was lacking, the capture of the Russian Black Sea naval base of Sevastopol which threatened the Turkish position on the Black Sea. The difficulty of the task had not been properly assessed, while the Allies lacked the necessary manpower. However, the steamships that took British and French troops to the Crimea were not matched on the Russian side by railways capable of moving large numbers of troops and ample supplies.

Landing to the north of Sevastopol on 14 September 1854, the 60,000-strong Anglo-French force faced a contested passage of the river Alma (20 September). Superiority in weaponry ensured that this frontal attack was successful, the poorly trained Russians suffering heavily from an absence of rifles and rifled artillery. The Allies then besieged the well-defended Sevastopol, with the French providing the majority of the force, although the siege was not fully effective, as some road links into Sevastopol stayed open. The Allies also had to face both particularly bad weather, which hit both supply routes and the living conditions of the troops, and attempts by the Russian army to disrupt the siege by attacks on Allied supply routes. These were the cause of the battles of Balaclava (25 October) and Inkerman (5 November), in which the Russians were blocked, albeit with heavy casualties.

This success gave rise to one of the key totemic images of the British military. The journalist William Howard Russell described the British infantry who successfully resisted a cavalry advance on the base of Balaclava on 25 October as a "thin red streak tipped with steel." The report led to Robert Gibb's painting *The Thin Red Line* (1881), although that made the engagement more dramatic than was the case. Balaclava also entailed the most memorable blunder, when a lack of clarity in passing on orders led to the charge of the Light Brigade into the face of Russian cannon. Despite heavy artillery support, Anglo-French land assaults in 1855 initially failed. The attackers lacked adequate experience in siege craft, and had to face a type of trench warfare that was different to earlier sieges. The Russians were supported by over 1,000 cannon, while the Allies fired 1,350,000 rounds of artillery ammunition. Such figures suggest that the Crimean conflict can be seen as the first industrial war. One British officer wrote to his beloved, "[N]ow I am so accustomed to the noise that I believe I could go to sleep in a battery when the enemy were firing at it."[14] Sevastopol, however, finally fell that September, ensuring that the peace settlement satisfied Anglo-French goals. Although operations in the Crimea engage the bulk of attention, the British and French also launched a major naval force into the Gulf of Finland in 1854, and this was responsible for attacks on Russian forts. Furthermore, Russian positions elsewhere, in the Baltic, and, with less force, in the White Sea and on the Pacific coast, were all attacked. However, the navy was unable to turn its command of the sea in order to win decisive advantage.[15]

Victory was won but at a heavy cost. The Crimean War offers an instructive parallel with World War One (1914–1918), both of which are generally seen in terms of folly, futility, and horror. In the former, attention focuses on the heavy casualties and mismanaged heroism of the charge of the Light Brigade at Balaclava, and on the horrific conditions in the siege of Sevastopol. The terrible conditions of the troops, especially a lack of adequate food, clean water, medical attention, shelter, and clothing, helped lead to very heavy losses from disease, and the administrative deficiencies were bitterly criticized in Parliament and the press. The Crimean War saw major advances in war reporting in the press, with news sent home by telegraph, and in war photography.[16] In both wars, there was also criticism of the caliber of the generalship. As in World War One, only a brief conflict was anticipated, and there were no adequate preparations, not least in strategic and tactical doctrine, for the struggle that was to arise. In the Crimean War, strategy occurred almost by accident and there was a lack of purposeful planning. At the tactical level, the British were fortunate that the Russians, still reliant on smooth-bore muskets, lacked modern rifles (the British had introduced them from 1851) and artillery. At Inkerman, attacking Russian columns, seeking to close to bayonet point, took casualties from the Enfield rifles of the British and were defeated. The percussion-lock rifle was more accurate and effective than the musket. The rifled barrel gave bullets a spin, which led to a more stable and thus reliable trajectory.

More generally, the multiple weaknesses of Russia as a military power were important to British success. On the British side, concern over the number of troops led to a recourse to foreign mercenaries. The deficiencies highlighted by the war, and the accompanying furor, led to a measure of reform that in part reflected impulses already present before the conflict. The consolidation of the War Office, Horse Guards, and Board of Ordnance, a key administrative development, began in 1854–1855 and there were improvements in the handling of logistics.[17] However, the relationship between the Secretary for War and the Commander-in-Chief, the key element in political-military links, remained unclear.

The other major challenge was the Indian Mutiny of 1857–1859, which led to the largest deployment of British forces between the Napoleonic Wars and the Boer War of 1899–1902. Victory was seen as crucial to British prestige and power in India. Many factors contributed to discontent among the Indian troops, and more generally in India. Given the strategic needs of British power, it is striking that a major cause of tension was the reluctance of many soldiers to serve abroad for caste reasons, and the newfound determination of the authorities to ensure that they were able to do so. This was understandable given the military resource India provided. For example, in 1838–1846, Indian troops had been very useful in the conquest of north Borneo and Labuan. The trigger for the rising was the British demand that their Indian soldiers use a new cartridge for their new Lee-Enfield rifles allegedly greased (to keep the powder dry) in animal fat, a measure that was unacceptable to Muslims and Hindus for religious reasons, although there was a concerted plan for mutiny with communications between the rebels long before the issue of cartridges. This was significant because of the low level of confidence between British officers and Indian subordinates: the army in India in 1857 contained about 232,000 Indian and 45,000 British troops. Most of the Indian troops in this army's largest section, the Bengal army (which comprised 135,000 Indian and 24,000 British troops), mutinied in May 1857, while there was also a large-scale civilian rising in north-central India. The garrison of Meerut mutinied on 10 May, and Delhi was seized the next day.

Fortunately for the British, much of the Indian army remained loyal (the Madras and Bombay armies, and about 30,000 sepoys of the Bengal army) and the rulers of Hyderabad, Kashmir, and Nepal provided assistance, helping ensure that the British outnumbered the rebels in many of the clashes in 1858. No major prince joined the rebellion, and it also had no foreign support: Afghanistan provided no support for the rebellion. Furthermore, the movement of British troops into the region, and the inability of the badly led rebels, who lacked effective coordination or indeed a clear program, to spread the rebellion, helped the British regain the initiative, storming Delhi and clearing the city in bitter street fighting in September 1857. Nevertheless, the campaign revealed serious flaws in the British military system, not least over transport and medical services. In the spring of 1858, the British overran the rebellious area, capturing Lucknow on 22 March, Jhansi on 3 April, and Kalpi on 22 April. Thanks to impressive generalship by Sir Hugh Rose, who understood the need for effective logistics, the rebellion in central India was ended in June with the capture of Gwalior and victory at Jaura-Alipur. Peace was officially declared by the Governor-General on 8 July 1858, although small-scale resistance continued, with a fresh rising at Multan in August 1858. However, the last battle was at the Sirwa Pass on 21 May 1859, on the frontier of Nepal. The defeated remnants fled into Nepal.

The Mutiny led, in 1858, by the India Act, to the end of rule by the East India Company, and, instead, to the direct administration by the British government of what was not left under dependent local princes, a system that continued until India gained independence in 1947. The British also became more cautious in their treatment of Indian opinion, not least in their willingness to consider unwelcome reforms. Caution owed something to the bitterness and racial violence of the struggle, and the long-standing images of cruelty it provided. For the British, this was the case with mutineers massacring women, children, civilians, and prisoners, as at Cawnpore in June–July 1857. In contrast, Colin Campbell's ability to lead a column to the relief of Lucknow in November 1857 became a totemic occasion of Victorian soldiering and served as a model for subsequent actions, while Henry Havelock and other commanders demonstrated Christian militarism.[18] However, there were alternative images of cruelty, with British troops killing captured mutineers, most dramatically by strapping them across the muzzles of cannon which were then fired. In modern India, the Mutiny was reinterpreted, somewhat anachronistically, as India's first war of independence or nationalism, and is now widely referred to as the "Rebellion."

Once the Mutiny was suppressed, India returned to its former role as a key support for British power elsewhere, including China. The separate local army, however, was now abolished, while the percentage of British troops among the forces in India was greatly increased, and the artillery became nearly all British. Furthermore, the Gurkhas and Sikhs, groups who had remained loyal, became increasingly important among the Indian troops, at the expense of Brahmins, many of whom had rebelled.

Also in the 1850s, Britain annexed Rangoon and southern (Lower) Burma, as the result of a war in 1852–1853 that proved easier, shorter, and less expensive than the First Anglo-Burmese War of 1824–1826. Awadh (Oudh) in India was annexed in 1856. Also that year, an expedition to the Persian Gulf in which Bushire was captured, led Persia to yield to British demands that its forces retreat from Herat in Afghanistan, an interesting contrast with present-day capabilities at a time of concern about Afghan security and Iranian (Persian) assertiveness. A war with China, begun in 1857, in which year Canton was captured, led, in 1860, to the Anglo-French occupation of Beijing, a major blow at the heart of Chinese power. The role of Sikh cavalry supported by Armstrong artillery showed the combination of imperial manpower and home industry in the spread of British power.

In the 1860s, the British annexed Lagos in West Africa (1861), although an expedition against the Asante farther west in 1864 was wrecked by disease. Another major African kingdom, Abyssinia (Ethiopia), was brought low in 1868. In a methodically planned campaign, an expedition entered the Red Sea, landed and marched from the coast into the mountains, a formidable logistical task, defeated the Abyssinians at Arogee, stormed the fortress of Magdala, and rescued the imprisoned British hostages who were the cause of the crisis, before withdrawing. Battlefield effectiveness was furthered by the new Snider breech-loading rifle, introduced in 1864. The campaign helped boost confidence in the military, and reflected the growing strategic importance of the region for British power, an importance that was to be furthered by the opening of the Suez Canal. The Abyssinian campaign drew on the resources of the empire in India, an example of the reinforcing nature of the British Empire at this time.

Expansion in New Zealand indicated the global reach of British power, but also that progress was far from easy. The Maori (many of whom did not resist) responded ably to British artillery and dug well-sited trench and *pa* (fort) systems that were difficult to bombard or storm, adopting layouts in order to increase the potential for their own muskets. The Maori inflicted serious checks on the British in the 1860s, but the availability of British, colonial, and allied Maori units, and the process of extending control, that included road and fort construction, ensured an eventual settlement on British terms. Operations in New Zealand, nevertheless, indicated the difficulties facing British imperial warmaking.[19] The conflicts of the period did not prefigure to any great degree the problems that were to be encountered in the twentieth century in holding colonies in the face of insurrectionary movements, not least because there was little need, as then, to fear foreign intervention, but there were some anticipations. Lieutenant-Colonel Lister wrote of an expedition in East Bengal in 1850 about the problems caused by "the facilities which their jungles afford, both materials and position, for throwing obstacles in the way of an advance or retreat."[20]

What might have been the major war of the period, that between Britain and the United States, did not occur. From 1815 until the revival of French naval strength from the mid-1820s, the Admiralty saw the American fleet as its most likely rival, but Anglo-American relations improved in the aftermath of the War of 1812–1815, and the two powers agreed in opposing Spanish attempts to reimpose control in Latin America and in suppressing the slave trade. In 1818, the frontier between Canada and the United States was agreed as far as the Rockies, while, beyond, the Oregon Territory was jointly administered. Nevertheless, there were tensions, including a dispute over the Maine frontier in 1838–1839, although the Ashburton-Webster Treaty of 1842 settled frontier disputes east of the Rockies. When risings occurred in Canada in 1837–1838, American sympathizers attacked, but the regular garrison overcame the challenge supported by extensive Loyalist volunteer activity, and war with the United States was avoided.[21] Although James Polk successfully campaigned for the presidency in 1844 on the platform of "54°40' or fight," in fact he was willing to partition the Oregon territory and settle the frontier in 1846 without British Colombia or Vancouver Island. Military expenditure in Canada and the number of troops there then fell. A 1859 border crisis over the San Juan Islands off Vancouver Island led to the deployment of local forces, but it was swiftly ended.

During the American Civil War (1861–1865), relations were tense, as the British government expressed sympathy for the Confederacy, and there was anger about the Union blockade, which hit British trade. In turn, the Union complained that British policy helped Confederate privateering. As tension rose, the British fleet in North American and Caribbean waters was strengthened and troops were sent to Canada, but caution prevailed and conflict was avoided.[22] Furthermore after the war, the Union forces did not turn to challenge British interests in Canada or overseas. Instead, Anglo-American differences were settled by the Treaty of Washington of 1871, and this permitted a reduction in the British military presence, with garrisons in Canada restricted to the naval bases of Esquimalt on Vancouver Island and Halifax, both important coaling stations for the navy.[23]

Meanwhile, the organization of the army was being transformed as a result of the Cardwell reforms. As Secretary of State for the Colonies (1864–1866), Edward Cardwell withdrew regular troops from the colonies for which the latter were not willing to pay, a key move toward colonial self-defense, and, as Secretary of State for War (1869–1874), he pushed through the ending of the purchase of commissions, instead insisting on appointment and promotion by merit and selection. This did not transform the social composition of the officer corps, which remained an admixture of landed elite and professional groups, with particular commitment derived from the extent to which, as in the navy, many officers were the sons of those who had served as officers. The failure to increase pay ensured that officers had to be men of means, while merit was construed in terms of seniority.[24] Peacetime flogging was abolished in 1869, while provisions were made for better military education, the retirement of officers and, under the Army Enlistment Act of 1870, the introduction of a short term of service. This did not make recruitment easier, as Cardwell had hoped, but it did lead to a larger reserve. The Commander-in-Chief was in theory brought under the close control of the War Office by the War Office Act of 1870. Infantry regiments were organized into two regular battalions, one on overseas station and another in a home barracks, a system designed to support the goals of imperial defense; and the regiments were linked by name to their county recruiting area. In this "territorialization," Britain was divided into 62 districts.

The merits of the reforms were contested, particularly by traditionally minded officers, not least George, 2nd Duke of Cambridge, the first cousin of Queen Vienna, who was Commander-in-Chief of the army from 1856 to 1895. His determination, connections, and experience helped ensure that the War Office Act did not have the impact that might have been anticipated. Furthermore, the new organizational system offered more for imperial punitive expeditions than for the emphasis on mass seen in the American and European warfare of 1861–1871. The latter, instead, suggested a need for the large-scale training and maneuvers the British lacked, and for which the Crimean War had revealed a major need. However, with their stress on professionalism, the Cardwell reforms meant the end of an *ancien régime* that no longer seemed appropriate in an age of general reform.

More generally, the emphasis was on change. The opening of the Suez Canal in 1869 transformed the geopolitics of British power, while the spread of steam power and ironclad warships ensured that Nelson's navy no longer set the model for naval conflict. The ability and readiness of the navy to achieve its goals depended on a willingness to respond to developments in naval technology that was an indication of the strength of the economy and the willingness to spend money on the navy. *Victoria*, launched in 1859, the largest wooden screw warship built, which mounted 131 guns, cost £150,000. Steam power, in which Britain led the world, was a key aspect of her industrial revolution, and transformed naval capability thanks to the harnessing of steam power to the cause of marine propulsion. The first warship, *Demologos* (Voice of the People), later renamed *Fulton*, was laid down by the Americans in order to provide protection for New York against Britain in the War of 1812 (although it was not in action before the peace), but the British rapidly developed a steam capability at sea. Their industrial capacity ensured that, even when other countries took the lead in technological innovation, Britain would be best placed to catch up and to develop what seemed appropriate. This flexibility enabled the navy to cope with the absence of any comparable lead in formal training or doctrine, while the deficiencies in formal training were more than compensated for by the experience that stemmed from the number and diversity of Britain's commitments. The navy at first leased small private steamships for use as tugs, purchasing its first in 1821. Eight years later *Columbia,* the first armed steamship in the navy, entered service, followed, in 1830, by *Dee,* the first purpose-built steam warship.

Early steamships suffered from slow speed, a high rate of coal consumption, and the problems posed by side and paddle wheels, which included their vulnerability to fire, and the space taken up by wheels and coal bunkers. This ensured that steamers would be outgunned in any clash with ships of the line, which helped explain the British reluctance to throw away their existing lead in sail warships by embracing the new technology.

Nevertheless, steam power replaced dependence on the wind, making journey times more predictable and quicker, and increased the maneuverability of ships, making it easier to sound inshore and hazardous waters, and to attack opposing fleets in anchorages. Steamers helped in the use of naval power to bring an end to the slave trade, particularly from West Africa. The ability of ships to operate during bad weather and on rivers was also enhanced by steam power. In January 1841, the *Nemesis,* a 700-ton, iron-hulled paddle steamer which had sailed round the Cape of Good Hope to China, destroyed eleven war junks near Canton. Far from being static, maritime steam technology developed rapidly, providing opportunities for the navy. In the 1840s, the screw propeller (placed at the stern) offered a better alternative to the paddle wheel, by making it possible to carry a full broadside armament. Screw steamers were also more mobile. The sloop *Rattler* launched in 1843, was followed in 1846 by the frigate *Amphion,* and the next year by the conversion of *Ajax,* a ship of the line, to screw propulsion. The French, whose naval ambitions and international moves in the 1840s alarmed Britain, were outspent in order to ensure that Britain had more steam ships of the line.

There were also developments in naval ordnance. In 1826, 32-pounders were introduced for all ships of the line, and in 1838 the shell gun was adopted as part of the standard armament. Firing exploding shells in place of the solid shot hitherto used, it was a serious threat to wooden ships. The new naval capability was shown when Acre was bombarded in 1840: steamers showed their ability to operate inshore, while a shell caused the explosion of the fortress's main magazine. This operation was a key step in the expulsion of Egyptian forces from Syria and Palestine.[25]

Shells helped lead to their antidote, armored warships. The first ironclad warship, the 5,630-ton *Gloire,* was laid down by the French in March 1858. A wooden frigate with 4.5-inch-thick metal plates, this was designed to challenge Britain, and five more ironclads were ordered in 1858. Worried that their naval lead was being destroyed, the British, in a major burst of expenditure, matched *Gloire* with an armored frigate, *Warrior,* laid down in May 1859. With its iron hull and displacement of 9,140 tons, this was a true iron (as opposed to ironclad) ship, with watertight components below, the first large seagoing iron-hulled warship. It could make 14 knots, compared with the *Gloire*'s 13, and carry 200 more tons of coal, thus having a greater range. Costing £377,000, the *Warrior* was a testimony to British manufacturing capability, which was a marked contrast to France where ironworking facilities were limited. Concern about France also led in 1859–1860 to a war scare that spurred the development of a large-scale Volunteer movement designed to protect the country against invasion.[26]

The shift to iron reflected not simply the vulnerability of wooden ships to shell fire, but also success in overcoming the problems that had delayed the use of iron, including its effect on magnetic compasses, the fact that iron hulls fouled very much worse than those that were copper bottomed, and the difficulties of securing sufficient consistency and quality in the iron. The ability to overcome these problems reflected the strength of the economy in the acquisition and application of relevant knowledge. Iron ships were structurally stronger and made redundant the wooden screw steamers built in large numbers in the 1850s. Britain's last wooden screw ship of the line entered service in 1861, and, having gained the lead in iron ships, the British retained it, ensuring a major advantage over the French.

There were also other advances in maritime technology. In the 1860s, high-pressure boilers were combined with the compound engine, improving the efficiency of steam power. Continuing strength in industrial capability and development in naval ordnance were shown with the development, in place of the early shell guns, of 7-inch Armstrong breech-loading rifled guns. In 1864, the modern self-propelled torpedo originated with the invention of a submerged self-propelled torpedo driven by compressed air and armed with an explosive charge at the head.

The practice of locating heavy guns in an armored casement began with the *Research* in 1864 and was followed in 1866 by the larger *Bellerophon,* a battleship protected by six inches of armor plating. In the absence of a major conflict, and with Queen Victoria (r. 1837–1901) still on the throne, it might seem difficult to point to a major turning point in military power, but the move away from a navy of smoothbore guns, wood, and sail broke with the pattern of centuries, and contributed to a more general sense of flux and novelty, if not uncertainty.

This shift also underlined the relationship between changing technology and international competition. Britain's dominance as a naval power had ensured an ambivalent response to new technology that might lead to its overthrow, for example submarines. Steam power, shell guns, and iron construction all appeared to offer opportunities to other powers and the last, in particular, was pushed hard by Napoleon III of France in a naval race with Britain in the late 1850s and 1860s. Combined with concern about his international ambitions, particularly in the Middle East and farther afield, this led to an upsurge in concern about defense. The development of French naval capacity led to major anxiety about the possibility of an invasion attempt. This encouraged an active buildup of the navy, as well as the construction of a new naval base at Portland. Fear of invasion also led to major defensive preparations in Britain, including the construction of impressive fortifications on the south coast designed, in particular, to protect naval bases, particularly Portsmouth, from attack: the fortifications were intended as part of an integrated defense system, the focus of which was naval power. There was also a major interest in volunteer home-defense forces, and this helped contribute to the growing acceptability and popularity of military service.

International developments, however, transformed the situation. Prussia's success against Denmark in 1864 and, even more, against Austria and its German allies in 1866, revolutionized the strategic situation in Europe and forced France to focus on the threat from a unified Germany. The defeat of France by the Germans in 1870–1871 accentuated an emphasis in French military expenditure on the army and fortifications. This underlined Britain's naval and imperial strength, as did the demobilization of much of the American navy in 1865 and the limited extent of American transoceanic imperialism prior to the 1880s. As yet, Germany, Italy, Japan, and the United States were not mounting a challenge in the naval or imperial category. There were still limits to British power. It would have been unwise to contest America's advance to the Pacific in the early nineteenth century or the German unification that had led, in 1866, to the annexation of Hanover (which was ruled by Victoria's first cousin); but the strength of other powers did not yet pose a serious challenge to British interests. There was concern about Russia's advance into Central Asia and the apparent threat it posed to the security of India, but the international situation appeared relatively benign and, with her rapidly growing economy, Britain could act as a major power without too great an impact on her public finances or society. This helped ensure that the navy in the 1870s displayed scant improvement in organization, technology, or doctrine,[27] while the army did not seek to emulate the capabilities displayed by the Prussians/Germans. The maneuvers held in 1871–1873 in response to the Franco-Prussian War were useful, but seen by critics as overly expensive, and were not repeated until 1898. The absence of a Chief of Staff or planning department made it difficult to shape change.

At the same time, the reputation of the military rose in part due to successes round the world and in part thanks to the sustained memorialization of victories in the Napoleonic War. More concretely, economic growth ensured that Britain was able to spend large sums on the military when its government chose. The Crimean War saw an abrupt shift from peacetime parsimony, with expenditure on the army and navy rising from £15.3 milllion in 1853 to £46.7 million in 1856. Much of this was met by higher taxation, though borrowing also rose. The ability to spend so much helped bring eventual success in the Crimean War, but from the late 1860s expenditure on the military as a percentage of central public expenditure declined. Britain was a great power on the cheap, a situation that was not to be sustainable.

CHAPTER 5

Growing Competition, 1871–1904

British military operations in this period were even more focused on the empire than in the years 1815–1871. There was no equivalent to the Crimean War with Russia of 1854–1856 and the conflicts with a "European" force were with the "Boers" of South Africa, settlers of Dutch descent (1881, 1899–1902). Like the Crimean War, these were hard struggles for Britain; but the Boer Wars should be located alongside other difficult wars for the empire, rather than being seen as a preparation for conflict with leading industrialized powers, which Britain had to face in 1914. If the empire set the prime task for the British military, it, however, did not preclude other concerns and, by the close of this period, they were increasingly shaping strategic tasking.

As with the previous period, tasking was very largely a matter of external commitments, except even more so. Domestically, Britain was largely peaceful and there was no mass activism threatening the state or its other agencies. The major growth of the police further lessened the need to rely on the army for domestic control, and this was important in the transition from popular antimilitarism to a more positive view of military service, soldiers, and officers, which can be linked to improvements in living conditions.[1] Although the army was still called out to aid the civil power, there was a lesser need for domestic-control tasks. This was true not only of England, but also of other parts of the British Isles. The opposition to the "clearances" by which workers without secure tenure were displaced from the land in "Highland Scotland" led to resistances in the 1880s, including the "Battle of the Braes" in Skye, but such disaffection could be handled very differently to the security issues in Scotland in 1689–1746. The police played the key role. The same was true of Ireland. Most Irish nationalism was nonviolent, and terrorist bodies, such as the Fenians and the Invincibles, were small scale.

The military itself was increasingly nonpartisan politically, with appointment and promotion owing little to shifts in national politics;

although patronage within the military was very important to promotion and field appointments, as with the "Ashanti Ring" (or "Wolseley Ring") of officers advanced by Sir Garnet Wolseley, who succeeded the hostile Cambridge as Commander-in-Chief in 1895, serving until 1900. This network competed with the protégés of Lord Roberts, the head of the Indian army, and Wolseley's successor. Wolseley loathed politicians and wanted a larger army, but British politics were such that his views were without important political consequences. Indeed, as Commander-in-Chief, Wolseley faced what he saw as greater government control, as administered through the civilians in the War Ministry. The linked concerns of finance and army size underlined the military's dependence on the politicians.[2] The navy was in a similar position. The key tensions there were within the service, rather than between the Admiralty and the politicians.

Around the world, this was a period of striking expansion, with major conflicts in Africa and South Asia. Repeated pressure was one of the characteristics of British power, and, having failed against the Asante of West Africa (modern Ghana) in 1864, the British mounted another expedition in 1873–1874. The Asante were outgunned by seven-pounder artillery, Gatling guns (an early machine gun), and breech-loading rifles, and defeated at Amoafu, the advancing British square firing repeatedly into the surrounding vegetation. The Gatling gun was taken to the Asante War, but not used in field operations. The Asante capital, Kumasi, was then seized and burned down. Ably commanded by Wolseley, who was described in 1874 by the Conservative leader Benjamin Disraeli as "our only soldier," the well-prepared British force also benefited from the assistance of African peoples, especially the Fante. The campaign was as much a battle against the elements as one against African foes. Rapid success helped ensure that the cost of the war to the British government was limited and this increased its acceptability to an administration very concerned about expenditure.

The British were less successful five years later in South Africa, when they attacked the strong kingdom of the Zulus, a powerful native state. However, a multicolumn advance failed because the columns were unable to offer mutual support, and the Zulus brought overwhelming force against one of the columns. At Isandlwana, on 22 January 1879, a 20,000-strong Zulu army defeated a British force of 1,800, of whom only 581 were regulars. The British had only two seven-pounder guns, and their camp was not entrenched, a key factor in the British defeat, as was the failure to concentrate British firepower and the Zulu advance in such a disciplined fashion. The Zulus enveloped the British flanks, but, thanks to the British Martini-Henry rifles, Zulu casualties were very high.[3] The Zulus, who did not want rifles, referred to the British as cowards because they would not fight hand-to-hand. The British were also defeated at Intombi Drift and Hlobane. However, the British went on to defeat the

Zulus at Gingindlovu, Khambula, and, decisively, Ulundi (4 July) in 1879. At each, heavy defensive infantry fire from prepared positions, supported by artillery, stopped Zulu attacks before they could reach the British lines, and British cavalry then inflicted heavy losses as the Zulus retreated. At Gingindlovu and Ulundi, Gatling guns were used on the four corners of a square defensive arrangement. The first combat use of the Gatling gun was at the Battle of Nyezane River (22 January 1879).[4]

The British also encountered difficulties in Afghanistan, which they invaded in the Second Afghan War (1878–1880), in an effort to block Russian influence. Prefiguring the situation in much warfare in the later stages of the empire, the British found it easier to advance and hold positions than to end resistance, let alone stabilize the situation. In 1878, a force advanced on Kabul and defeated the Afghans at Peiwar Kotal. The following May, the Afghans accepted British control over the frontier passes and dominance over Afghan foreign policy; but, in September 1879, the newly installed British Resident and his staff were killed and a fresh advance proved necessary. The British were victorious at Charasia Ridge and entered Kabul, but it was difficult to win a lasting success, not least because of the fractured nature of Afghan politics, which made it hard to find an effective central authority with whom to make peace. The British position outside Kabul was soon embattled, although the defense during the siege was well-handled and the relief was a great success. However, at Maiwand (27 July 1880), an 11,000-strong Afghan force under Ayub Khan, armed with British Enfield rifles and with 30 well-handled cannon, including three rifled 14-pounder Armstrong guns, defeated a 2,500-strong British brigade, killing 962: the British artillery was outgunned and part of the infantry gave way after five hours, leading to a harrowing defeat. The British garrison at Kandahar was then invested. The flavor of difficult imperial conflict can be captured in the correspondence of the Reverend Alfred Cane. Of a sortie against the village of Deh Khoja, he noted,

> we began by shelling the place. There was no reply so 800 of our infantry advanced to the attack when at once a galling fire was opened on them from loop holes round the village. Our men rushed on and entered the village on the south side but only to find it filled with armed men firing from the windows, doors and roofs. It was a hopeless task...had to return in hot haste under the same heavy fire.[5]

It proved necessary to send a relief expedition, and this was successfully accomplished by Sir Frederick Roberts. His crushing of Ayub Khan outside Kandahar proved the last major action of the war. Nevertheless, the political and logistical problems of operating in Afghanistan challenged the efficacy of the forward policy which the government of India had been pursuing, and encouraged the British to draw back and, instead, seek to stabilize their position on the "North-West Frontier" of British India, which meant, in modern terms, on the Pakistani side of the Afghan-Pakistan border. Ironically, in 2006, British forces were again deployed near Kandahar.

Egypt proved less problematic militarily than Afghanistan, but it was to lead Britain into serious difficulties in Sudan. Protecting British interests in Egypt in 1882 led to a bombardment of Alexandria on 11 July followed by an invasion in which the largest force sent from Britain between the Crimean and Second Boer wars secured a rapid victory. The Egyptian army was routed by Wolseley at Tel-el-Kebir on 13 September.[6] After a night march, the British attacked the Egyptian earthworks at dawn without any preliminary bombardment. Wolseley preferred to try to gain the advantage of surprise, and his infantry attacked using their bayonets. Gaining the initiative was worthwhile, because Wolseley retained control of his maneuverable force, while in combat they displayed cohesion, discipline, and high morale. As a sequel to the battle, a rapid cavalry advance seized Cairo and a quasi-protectorate over Egypt was established. The contrast with failure in 1807 was striking, and, more generally, reflected a rise in British capability in conflict outside Europe.

However, Muhammad Ahmad-Mahdi's Islamic revivalist rising in Sudan destroyed Egyptian control there. A British attempt to relieve the garrison under Major-General Charles Gordon at Sudan's capital, Khartoum, failed in 1885, with Gordon being killed on 26 January in what was presented as a totemic moment of British manliness and heroism.[7] He died two days before the arrival of the relief force which had battled its way forward. Conflict continued, culminating in a large-scale British intervention in Sudan from 1896. At Atbara, on 8 April 1898, advancing British troops outgunned the Mahdists, who had no artillery, and successfully stormed their camp. The Anglo-Egyptian forces under Major-General Horatio Kitchener lost 81 killed and 487 wounded, and their opponents 3,000 and 4,000, respectively. The Mahdists, under the Mahdi's successor, the Khalifa Abdullahi, relied on a strategy and tactics that played to the British advantage, not least by permitting force concentration and the use of firepower. Instead of employing the potential of the Sudan's vast extent for defense, by threatening the communications of the British forces or making them advance farther into the interior, the Mahdists engaged in a large-scale battle to defend the capital. At Omdurman, the decisive battle, on 2 September 1898, British rifle, machine guns, and artillery fire, including from high-angle howitzers, devastated the Sudanese attackers, Winston Churchill, who took part in the battle, writing, "It was a mere matter of machinery." Including on his river gunboats, Kitchener had 80 pieces of artillery and 44 Maxim guns. The British infantry had Lee-Metford smokeless magazine rifles. Having defeated the Sudanese attack, Kitchener's men then advanced. In the second stage of the battle, the Sudanese showed more resilience than had been anticipated, but they were outfought. The Anglo-Egyptian forces lost 49 killed and 382 wounded, and their opponents about 11,000 and 16,000, respectively. Abdullahi was subsequently defeated and killed by a British cavalry force at Umm Diwaykarat in November 1899, and British authority became the key element in Sudan, although the sultanate of Darfur was not brought under control until World War One.

Elsewhere in Africa, there was major expansion in West Africa, where the British occupied the interior of the Gambia in 1887–1888; campaigned successfully against the Asante in 1895–1896, and annexed Asante in 1901 after a rebellion had been crushed; captured Benin; defeated the Yorubas in Nigeria; and established the Protectorates of northern and southern Nigeria in 1900. In southern Africa, the British overran what they renamed Rhodesia, and suppressed a rebellion by the Ndebele and Shona in 1896. Soldiers were exposed to a variety of difficult environments, and by 1902 their collective experience covered much of Africa.[8] By 1900, the British had an empire covering a fifth of the world's land surface and including 400 million people.

Expansion reflected a range of factors. An ability to win local support was a key element, and one that is underrated in the nationalist historiographies of the modern world. The support included the alliance of local rulers, as in India, Malaya, and Nigeria, as well as the backing of some regional potentates in the invasion of Abyssinia in 1868. The ability to recruit large numbers of indigenous mercenary soldiers was also crucial, although their role varied. About half of the force that attacked the Zulus in 1879 were Africans in the Natal Native Contingent. The officers were White colonists. The African horsemen were especially useful. However, the role of the Natal Native Contingent was fundamentally one of supplying labor: only one rifle was issued to every tenth man, and he was only given ten cartridges.[9] In contrast, at Omdurman, the Sudanese brigade in Kitchener's force played a crucial role, in Nigeria the British benefited from the West African Frontier Force they established, and, when they successfully invaded Hunza on the North-West Frontier in 1891, it was with 1,000 Gurkha and Kashmiri troops under 16 British officers. Ten years later, when an expeditionary force was sent into the interior of British Somaliland in order to confront the rising by Sayyid Muhammad 'Abdille Hassan, who in 1899 had declared holy war on Christians, it consisted of 1,500 Somali troops and 21 British officers. Indian troops were also important in British operations in Somaliland. More generally, the ability to win native support was in part a product of local rivalries, which greatly helped the British in many cases. In addition, they came to the task of fighting in Africa with considerable experience, particularly in South Asia, of treating with non-Western peoples and of fighting outside Europe. This experience encompassed the recruitment, training, and use of local levies and allied forces, the development of logistical capability, and coastal operations using coastal and river vessels.

These factors took precedence over new technology, though it would be wrong to ignore the role of the latter, and not only in combat. The poet Hilaire Belloc observed, "Whatever happens we have got/The Maxim Gun; and they have not" (*The Modern Traveller*, 1898). Indeed the Maxim (machine) gun, introduced in 1883, was important, although, across much of Africa, the breech-loading rifle was more valuable, because it was more suited for the dispersed fighting that was characteristic of much conflict. The Martini-Henry, a single-shot breech-loader, was replaced by the Lee-Metford, a more effective magazine rifle. Artillery was also significant, although, in the mountainous terrain of the North-West Frontier it was difficult to move and use effectively. As was characteristic of military activity, however, there was a process of challenge and response, and a practical engineered solution was devised: mobile screw guns were found best. Light and carried in sections, they could be screwed together for firing. Artillery was a key force multiplier in attacking positions: the walls of Kano in Nigeria were breached within an hour in 1903.

Military interest in the nature of colonial warfare rose. Colonel Callwell's *Small Wars: Their Principles and Practice*, published in 1896, appeared in its third edition in 1906, and there was also extensive and sympathetic popular accounts, such as John Frederick Maurice's *A Popular History of the Ashanti Campaign* (1874). Maurice, who had been Wolseley's private secretary during the Asante campaign, went on to be a professor at the Staff College. Newspapers spent heavily on telegraphy to receive reports of conflicts, such as the Zulu War of 1879.

Technology was also important in the more general projection of power. Steamships, railways, and telegraph lines combined to provide mobility and enhanced control and command, with improved logistics a vital product. Steamships permitted the movement of military resources, making it possible to respond to crises and thus to hold the empire with a relatively modest number of troops. The distribution of forces, in particular colonies, thus reflected the chronology of concern, as in New Zealand where it rose in 1864–1865. Railways were used in deploying troops and supplies toward areas of operation as in Sudan in the 1890s (the 383-mile-long Sudan Military Railway was built across the bend of the Nile), or on the North-West Frontier when moving troops against the Waziris in 1897. The rising by the Métis (mixed-blood population) of Manitoba in 1885 was followed by the dispatch of over 4,000 militia along the Canadian Pacific Railway; which was rewarded by the renewed government subsidy that permitted the completion of the railway. The militia suppressed the rising.[10] Road construction could also be important as in New Zealand in the 1860s, when troops were used to extend the Great South Road from Auckland over the hills south of Drury in the face of

Maori opposition. By 1874, a road had been finished between Tauranga and Napier separating two areas of Maori dissidence. The telegraph was used to issue instructions for troop movements, for example the dispatch of troops from India to Abyssinia in 1868 and from Sri Lanka to Natal during the Zulu War. Furthermore, the construction of an infrastructure of sanitation, offering pure water, effective sewage systems, and sanatoria, greatly increased the survival rates of troops, and thus the viability of a sustained military presence in the colonies.

Politics and technology did not mean, however, that there was no conflict, much of it brutal and devastating. This was captured in the letters and diaries of Donald Alexander MacAlister, who served as a transport officer with the field force sent against the Aros of southeastern Nigeria in 1901–1902, one of the many colonial campaigns that are now largely forgotten,

> We have to trek through the jungle in single file. In order to prevent flank attacks, flankers are sent out who cut paths through the jungle parallel… We are 1,500 men against 80,000. However the blacks do not combine so that all the column do is to attack village after village (22 November 1901).
>
> The burning of the town was very exciting and Stewart and myself were the first to apply matches but we had to go through to see if the road was freed of enemy. Our carriers and bushmen have cleared the bush all round and everywhere trees are being felled and the ruins of the huts pulled down …We had the Maxim pouring into the bush this morning. There must be a great deal of dead…As I write the millemeter gun pouring case shot into the bush. It is a glorious day (25 December 1901).
>
> The Colonel has given us all a little lecture on biffing natives. He said we must *not* biff them. A case was brought to his notice where Fox…had so mashed one man that his eye had to be removed and other things. I am glad to say I have not found it necessary to do much biffing but a native sergeant who was very impudent on the matter of keeping silence the other evening when I told him to stop his clatter got a hard one in the ribs and laid himself up for 2 days…This morning I went on a small punitive column. The enemy who had surrendered refused to make roads. We marched on Okerojee farm and took all livestock and captured everybody and looted the place. One of the enemy killed. (2/4 January 1902).
>
> The size of Iboum is much reduced. It is now a small fortified place with everything outside the walls leveled to the ground…The natives have been crowding in with guns of all kinds and some of these guns are very fine specimens of Sneider. The bulk of those brought in lately could if properly handled have done us a good deal of damage. They have all been broken up and burned. (12 January 1902).
>
> If a native breaks our laws his house is burnt down—very simple. (2 February 1902).[11]

Atrocities had also been committed in Zululand and Sudan. This was the cutting edge of the emphasis on control that became more prevalent in British (and non-British) imperialism. In contrast to earlier periods of expansion in Asia and Africa, sovereignty became more crucial than informal influence. In part, this was because the profit motive was subordinated to geopolitics. In what the *Times* termed in 1884 the "Scramble for Africa," much British expansion from 1880, as earlier, arose directly from the response to the real or apparent plans of other Western powers, although, in the case of the response to Russian expansionism, this had been a key element in British policy in South Asia from the 1830s. The search for sources of raw materials and for markets for British goods was also important.

Instead of open conflict with other Western powers, Britain tried to preempt her rivals by grabbing territory. The doctrine of "effective occupation," developed at the Berlin Congress of colonial powers in 1884–1885, encouraged a speeding up of the process of annexation. Concern about French ambitions led to the British capture of Mandalay in 1885 and the annexation of Upper Burma the following year, although much of it was only brought under limited control and a serious popular insurrection across Burma lasted several years and required harsh measures to create a semblance of order. Similarly, French and German expansion in Africa led Britain to take countermeasures, although economic factors also played a role. Expansion into Somaliland and Sudan was in part a response to concern about French schemes, which, in the Fashoda Crisis of 1898, nearly led to war over Sudan; while German moves in East Africa led the British into Uganda in the 1890s. In turn, such activity led to pressure for fresh initiatives, a memorandum of 1904 on the situation in Somaliland, where the British were at war with Mullah Sayyid Muhammad, noting "in so much as passive defence, unless combined with active offence, is a costly policy, rarely leading to decisive issues, active operations outside the active sphere of the Protectorate were deemed essential to ultimate success."[12] The guerrilla tactics of the Dervishes indeed proved a major problem but, by the end of 1904, large-scale and expensive British offensives had hit their strength and morale and, in 1905, the Dervishes agreed to a peace that lasted until 1908.

Widespread public commitment to the cause of the empire led to a growing sense of imperialist military mission. This aspect of muscular patriotism and, indeed, Christianity, contributed greatly to the improved public image of the army in late-nineteenth-century Britain. For long, this image had been well below that of the navy, but positive views of the role of the army became more pronounced. They were reflected in the press, in paintings, and in the cult of heroism associated in particular with the Victoria Cross (VC), an order for conspicuous gallantry instituted in 1856. The heroes were much honored, not least in June 1857 when Queen Victoria made awards to 62 individuals in a ceremony in Hyde Park.[13]

The actions of VCs were much reported in the press, and the extent to which the order was granted to heroes of all ranks attracted particular attention.

Expansionist imperialism led, however, to a serious challenge to the army during the Second Boer War of 1899–1902, and this resulted in grave political and public concern about military preparedness and, indeed, competence. Although the strains of the conflict and its impact on Britain's military reputation were to be far less than those of World War One (1914–1918), the latter was yet to occur, while the problems and faults of the world war were, unlike the Boer War, shared by other states. The British had already experienced the skill of defensive Boer firepower at the Battle of Majuba Hill in the First Boer War (27 February 1881), which had led them to acknowledge Boer independence. An officer present at the battle recorded the problems caused by "bullets from an enemy we could not see" and, as a result, that "the Boer fire so completely dominated ours": 267 of the 555 strong British force, including the commander, Sir George Colley, were casualties.[14]

The second war proved more difficult than had been anticipated because the Boers took the initiative. Their effective use of the strategic offensive was combined with the successful employment of a tactical defensive in which they made good use of their smokeless, long-range Mauser magazine rifles and their superior marksmanship. This led to heavy casualties for the British, whose fighting methods proved inadequate. For example, artillery was still sited in the open, as it was thought that this was the best way to get range. Such a deployment, however, ignored the vastly improved rifles available to the Boer infantry, and the gunners were shot down. Furthermore, the Boer use of trenches, as at Magersfontein, limited the impact of artillery. Limitations in officer training were also revealed by the fighting. In December 1899, the British were defeated at Stormberg, Magersfontein, and Colenso (9–15 December, "Black Week"), and their positions at Kimberley, Ladysmith, and Mafeking were besieged. British generalship proved deficient, a failing blamed on Wolseley, who was held responsible for failing to prepare the army, and forced into retirement as Commander-in-Chief. In practice, the politicians bore part of the responsibility, not least for underestimating the Boer challenge and not planning for war (or funding preparations) accordingly.[15] These sieges, however, led to a loss of Boer momentum that threw away the initiative gained by beginning the conflict, although, in January 1900, the British were also defeated at Spion Kop.

Boer firepower forced a rethink in tactics, prefiguring the process that was to occur during World War One. In 1900–1902, the British developed an appropriate use of cover, creeping barrages of continuous artillery fire, and infantry advances in rushes, coordinated with the artillery, although there was much tension over tactics. Colin Ballard of the 9th Foot, preferred charging the Boers to firing "at them at 5000 yards range...hard riding is now the game and is worth more than all the shooting and manoeuvring we have learnt at Aldershot."[16] More effective generalship, under Lord Roberts and his Chief of Staff, and later successor, Horatio Kitchener, also changed the situation in 1900. The British were able to seize and maintain the initiative, while the Boer field army proved less effective than their commandos. Indeed, their army under Piet Cronje was trapped and forced to surrender at Paardenberg on 27 February 1900. Roberts pushed on to capture the major towns, Bloemfontein (13 March), Johannesburg (31 May), and Pretoria (5 June), and to overrun Transvaal.

British victories contributed to the crucial political dimension, by hitting Boer morale and exacerbating their divisions: aside from tensions between Transvaal and Orange Free State, there were political, social, and religious rifts. The political dimension was more significant than is usually allowed for. It was also seen in Britain. There, the high costs of the war, including not only unexpected defeats but also a fiscal crisis that led to a major rise in income tax as well as government borrowing, badly hit national confidence. However, Roberts' successes in 1900 contributed to an upsurge in patriotic sentiment and helped the government in the "khaki election" held that October. The opposition Liberals were publicly divided over the merits of the war and only 184 were elected to Parliament, while no fewer than 163 government supporters were elected unopposed. Conservative victory ensured that the war would be pursued.

Wider strategic issues were also important in the course of the war. Not engaged in any other major struggles, the British were able to focus military and financial resources on the conflict, which was a testimony to the strength of the imperial and economic systems. Britain's empire and dominions, particularly Australia, Canada, Cape Colony, and New Zealand, also sent troops, looking toward their key contributions they were to make as Britain's allies in the two world wars. The use of these troops built on their role in local operations in recent decades. For example, in New Zealand, the conflict with the Maori Te Kooti in 1868–1872 was waged by local colonial and loyal Maori forces as only one British regiment had been left in New Zealand. More generally, the Armed Constabulary played a key role in overawing Maori dissidence. The sense that they had earned full membership in the empire through blood sacrifice arose from the Boer War and was strengthened by World War One. In the Boer War, the colonial commanders were given considerable independence. However, due to the dispatch of much of the regular army, as well as reservists, yeomanry regiments and volunteer service companies, from Britain, the army was left below normal strength in the British Isles.

This gave rise to a sense of manpower crisis, and to pressure for the introduction of conscription, which fed through into postwar interest in military reform. The decision to allow auxiliary forces—militia, yeomanry, and volunteers—to serve abroad yielded over 100,000 men for service in South Africa but also reflected the seriousness of the situation as well as the strength of popular patriotism.[17]

Unchallenged control of the South African ports also allowed Britain to bring its strength to bear, while the railways that ran inland from the ports facilitated the deployment of military resources, although it also proved necessary to use wagon trains. The navy also ensured that foreign intervention was not possible, not least by blockading Delagoa Bay to prevent supplies from reaching Transvaal via the neutral Portuguese colony of Mozambique.

Once Transvaal had been overrun, Boer forces concentrated on dispersed operations in which their mounted infantry exploited their mobility and knowledge of the terrain to challenge British control. In response, the now vastly more numerous British adopted counterinsurgency practices that were also to be used in the 1950s against Communist insurrection in Malaya. They relied on composite columns and on an extensive system of fortifications: a blockhouse system of barbed-wire fences and small positions. Furthermore, the British employed scorched earth policies and reprisals, Malcolm Riall recording in April 1901, "H Company go off to burn and destroy a farm close by as a carabinier has been shot by a Boer sniping from there."[18] To deprive the guerrillas of civilian support, the British ravaged their farms and moved their families into detention camps. A total of 27,927 Boer civilians died there from disease, and the camps were criticized in Britain, but they were less emotive an issue than was subsequently suggested by the misleading comparison with Nazi Germany implied by the use of the term concentration camps to describe the policies of both. A final and decisive drive against the Boers in Western Transvaal in April 1902 led them to capitulate by the Treaty of Vereeniging.[19] The subsequent political settlement led to a South Africa in which the Boers played a key role within a white ascendancy that thwarted black aspirations. Although reconciliation between Britain and the Boers was limited, it was sufficient to enable most Boers (or Afrikaners) to support Britain in both world wars, and this was a key military resource for the British in Africa. An anti-British Boer rising soon after World War One began in 1914 was swiftly suppressed.

The years immediately after the Second Boer War saw both the continuation of earlier military trends and new developments. Imperial power was manifested on and beyond frontiers, as well as within territories over which power was claimed. In 1903, the army of the Emirate of Sokoto was smashed at Burmi in Nigeria, with vastly disproportionate casualties. The

Caliph and his two sons were killed and resistance in northern Nigeria came to an end. The following year, a force advanced from India to Lhasa, the capital of Tibet, in order to thwart alleged Russian influence and dictate terms. En route, at Guru, it opened fire on Tibetans who were unwilling to disarm, and, in large part owing to their two Maxim guns, four cannon, and effective rifles, the British killed nearly 700 Tibetans without any losses of their own. Lhasa was occupied, but with winter coming, it was necessary to accept treaty terms that were not as good as the British government had hoped. In Kenya, in 1905, the field force sent to suppress resistance among the nomadic Nandi used its ten Maxims to cause heavy casualties. In a subsequent expedition, 407 Embu were killed, but only two among the field force.

As the British crossed the Himalayas on the way to Lhasa, however, ministers and commentators were having to consider a threat nearer home: Germany. German unification in 1866–1871 had produced an assertive state that was increasingly regarded as a challenge. Alongside worries about her intentions in Europe, came concern about German naval expansion, which was clearly aimed at Britain, and her colonial ambitions, particularly in Africa but also in the Pacific. Worry about Germany had a profound impact on British foreign policy and military plans. Britain moved from a position of "splendid isolation," or nonintervention in Continental European quarrels, into one of alliance commitments designed to strengthen her relative position. Alliance in 1902 with Japan, whose navy was developed with British advice, was followed by an *entente* with France in 1904. This was an understanding, not an alliance, but it was increasingly to affect foreign policy and military planning. In addition, concern about German intentions was to lead to a naval race in which Britain built a new class of battleship, the *Dreadnought,* the first of which was launched in 1906. This was a key aspect of the engagement with the potential offered by technological advance in order to maintain competitive edge. Britain won the naval race, but it put serious pressure on public finances.[20]

Furthermore, a series of conflicts, not just the Second Boer War, but also the Spanish-American (1898) and Russo-Japanese (1904–1905) wars, led to concern about the appropriateness of the British army for possible warfare with other Western powers. It was fortunate for Britain, in this more troubling situation, that relations with the United States were acceptable. The United States had become a more active imperialist power from the 1880s and built a major navy, but Britain managed her disputes with the United States in the Pacific, North America, and South America skillfully. American hegemony in the Western Hemisphere was accepted, in part by being more conciliatory over the Canadian frontier than the Canadians would have preferred. American expansion in the Pacific was also accepted, even if, as with the gain of Hawaii, it led to the overthrow of British interests. In turn, the Americans did not seek to overthrow the British Empire. In 1908, the Committee of Imperial Defence and the Foreign Office concluded that the possibility of war with the United States was remote. This was just as well, as by then, concern about Germany had become more acute.

Part III: Imperial Partner, 1904–

CHAPTER 6

Serious Pressures, 1904–1933

The military history of this period is understandably dominated by the traumatic experience of World War One (1914–1918). Aside from the war itself, there is an understandable tendency to treat the preceding years in terms of preparation and the subsequent period in terms of learning lessons. This is understandable, but it risks detracting from other narratives that repay continued attention, even if their relative attention is shadowed by the world war. Two narratives in particular deserve attention, the political role of the military, and its importance in imperial control.

In contrast to the situation in most European states, the military was only a factor in politics in defense of legal authority and in support of government. This was the situation in 1910–1911, when the army was willing to act against strikers. In 1910, sabotage by striking miners in South Wales led to the deployment of troops to enforce order (although the Home Secretary, Winston Churchill, was criticized for holding the troops back and allowing the rioters to destroy property), while, in 1911, a general rail strike led to the same, and two strikers were killed in Liverpool. In response to large-scale strikes in Glasgow in 1919, 12,000 troops were deployed, as were tanks. In 1921, strikes led the General Staff to think of bringing in troops from foreign postings and to consider calling out reservists.[1] Furthermore, there were extensive troop movements at the time of the General Strike of 1926, although no use of force. More generally, it is possible to present a benign account of the role of the military, and to note its noninterference in civilian politics even in periods of real, or apparent, political and economic crisis, such as 1910–1911, 1926, and 1931.

A less positive interpretation, however, could also be advanced. First, there were episodes in which control by the government was challenged. Potentially the most serious occurred in March 1914. In the "Curragh Mutiny," Brigadier-General Hubert Gough and 59 other officers of the 3rd Cavalry Regiment stationed near Kildare at the Curragh Barracks resigned their commissions rather than impose Home Rule in Ireland. This was the policy backed by most Catholic Irish nationalists and one, crucially, supported by the Liberal government of Britain, which was dependent in Parliament on the support of these nationalists. No orders had yet been given, so there was no "mutiny," and the crisis was defused when the War Office promised that they would not be ordered to do so and refused to accept the resignations. However, there was no Cabinet authorization for this assurance given by the Secretary of War and the Chief of the Imperial General Staff, and they were both obliged to resign, while the Prime Minister, Herbert Asquith, repudiated the assurance. The crisis was a serious one as many Ulster Protestants, encouraged by the opposition in Britain, were preparing to resist Home Rule by force. The outbreak of World War One shifted attention from Ireland, and Home Rule was shelved, but, had that not been the case, the Curragh Mutiny suggested that the government would have encountered problems in using the army to impose an unwelcome solution on Ulster. This might well have divided and politicized the armed forces, and, at the least, the episode suggested the conditionality of military obedience.

Disaffection of a very different kind was pronounced in 1919, as widespread anger within the military about delays in demobilization after World War One combined with left-wing opposition to intervention in the Russian Civil War. This led to governmental anxiety about the military, and concern within the latter concerning the impact of political developments and agitation. The abandonment of the intervention, combined with demobilization and the end of conscription in 1919, eased tensions, but military loyalty remained a sensitive issue. In 1924, there was a serious political controversy when John Campbell, editor of the *British Worker*, published a piece pressing soldiers never to shoot at strikers. The Labour government's hesitation about prosecution led to a vote of no confidence in the House of Commons. In September 1931, pay cuts imposed by the National Government led to the Invergordon Mutiny, in which sailors of fifteen warships of the Atlantic fleet based at Invergordon, refused to go on duty. The Admiralty's willingness to revise the cuts ended the crisis in the fleet, but the episode helped cause a run on sterling in the foreign exchange markets, and the currency had to come off the Gold Standard.

Aside from these detailed episodes, it can be suggested that the social structure and "politics" of the military, and its general assumptions, had detrimental consequences in both war and peace. For example, many of the generals of World War One, such as Field Marshal Haig, Commander-in-Chief in France from 1915, had a conviction of the value of the attack that in part arose from their social and cultural attitudes; although there were also important political and strategic reasons for such a focus. Similarly, the Admiralty's unwillingness to adopt A.J. Pollen's advanced gunnery system in the 1910s has been attributed to political and religious dislike for Pollen, as well as a more general distaste for the technical values presented by Pollen's automated system with its use of analog computers. This challenged the role of gunnery officers and the nature of service cohesion and identity. These and other issues may not appear to have much of a role in a history of this type, but they serve as a reminder that a conflict-based account of military history can detract not only from an understanding of the wider roles of the military but also from an appreciation of its assumptions and development. Crucially, in contrast to many states, including monarchies such as China, Portugal, and Turkey, the military was not an agency for political transformation and enforced modernization. Instead, the officer corps saw itself as a force for stability, and this view was not seriously challenged either from within this corps or from the ranks. A report of 1938 was more generally true of much of the military, "The cavalry regiments...attract officers from families which in the past have preserved the feudal conception that the holding of estates carries with it a liability for defence of the kingdom."[2]

One important aspect of the military was the commitment to imperialism. This was not only a matter of the major role of the Indian Army in British power, and the careers of individual commanders and particular regiments, but also a more general cultural commitment in the sense of the nature of army life and the place of the military. The concern about Germany that culminated in World War One might appear to represent an end to this set of assumptions, but the degree to which they reemerged in the 1920s and 1930s is striking. In part this was because the war led the empire to reach its widest extent, creating new commitments that had to be defended. It was also the case that some prewar problems continued, for example in Somaliland, while the war itself led to extensive campaigning outside Europe, in both Africa and the Middle East.

Clashing commitments acted on a changing military. The Second Boer War had suggested that much needed improvement. In part this was not directly a matter of military arrangements, for concern about the health of army (and police) recruits helped inspire a drive for social reform designed to strengthen the people. This was very much within a context of international competition, and reflected a wide understanding of defense issues that needs to be retained in any military history. There was also anxiety about the effectiveness of military arrangements, not least because the British tradition of volunteer service ensured that military thinkers faced the dilemma of how to fight a future mass-army war. The Second Boer War had been followed by a rush of comments and proposals, but it proved difficult to produce coherent and acceptable policies.

From 1904, however, the situation improved. Mindful of German developments, which then enjoyed considerable prestige, the Esher Committee of 1904 recommended the foundation of a General Staff. In 1905, Richard Haldane became Secretary of State for War, a post he held until 1912.

The policy level had already been enhanced with the establishment of the Committee of Imperial Defence in 1902, a development in some respects anticipated by the Hartington commission of 1890. Command and planning structures were strengthened under Haldane with the institutionalization of a General Staff and the creation of the post of Chief of the General Staff (rapidly changed to Chief of the Imperial General Staff). The General Staff was designed to ensure a trained body of senior officers across the army, and this led to staff tours and conferences, but much of the officer corps was unsympathetic, not least when assumptions about criteria for promotion were challenged. The effectiveness of the system was less than that of its German counterpart, but the contrast between the Second Boer War and the deployment and operations of the British Expeditionary Force (BEF) in Belgium and France in 1914 suggested a marked rise in efficiency.

Haldane was also very concerned about numbers, not least in response to the possibility of war with Germany and it was also necessary to maintain imperial garrisons. Conscription was regarded as at odds with the country's liberal traditions, and was not seen as viable, but Haldane was responsible for the peacetime organization of what could be a wartime BEF. In support of this, Haldane sought to modernize the second-tier forces represented by the militia and Volunteers. They were reorganized, the militia becoming a Special Reserve designed to provide drafts for the regular army, while the Volunteers and Yeomanry became a Territorial Force, the basis of what, in 1921, became the Territorial Army. Although there was an option of volunteering to serve abroad once mobilized, this force was essentially a home defense force designed to free the regulars for service abroad. As part of the Territorial Force, Haldane, in 1909, established the Voluntary Aid Detachment, a nursing body that was the first time that women were given peacetime military organization. The development of reserve forces rested in part on a sense of international competition but also on a more general feeling that manliness was best developed and shown through military training. This was linked to a very positive image of the military.[3] There were also organizational reforms in the Dominions, for example in New Zealand in 1909–1911.

Organizational reforms were accompanied by changes in doctrine and tactics, although, not without controversy. Ian Hamilton, the Inspector General of Overseas Forces, felt that the cavalry training regulations of 1907 had ignored the lessons of the Boer War and led to a misplaced confidence in shock tactics and in charging infantry and artillery, a practice derided by the playwright George Bernard Shaw in his *Arms and the Man* (1894). He suggested to the Royal Commission on the War in South Africa the value of equipping soldiers with entrenching tools, and also proposed wheeled shields for the infantry. Hamilton had been criticized by the War Office when his reports from the Russo-Japanese War, where he headed an observer mission, disparaged the role of cavalry. In practice, the cavalry regulations emphasized the value of tactical versatility, not least dismounted tactics and the use of the rifle.[4] More generally, there was also considerable interest in improved weaponry. The Vickers-Maxim machine gun, adopted by the army in 1912, fired 250 rounds per minute. A new service rifle, the Lee-Enfield, was adopted for all ranks.

At sea, there were major developments in surface sea power, as well as a fundamental advance in submarines. The first focused on *Dreadnought*, a battleship launched in 1906 that was to be the first of a new class of all-big-gun battleships, its guns able to fire two rounds per minute, and the first capital ship in the world to be powered by the marine turbine engine. Completed in fourteen months, her construction reflected the industrial and organizational efficiency of British shipbuilding. *Dreadnought* was faster and more heavily gunned than any other battleship then sailing, and made earlier arithmetics of relative naval power redundant. This encouraged the Germans to respond with the construction of powerful battleships, launching a naval race with Britain. By the outbreak of the war, Britain had 21 dreadnoughts in service compared to the Germans' 14. Furthermore, 12 and 5, respectively, were under construction in a naval race that Britain had won. The British also had the largest number of submarines (89) then, despite having only launched their first one in 1901. However, many of these submarines were of limited value, in part because they were designed for harbor defense. More seriously, insufficient thought was given to the defense of warships and merchantmen against submarines. In organizational terms, however, the Admiralty made major advances in the collection and processing of information, so as to be able to provide coherent central control of naval resources.[5]

Change was also coming from another direction. Manned heavier-than-air flight led the press baron, Lord Northcliffe, to remark, "England is no longer an island." Flight had had an earlier role in warfare with balloons, but its capability was now transformed. In 1909, Louis Blériot made the first airplane flight across the English Channel. That year, and in 1913, there was grave concern about the possibilities of an air attack and the bombing of defenseless strategic targets and cities. In 1911, Britain established an air battalion, and in 1912 the Royal Flying Corps.[6] By 1914, Britain had 113 military airplanes, although Russia, Germany, and France each had more. The focus was on airplanes as a means of reconnaissance and artillery spotting. Indeed in 1909, when the Chief of the Imperial General Staff sought views on the likely effectiveness of airships (hydrogen-filled balloons powered by a motor) and planes, he met with a skeptical response from Hamilton, who was unimpressed about the possibilities of bombing, "The difficulty of carrying sufficient explosive, and of making a good shot, will probably result in a greater moral than material effect."[7]

Meanwhile, military planning shifted direction. The First Moroccan Crisis (1905–1906), provoked by Germany, increased concerns about German intentions. From 1906, the service attachés in Berlin were united in agreeing that the German armed forces were preparing for attack, although there was a lack of agreement over the danger to Britain. 1913–1915 was seen as the likeliest period for this aggression. The intelligence reports were widely distributed throughout government and the armed forces, contributing to a coordination of foreign and defense policies.[8] The Moroccan Crisis was followed by Anglo-French staff talks aimed at dealing with a German threat, and their consequences were to play a major role in leading Britain toward World War One. In 1907, military maneuvers were conducted for the first time on the basis that Germany, not France, was the enemy, while, that year, fears of Germany also contributed to an *entente* with France's ally Russia. Thus, in its focus on Europe, Britain moved close to a power with which it had competed for hegemony in South Asia for decades. Henry Wilson, the Director of Military Operations from 1910–1914 and a strong francophile, produced the plans that enabled the BEF to deploy to France speedily when Britain and Germany went to war in 1914.

Britain was a long-standing guarantor of the neutrality of Belgium, but, largely heedless of the British response, and determined to strike at France across a broad front, Germany invaded Belgium uniting most of the British government behind war. This conflict was to be terrible for Britain. It was widely, but erroneously, assumed that the conflict would be short. Furthermore, World War One was crucially different from Britain's experience of conflict since the Napoleonic Wars because of its seemingly intractable character, the threat to the British home base, the possibility that Britain might lose, with very serious consequences, and the massive quantity of manpower and resources that the war required and destroyed, and if each of these echoed the experience of the Napoleonic War, that was an experience outside that of those alive in 1914. Furthermore, Britain took a greater role in the land conflict in World War One than it had done in the Napoleonic Wars.

The confidence of the war's outbreak was followed, after the failure of the combatants in the First Battle of Ypres to win on the remaining open flank in Flanders,[9] in October–November 1914, by the emergence of stalemate. The troops were not going to be "home by Christmas." Furthermore, vast numbers were to be required, a demand that put a considerable strain on British and imperial society, as well as on military institutions and practices. The BEF, known as the "Old Contemptibles," was largely destroyed in the initial campaign, and was replaced by the creation of the New Army. Far greater in size, this force enabled Britain to fight on many fronts, but it posed major challenges for training, command, and supply. Between August 1914 and December 1915, 2.5 million men volunteered, but the demands of war proved inexorable and, despite considerable political reluctance, conscription was introduced in 1916. The Military Service Act of January 1916 introduced conscription, a measure that really drove home the impact of the war, for single men and, in response to a sudden surge in weddings, the married followed in April. This measure was seen as opposed to the Liberal tradition of civil liberty and was forced on Herbert Asquith, the Liberal Prime Minister, by David Lloyd George, the most dynamic Liberal minister and by the Conservative coalition partners. In December 1916, Asquith was to be replaced by the more forceful Lloyd George.[10] Conscription also became an issue in the Dominions as replacement needs ceased to be met by volunteering. In December 1916, it was introduced in New Zealand, although volunteering also continued. Canada followed in 1917. As in Australia and Ireland, conscription in Canada proved a divisive issue, reflecting ethnic and regional divisions, as it did not do in Britain.

The campaigning was for long intractable, particularly on the Western Front in Belgium and France. The concentration of large forces in a relatively small area, the defensive strength of trench positions, especially thanks to machine guns with their range and rapidity of fire, and to quick-firing artillery, but also helped by barbed wire and concrete fortifications, ensured that, until the collapse of the German position in the last weeks of the war, the situation there was essentially deadlocked. Fifty-eight percent of British battlefield deaths were from artillery and mortar shells, and just below 39 percent from machine-gun and rifle bullets. In attacking German positions, it proved very difficult to translate local superiority in numbers into decisive success. It was possible to break through trench lines, but difficult to exploit such successes. As yet, airplanes and motor vehicles had not been effectively harnessed to help the offensive. Furthermore, once troops had advanced, it was difficult to recognize, reinforce, and exploit success: until wireless communications improved in late 1917, control and communications were limited. Frontal attacks, particularly at Loos (1915), the Somme (1916), and Arras and Passchendaele (1917) led to heavy casualties, not least when a strategy of attrition came into play, as at Passchendaele, a hell of shells and mud. The Germans had dug in having seized much of Belgium and part of France, and this put the Western Allies led by Britain and France under the necessity of mounting offensives. Another reason was provided by the wish to reduce German pressure on their ally Russia and to prevent it from being knocked out of the war, as it was to be in 1917. Furthermore, there was a conviction that only through mounting an offensive would it be possible for the Allies to gain the initiative and, conversely, deny it to the Germans, and that both gaining the initiative and mounting an offensive were prerequisites for victory, which, indeed, was to be the case in 1918.

More specifically, in early 1915, it was widely believed that the stalemate of the winter reflected the exhaustion of men and supplies in the previous autumn's campaigning, and that it would be possible, with fresh men and munitions, to restart a war of maneuver. It was not generally appreciated that stalemate and trench warfare reflected the nature of war once both sides had committed large numbers and lacked the ability to accomplish a breakthrough. Furthermore, the strength of the German defensive positions was not appreciated. German lines were carefully sited on favorable terrain, while Allied lines were sited on the Germans, which gravely hampered Allied offensives.

Similarities between attacks at the tactical level did not mean a similarity in operational and strategic circumstances, planning, and political contexts. The *ad hoc* attempts in 1915 to ensure a strategic breakthrough on the Western Front by frontal attacks were designed to overcome the problems posed by trench warfare by compressing the front of attack. In January 1915, Arthur Balfour, a member of the Committee for Imperial Defence, argued

> that the notion of driving the Germans back from the west of Belgium to the Rhine by successfully assaulting one line of trenches after another seems a very hopeless affair, and unless some means can be found for breaking their line at some critical point, and threatening their communications, I am unable to see how the deadlock in the West is to be brought to any rapid or satisfactory conclusion.[11]

In 1916, instead, there was a more coherent and ambitious grand plan for a series of concerted assaults by the Allies on all major German fronts. Designed to inflict sufficient all-around damage on the German army, not least by forcing them to use up their reserves, to permit follow-up attacks that would achieve the long-awaited breakthrough, this strategy was derailed by the preemptive German assault on French-held Verdun in February 1916. This obliged the British to take a greater share in the eventual Anglo-French attack on the Somme in July 1916. The attack was poorly prepared, both in the sense of inadequate supporting firepower and in the definition of attainable objectives.

The relative stability of the trench systems made it worthwhile deploying heavy artillery to bombard them. The guns could be brought up and supplied before the situation changed, as it did in maneuver warfare. It was also necessary to provide artillery support in order to batter an enemy's defensive systems. Artillery was designed to cut casualties among the attacking infantry, although it may, instead, simply have fulfilled its role of increasing casualties among the defenders. Whereas, on the Somme in 1916, the guns had been spread too widely to be effective, the British used 2,879 guns—one for every nine yards of front—for their attack near Arras in April 1917.

The impasse was broken in 1918. American entry into the war against Germany in 1917 greatly altered the strategic situation, but by 1918 the Americans had only taken over a part of the front line. Their role would have been far greater had the war continued into 1919. As a result, it was the British contribution that was crucial in 1918, not least because Russia was knocked out of the war that year by the Germans, while the French had been gravely weakened by earlier casualties. The British blocked the last German offensive in the spring, and, in July–November, with French and American support, launched a series of attacks in which they outfought the Germans, overrunning their major defensive system in September. The development of effective artillery-infantry coordination, and of far more sophisticated fighting practices and more varied unit structures than in 1916, played a large part in this success; although later attention tended to focus on the novelty of massed attacks by tanks. More generally, the Germans had lost their superiority in weapons systems.

Tanks, which were first used in September 1916, and in the development of which the British played the key role, were valuable, not least in overcoming one of the major problems with offensives against trenches: the separation of firepower from advancing troops, and the consequent lack of flexibility. By carrying guns or machine guns, tanks made it possible for advancing units to confront unsuppressed positions and counterattacks. They offered precise tactical fire to exploit the consequences of the massed operational bombardments that preceded attacks. However, tanks also had serious limitations, especially in durability, but also in firepower and speed. The light infantry mortar in practice was more effective, more reliable, and more capable of providing flexible infantry support than the tank, which was underpowered, undergunned, underarmored, and unreliable. Moreover, it was difficult for the crew to communicate with each other, let alone anyone outside the tank, and this made it harder to get a tank to engage a target of opportunity. The value of tanks was also affected by the difficulty of providing sufficient numbers of them, which reflected their late arrival in wartime resource allocation and production system. German success in antitank measures was also important. To operate most effectively, tanks needed to support, and to be supported by, advancing infantry and artillery, a lesson that had to be learned repeatedly during the century in the face of pressure from enthusiasts for tanks alone. Instead, on the Western Front in 1918, well-aimed heavy indirect fire, ably coordinated with rushes by infantry who did not move forward in vulnerable lines, was the key to tactical success. The British army had 440 heavy artillery batteries in November 1918, compared to 6 in 1914.

Success elsewhere was also important. The navy retained control of home waters, checking the German fleet at the Battle of Jutland in the North Sea (31 May 1916). The largest battleship clash in history, this was mishandled as a result of the caution of the British commander, Admiral

Sir John Jellicoe, and problems with fire control and the unsafe handling of powder, and the British lost more warships; but the German ships were badly damaged in the big-gun exchange, and their confidence was hit by the resilience and size of the British fleet. On 4 July 1916, the German commander at Jutland, Vice-Admiral Reinhard Scheer, suggested to Wilhelm II that Germany could only win at sea by means of using submarines. After very heavy shipping losses, the German submarine menace was overcome, in part through the belated introduction of convoys in May 1917. Britain was therefore able to avoid blockade and invasion, to retain trade links that permitted the mobilization of British and Allied resources, crucial links with the United States, and to blockade Germany. Submarines were a new type of old challenge, the commerce raider, and, in some respects, were less of a challenge because the latter had benefited from France's many anchorages, while the Germans had only limited access to the high seas, not only because it had fewer anchorages but also as Britain could try to block the English Channel and the North Sea through anti-submarine measures, particularly minefields. In World War One, submarines proved a more serious threat than German surface raiders because it was very difficult to detect them once they submerged, and depth charges were effective only if they exploded close to the hulls. Furthermore, reflecting the possibilities for warmaking of a modern industrial society, the specifications of submarines, their range, seaworthiness, speed, and comfort, and of the accuracy, range, and armament of their torpedoes, greatly improved.

The impact of these developments was accentuated by inexperience in confronting submarine attacks and the limited effectiveness of antisubmarine weaponry. These increased the vulnerability of British trade and the danger that Britain might succumb to a form of blockade. Submarines promoted the German cause most effectively not by destroying warships but by sinking merchant vessels; during the war the Germans sank 11.9 million tons of Allied shipping, mostly commercial, at a cost of 199 submarines. In 1915, the Germans launched unrestricted submarine warfare as part of a deliberate campaign to starve Britain into submission, only for this to be stopped as likely to provoke American intervention. A continuing desire to deliver a knockout blow led on 2 February 1917 to the resumption of such warfare, but it helped bring the United States into the war on 6 April. The initial rate of Allied shipping losses was high enough to make defeat appear imminent. From February to April 1917, 1,945,240 tons of shipping were sunk with only nine German submarines lost. As a result, there was pessimism among British military leaders about the chances of success. However, despite inexperience in antisubmarine warfare, American entry into the war made a key difference, as it was again to do in 1941. In 1917, the United States had not only the world's largest economy but also the third largest navy (after Britain and

Germany). From May 1917, American warships contributed to antisubmarine patrols in European waters, just as the dispatch of five American battleships to Britain in late 1917 contributed decisively to the outnumbering of German surface warships.

Internal strategy was also crucial and, as so often, the branch of strategic policy that tends to be neglected in military history. As in World War Two, a major attempt was made to manufacture imported goods at home and to increase farm production, so as to reduce the need for imports. As more generally in World War One, activity focused on government and led to an increase in its power. With the Food Production Act of 1917, the government imposed a policy of increasing the amount of land that was plowed, rather than under grass, because it was more efficient to feed people directly with cereals (the price of which was now guaranteed), from the land, rather than indirectly via meat and milk. For example, in Wales the percentage of tillage rose by over 40 percent. Production of meat and milk in Britain fell, but County Agricultural Executive Committees oversaw a 30 percent rise in national cereal production. Statistics, however, can be misleading, as the rise in food production in 1917–1918 was a recovery after a major fall in 1916, and, despite the attempts of the Board of Agriculture to claim the credit, the recovery owed much to better weather.

In military terms, the introduction in May 1917 of a system of escorted convoys was a key measure in the war for Britain's trade. Convoys cut shipping losses dramatically, reducing the targets for submarines, and led to an increase in the sinking of German submarines. The monthly tonnage of shipping lost by Britain fell from 630,000 tons in the first four months of the unrestricted submarine attacks in 1917 to below half a million tons in August 1917. Only 393 of the 95,000 ships that were to be convoyed across the Atlantic were lost, including only three troop transports. The German defeat was demonstrated by the large number of American troops safely shipped across the Atlantic.

Thanks to naval dominance, amphibious capability, and imperial support, the German colonies in Africa were overrun (although resistance in German East Africa continued until the close of the war),[12] the Suez Canal and oil supplies in the Persian Gulf were both protected from Germany's ally Turkey, and the Turks were eventually driven from Palestine (now Israel and Palestine) and Mesopotamia (now Iraq). Reference to Britain has to be understood to mean the British Empire. Australia, Canada, India, New Zealand, and South Africa in particular made key contributions. The Canadians were particularly important on the Western Front,[13] while Australian, New Zealand, and Indian forces took a major part of the war with Turkey. Indian and South African units were important to the conquest of Germany's African colonies, while in 1914 an expedition from New Zealand captured the wireless station on German Samoa.

The war also represented an opportunity, but, even more, a need, to expand imperial control in order to contain possible discontent, preempt exploitation by rivals, and tap resources. For example, in the Islamic world, Egypt was made a protectorate in 1914, while, in 1916, Qatar became independent from Turkish rule under British protection. In Sudan, British control increased with the conquest, in 1916, of the territory of Darfur, whose Sultan, Ali Dinar, had heeded Turkish calls for Islamic action. Aircraft and light lorries were used to provide speedy firepower and mobility in Darfur. In Somaliland, the equivalent was the local Camel Constabulary organized from late 1912. This provided mobility and tactics appropriate to the environment, and, although a large Dervish force defeated the Camel Constabulary at Dulmadobe in 1913, killing its commander Richard Corfield, the Camel Constabulary was increased in size and was able to exert pressure on its opponents. During World War One, there were not the troops to spare for a major offensive, but there were successes, including the capture of the Dervish fort at Shimberberis in February 1915 and the naval blockade became more effective, hitting the supply of arms and ammunition to the Dervishes. Furthermore, the Turkish failure to break through into Egypt and their defeat in Arabia meant that the Dervishes did not receive the foreign assistance they wanted. As elsewhere, pan-Islamic opposition to Britain was an aspiration not a reality. Farther south, in Jubaland (part of British East Africa, the basis of Kenya, but, in 1924, ceded to Italy, and added to Italian Somaliland), where the British had established a post at Serenle in 1910 and mounted an expedition in 1913–1914 to increase their power, the local Awlihan clan attacked Serenle in 1916 killing the British official and most of his garrison. In response, in 1917, a punitive expedition defeated the Awlihan, seized most of their firearms, and captured most of their elders. The British expedition benefited from the support of the Italians in Somaliland. More generally, the deployment of British power in Africa was helped by the extent to which most of the continent was ruled by allies in the world war.

On the Home Front, there was a major transformation, as the war also saw the first air attacks on Britain. From January 1915, Zeppelins (German airships) bombed Britain. The material damage inflicted was relatively modest, but attacks on civilians were a preparation for a new type of total war. A total of 51 Zeppelin attacks on Britain (208 sorties) during the war, dropped 196 tons of bombs, which killed 557, wounded 1,358, and caused £1.5 million worth of property damage.

Reconnaissance, however, was the most important function of airplanes, and, even at the close of the war, many aircraft in service were reconnaissance and observation planes. The Turkish columns advancing on the Suez Canal in 1915 were spotted by British planes. Planes came to replace the reconnaissance functions of cavalry. Aerial photoreconnaissance also developed, leading to the production of accurate maps. Tactical reconnaissance was also significant, especially artillery spotting, although the balloon was the most important means of aerial observation in the war and played a key role in artillery direction. Aerial combat helped deny these opportunities to opponents, and air-superiority operations were therefore seen as having value for conflict on the ground, making it difficult for opponents to plan attacks effectively.

Airplanes were also used for bombing. In September and October 1914, the Royal Naval Air Service conducted the first effective strategic bombing raids of the war, when planes carrying 20-pound bombs flew from Antwerp to strike Zeppelin sheds at Düsseldorf and destroyed one airship. Strategic bombing was also directed against civilian targets. In 1917, as a match to German unrestricted submarine warfare, twin-engined Gotha bombers flew over the North Sea, beginning airplane strategic bombing of Britain with attacks on London. This encouraged the establishment of the Royal Air Force on 1 April 1918. It was designed to surmount the deadlock of the trenches by permitting the destruction of the enemy where vulnerable,[14] but the actual damage inflicted by British bombing raids in 1918 was minimal, and many planes were lost.

Ground attack also developed as part of the enhancement of airplane military effectiveness during the war. This technique was used at the Somme in 1916 and, in a more sophisticated fashion, in 1917, both at Passchendaele and in support of tanks at Cambrai. In 1918, German supply links came under regular attack, inhibiting their attacks, while the British used air strikes in their advance in Palestine and their submarine patrols increased German losses. At the same time, antiaircraft capability increased considerably, providing another instance both of the action-reaction cycle of military advances, and of the increasing specialization of military power.

The ability of airplanes to act in aerial combat was also enhanced. Increases in aircraft speed, maneuverability, and ceiling made it easier to attack other planes. Synchronizing gear enabled airplanes to fire forward without damaging their propellers. There was also a development in tactics. Airplanes came to fly in groups and formation tactics developed. Airplanes also became the dominant aerial weapon: their ability to destroy balloons and airships with incendiary bullets spelled doom for these, especially Zeppelins.

Airplane production rose swiftly. In 1914 the Royal Aircraft Factory at Farnborough could produce only two airframes per month, but their artisanal methods were swiftly swept aside by mass production, and by 1918 Britain had 22,000 airplanes. Air power also exemplified the growing role of scientific research in military capability: wind tunnels were constructed for the purpose of research, and strutless wings and airplanes made entirely from metal were developed. Engine power increased and size fell, and the speed and rate of climb of airplanes rose.

The sense of what air power could achieve also expanded. In 1915, the Committee of Imperial Defence considered using long-range planes, based in Britain's ally Russia and dropping incendiary bombs, to destroy German wheat and rye crops.[15] However, this was not feasible. The war also ended before it was possible to use the large Handley Page V/500 bombers to bomb Berlin. More generally, at this stage, many of the hopes of air power were based on a misleading sense of operational and technological possibilities. The British exaggerated what their bombers had achieved, leading to a misrepresentation of the potential of strategic bombing in subsequent discussion.[16] In aerial combat, the Germans did not lose in the air as they were to do in World War Two, and this, in large part, indicated the relatively more limited capability of World War One aircraft.

If air power was one aspect of modernization, another was provided by the impact of the war on government. This was not only a case of its powers expanding, but also of changes in its very processes designed to ensure that it was able to manage war effectively. There had been no comparable pressures during the wars of the empire of the previous century, but the situation was transformed by the multiple problems of developing, sustaining, and coordinating power during an industrial world war. The crucial break occurred after Lloyd George became Prime Minister in December 1916. His predecessor Asquith's Cabinet had been unwieldy, the management of the war seemed inadequate, and this led to pressure for a small War Committee to direct the war effort. Lloyd George, Britain's first modern presidential-style Prime Minister, created a War Cabinet of five members. Meeting every other day, this body was given a secretariat, and was made responsible for creating and coordinating policy, corresponding directly with government departments. Lloyd George gave unity to government by controlling the executive authority of the War Cabinet. In 1940, Churchill was to revive Lloyd George's position with a similar War Cabinet.

In 1918, Germany was defeated in the fighting, not "stabbed in the back" by domestic opposition (as German right-wingers later claimed), but postwar euphoria was limited in Britain. The war had seen strong patriotism, and a widespread conviction that it had to continue until Germany could be driven from Belgium; but the discontent of many soldiers led to thousands of court-martials, while shell shock affected large numbers. Several war poets presented the war as an epitome of military futility and incompetence, and Richard Aldington, who had been affected by gas and shell shock, denounced society in his antiwar novel *Death of a Hero* (1929). Such views, however, found scant echo in public opinion which in the 1920s emphasized the patriotic themes of the war,[17] or in the inscriptions on the numerous war memorials erected after the conflict. The last were, and are, one of the more eloquent testimonials to the heavy cost and loss of this war. For example, 10 percent of male Scots between 16 and 50 were killed. At the Somme in 1916, the New Zealanders suffered 40 percent dead or wounded in 23 days' operations, while, at Passchendaele on 12 October 1917, they had the heaviest casualties of any one day in their military history: over 600 dead and 2,000 wounded. Confirmed British and empire military dead came to just below 1 million, a figure which was to give rise to the idea of a "lost generation." The recovered memory of the conflict has conditioned the public imagination of war ever since in Britain, and its grasp remains strong to the present day and has been much ventilated on television. There is insufficient stress on the variety of individual response. For example, Captain P.L. Wright and Private J.T. Darbyshire of the First Buckinghamshire Battalion of the Oxfordshire and Buckinghamshire Light Infantry left very different accounts in both tone and content,

> the condition on the ground was such as to render the chances of a successful attack exceedingly small, if not impossible, but the progress made actually was considerably greater than expected, though casualties were high. [Wright]
>
> At 4am Oct 9 we were relieved by the Woster Regt who went "over the lid" we raced like hares along the duck board to try to get away before the barrage opened, but we were caught in it and several of the fellows who had been in England training with me met their end "God rest their souls in Peace" left in the land of desolation [Darbyshire].[18]

The high losses reflected not so much the futility of war, or of this war, as was subsequently claimed by critics, but, rather, the determination of the world's leading industrial powers to continue hostilities almost at any cost. More specifically, casualties were high because of the willingness to attack, combined with the advantage weapons technology gave the defense and the value of defense in moderate depth, given the constraints on offensive warfare and the numbers of troops available for the defense.

These issues were to dominate much subsequent military thought, as commentators, planners, and tacticians considered how best to avoid a repetition of the casualties of trench warfare; but the immediate postwar years saw the military facing challenges that were very different to those of the world war. Outside Europe, Britain faced imperial policing issues, leading, most spectacularly, to the Amritsar massacre of April 1919 when General Dyer ordered troops to fire on a demonstrating crowd, causing nearly 400 fatalities. Across the empire, unwelcome British policy initiatives could lead to a violent response, as, in the 1920s, with a direct tax on livestock in British Somaliland, which had to be abandoned. Prewar problems also recurred, for example in Somaliland, where, having seen their position in the interior collapse in 1910–1912, the British had taken the initiative again from late 1912. An intelligence report of 1919 noted the need to respond to new challenges, but in a very different manner to that posed on the Western Front,

> The large increase in the number of rifles in the Mullah's possession and the consequent discard of the spear...We may expect the Dervishes to take up defensive positions which they will defend stubbornly behind cover without exposing themselves. We must be ready to carry out attacks against most difficult positions and up narrow and steep-sided valleys, to employ covering fire and frequently to capture the heights or the key to the position before it will be possible to make any headway. It will also be necessary to employ artillery, firing high explosive-shell, if the various Dervish strongholds are to be captured without very heavy casualties. In short, whereas in the past the training of troops in Somaliland could, in the main, be carried out with a view to meeting one form of savage warfare, namely the Dervish rush in bush country, troops must now be trained to readily adapt themselves to a more varied form of fighting which will in some degree resemble hill warfare in India.[19]

In the event, a combination of the Somaliland Camel Corps and the Royal Air Force's (RAF's) Z Force brought the necessary combination of force and mobility. Naval support was also important in what was an impressive combination. Launched in early 1920, it saw the Dervishes routed. Their stronghold at Taleh was bombed and Mullah Sayyid Muhammad fled into the Ogaden (which the British recognized as part of Ethiopia). He was dislodged from there by a British-approved attack by tribal "friendlies," the Isaqs, and fled, dying of illness. The opposition to Britain collapsed without his charismatic leadership. Another instance of a resumption of earlier problems was provided by the Third Afghan War in 1919, in which, in response to Afghan attacks, the RAF bombed Jalalabad and Kabul. Furthermore, recent extensions of imperial authority led in some cases to revolts that posed serious issues, particularly those in Egypt in 1919 and Iraq in 1920–1921. There were also Arab riots in Palestine in 1920–1921.

There were also more novel conflicts. In the Russian Civil War, the British were one of the leading powers among the fourteen countries that intervened against the Communists. British forces were sent to the Baltic, the Black Sea, and the Caspian, and to Archangel and Murmansk in northern Russia. Aircraft and tanks were used by British forces. This was an unsuccessful intervention, abandoned in 1919, although British action was important in securing the independence of the Baltic Republics: the navy played a key role in the Baltic.

Closer to home, there was also failure in Ireland, which showed both the effectiveness of terrorism and the difficulties of responding to guerrilla warfare. Conflict began in 1916 when a general rising was planned by the military council of the Irish Republican Brotherhood. Aside from the rising in Dublin, there was supporting action in different parts of Ireland, but, due to divisions in the leadership, nothing of note. This helped ensure that the rising in Dublin on Eastern Monday (24 April) would fail militarily. Instead, it became merely a bold gesture. About 1,200 rose and seized a number of sites, but they suffered from bad planning, poor tactics, and the strength of the British response, which included the uncompromising use of artillery. The insurgents were forced to surrender unconditionally on 29 April. The firm British response, however, served to radicalize Irish public opinion. Martial law was declared, and a series of trials, fifteen executions, and numerous internments provided martyrs for the nationalist cause. The Irish Volunteers were swiftly reestablished and, by the end of 1917, began public drilling exercises. Political support for independence grew. A government proposal to introduce conscription in 1918 was very unpopular, and the war undermined support for the Home Rulers, who had sought autonomy within the empire.

Instead, in 1919, the Irish Volunteers, soon to rename themselves the Irish Republic Army (IRA), began terrorist activity. They were opposed to conventional politics, which they saw as likely to lead to compromise. The British refusal to accept independence precipitated a brutal civil war in 1919–1921, in which terrorism and guerrilla warfare destroyed the British ability to maintain control. In tones that were to become familiar from counterinsurgency operations elsewhere, Lieutenant-General Sir Philip Chetwode, Deputy Chief of the Imperial General Staff, claimed that victory was possible, but only if the army was given more power, including control of the police, and the full support of British public opinion,

> The full incidence of Martial Law will demand very severe measures and to begin with many executions. In the present state of ignorance of the population in England, I doubt very much that it would not result in a protest which would not only ruin our efforts, but would be most dangerous to the army. The latter have behaved magnificently throughout, but they feel from top to bottom that they are not supported by their countrymen, and should there be a strong protest against severe action it would be extremely difficult to hold them.[20]

Possibly Chetwode was correct, and, with a tough policy, the rebellion could have been put down, but public opinion would not have stood for it. Instead, there was a British withdrawal from much of Ireland, and a partition between a self-governing Irish Free State, and a mainly Protestant Northern Ireland, which remained part of the United Kingdom. This partition was opposed by much of the IRA, the anti-Treaty forces known as the Irregulars. They were unable to accept a settlement that entailed anything short of a united Ireland. The Irregulars mounted a terrorist campaign in Northern Ireland in 1921, and also fought the newly independent government in the South in 1922–1923, in what was a more bloody conflict than that of 1919–1921. The IRA, however, was beaten both north and south of the border and, thereafter, IRA terrorism remained only a minor irritant until the late 1960s.

Military commitments in the 1920s focused on the empire, and this affected the process of lesson-learning from World War One. When, in 1923, France and Belgium sent troops into the Ruhr, the key economic zone, in an attempt to enforce the payment of reparations (money owed as part of the peace settlement), Britain did not take part. In the 1920s, with Germany largely disarmed (the Versailles peace settlement had restricted it to an army of only 100,000 men, with no advanced weapons), the Soviet Union absorbed by internal issues, and relations with France and the United States cordial, a recurrence of large-scale conflict between regular forces appeared unlikely. The Washington Naval Treaty of 1922 and the London Naval Treaty of 1930 represented international agreement on the size of surface navies, and appeared to end the prospect of naval races. The first established a 5:5:3 ratio in the capital ship tonnage of Britain, the United States, and Japan, and the second extended the agreement. Thus, despite tensions, there was to be no naval race between Britain and the United States: Britain accepted naval parity with the United States. The Locarno Treaty of 1925 appeared to indicate that Germany could be readily reassimilated into the international system.

Nevertheless, there was intellectual enquiry about the nature of war winning and much interest in the potential of tanks, and, in general, in the potential of new weaponry in a context of rapid changes in effectiveness. General Sir Archibald Montgomery-Massingberd commented in 1929 on the need to develop vehicles able to withstand the rocky terrain of India, "[T]hings advance so quickly now that things which seemed impossible a year or two ago are already practically accomplished."[21] In 1923, General Rawlinson, the Commander-in-Chief India, called for a "centre to train all ranks in the scientific use of automatic weapons."[22] There was considerable uncertainty over the extent to which tanks should play a role in force structure and doctrine.[23] This was a problem that partly arose from differences over the assessment of their role in 1918, and this was accentuated because Plan 1919 was not mounted. The extent to which large-scale tank attacks were not mounted in the last two months of the war encouraged officers who emphasized the role of more traditional weaponry, particularly artillery.[24] It was also difficult to gauge how far the developing specifications of tanks altered operational capability options. Moreover, as Montgomery-Massingberd, the head of Southern Command, wrote in 1928, of developments with tanks, "The whole question is one of money."[25] This was acute not only because of problems with public finances and the range of imperial commitments, but also due to demands from other services, not only the navy, but also the air force.

Air power was not only a new source of expenditure, but was also seen as a war-winning tool able to avoid the drawn-out attritional character of conflict on the ground seen in World War One. Air power was presented as the best way to overcome the impasse of trench warfare and to deliver the effective total war that was required. This was the view not only of experts but also of the wider public. In John Galsworthy's novel *A Modern Comedy* (1929), Sir Lawrence Mont wonders how the English nation could exist with "all its ships and docks in danger of destruction by aeroplanes." Airmen argued that bombers would be able to destroy opposing economies and, more particularly, that large bombers would be able to fight off fighter attack and thus not require fighter escorts. As a consequence, the RAF had twice as many bombers as fighters for most of the interwar period. These bombers were seen not only as likely to be effective in war, but also as a deterrent against attack, although the Air Ministry was more moderate in its claims than independent air enthusiasts.[26] Priorities were not changed toward fighters until 1938. The creation of the RAF was a major institutional change in the organization of the military. It institutionalized a commitment to air power. As a result, there was pressure from the army to end the independence of the air force and, instead, to give both army and navy their own air forces.

The Fleet Air Arm was under the RAF, not the Admiralty, and the latter remained committed to the battleship. Nevertheless, despite financial stringency, there was an important commitment to naval air power, in the development of which Britain had led the way. Raids by aircraft launched by early carriers had been staged in the last stage of World War One, and soon thereafter during the Russian Civil War. There was no experience with conflict between aircraft carriers, but considerable confidence in their potential. In 1920, Rear Admiral Sir Reginald Hall MP argued in the *Times* that, thanks to aircraft and submarines, the days of the battleship were over. The number of planes in the Fleet Air Arm rose to 144 by the end of the 1920s, and five new carriers entered service in 1922–1938, while, by 1933, hydraulically reset transverse arrester gear was in use to handle landing. Aside from being used in the Russian Civil War, carriers were sent far afield, the *Argus* being stationed near the Dardanelles during the Chanak crisis, a confrontation with Turkey, in 1922. There was a carrier on the China station in the late 1920s (first *Hermes* and then *Argus*), and another, *Furious*, took part in the major naval exercises in the late 1920s.[27]

In the 1930s, however, the lead in naval aviation was increasingly taken by the United States and Japan, in part because they would be the key powers in any struggle for control of the Pacific. In contrast, no naval power was as acute a threat to Britain in the 1920s, while, in the 1930s, the need for deep-sea air capacity in war with Germany appeared lessened by the vulnerability of German naval power to land-based air attacks. The lesson of World War One appeared to be that the Germans could be bottled up in the North Sea. In 1940, however, they were to transform the situation by seizing Norway and France, and by basing warships, submarines, and aircraft in both.

Bringing ethical issues about air power into interwar organizational questions, General Milne, the Chief of the Imperial General Staff, wrote of

> the highly organized and unscrupulous propaganda of the Air Staff...the separation of the Air Staff from the General Staff which prevents problems of defence being considered as a whole, and with a proper sense of proportion as to their cost...the Air Staff have found it necessary, in order to find support for their separate and independent existence...to devise a special form of so-called air strategy...there appears to be two principles or catch words upon which it is based...attack against the nerve centers of an enemy nation...and the moral effect of the air arm. In dealing with problems of war on a large scale against civilized countries the former term is usually employed. The objectives of such strategy are the centres of production—nominally of munitions, which, be it marked, is a term of very wide significance. In effect this new form of strategy takes the form of attack against civilian workers, including their women and children. The hitherto accepted objectives of land and sea warfare have been the armed forces of the enemy, and whether or no we as a nation are justified morally in adopting a military policy which is so totally at variance with the accepted dictates of humanity, there is no doubt that we should be the first to suffer if the next war were to be waged on such principles.[28]

Army pressure was unsuccessful, but, as a reminder of the imperial focus of military tasking, the RAF spent the 1920s protecting distant interests, in 1928, bombing the Wahabi tribesmen of Arabia who threatened Iraq and Kuwait. However, in 1922, the General Staff of the British Forces in Iraq observed, in a military report on part of Mesopotamia, "Aeroplanes by themselves are unable to compel the surrender or defeat of hostile tribes."[29]

CHAPTER **7**

Multiple Challenges, 1933–1968

Never before has it been in such a perilous position.
—William Joyce, "Lord Haw Haw," Nazi radio propagandist, on Britain,
28 December 1941

The threat from major states with competing ideologies dominated British military history from the rise of Hitler to power in Germany in 1933, until the end of the Cold War with the fall of Soviet power in 1989–1991. These threats led to a marked shift in priorities. Commitments to the empire, which had dominated force structure and planning in the 1920s, remained important in the 1930s, and indeed affected strategy during World War Two (1939–1945), not least in Winston Churchill's determination that British forces should regain Malaya and Singapore from Japan, but these commitments took a secondary role in the war. After that, there was a revival in these commitments, particularly in the face of independence struggles, but imperial roles competed with the new strategic need to confront the Soviet Union in Europe and the North Atlantic, and the latter took precedence. In October 1964, Britain still had more troops "east of Suez" than in Germany (where, as part of its NATO commitment, Britain manned part of the front line against Soviet forces), but, in January 1968, the government announced that it was abandoning the military position east of Suez. An era of distant military commitment appeared at an end.

During this period of ideological confrontations, the military had to devote little attention to domestic control. There were homegrown Fascist movements in the 1930s, as well as Communist demonstrations, but neither were able to challenge the government seriously. Sir Oswald Mosley, the head of the British Union of Fascists (BUF), saw himself as a second Benito Mussolini (the dictator of Italy), but it proved easier to borrow the latter's black shirts as a party uniform, than to recreate the political circumstances that had permitted the Fascist seizure of power in Italy in 1922. The membership peaked at maybe 50,000 members in June 1934, and was singularly ineffective in a political culture that had little time for those seeking the overthrow of the system. The government used the police and the law, not the army, to contain both the BUF and the Communists, whose membership was still no more than 18,000 in 1939. The Public Order Act of 1936 banned political uniforms and paramilitary organizations and controlled marches. When World War Two broke out, there was no pro-German violence. Instead, the Fascist leaders were arrested, and their movement collapsed. In 1935, troops had been brought in to back up the police after sectarian riots in North Belfast claimed eleven lives, but such assistance was not needed in Britain, and that itself is part of its military history.

After World War Two, there was concern about Communist disaffection in Britain at a time of rising tension with the Soviet Union. The Labour government claimed that Communist conspiracies were behind strikes, for example the London dock strike of 1949, but Communism was contained, in part due to the avoidance of defeat and German occupation in the recent war, which ensured that the political system was stronger than in many Continental states. Aside from the docks, there was relatively little confrontation between government and trade unions, but, in the docks, troops and the Supply and Transport Organization were used to defeat strikes. More generally, the military responded to political and social changes within Britain without any particular problems or issues, and this despite the major disjuncture of moving, in 1939, from a volunteer service to conscription, and a conscription, moreover, that was maintained in the subsequent peace, only ending in 1963.

It was far less easy to keep order in the empire than in Britain, and the British faced particular problems, in the 1930s, in Palestine and in Waziristan on the Northwest Frontier of India, although there were also difficulties in other colonies requiring military action, including Burma and Cyprus. The Arab rising in Palestine in 1936–1939 led to the deployment of 50,000 troops, and that under the Faqir of Ipi in Waziristan to over 60,000 being deployed. He benefited from his ability to recruit support and take refuge in Afghanistan, but his peak strength was only 4,000 men, and, although his men had good rifles, they lacked artillery and machine guns. The British deployed about 50–60 armored cars, which were used mainly to escort road convoys, and proved quite effective in that limited role. A handful of light tanks also went for an occasional trundle on open ground, but could get nowhere near the kind of mountainous terrain on which the principal engagements took place. The campaign also revealed the limitations of British communications, as the tribesmen cut telegraph lines. Wireless (radio) was still in its infancy in the British forces, only the largest bases and headquarters having reliable wireless communications, so most signaling below brigade level was carried out using old-fashioned colored flags, the heliograph, and dispatch riders. Success was consolidated by new roads, which permitted a more rapid response to renewed opposition, but guerrilla opposition continued until 1943 (and the Faqir was never captured), and the region was subdued as much due to tribal rivalries and to financial inducements, as to superior British numbers and firepower. This very much reflected continuities of conflict in the region that, indeed, were to be seen anew there in the early 2000s.

Imperial commitments affected the ethos, structure, and doctrine of the British military. For most of the period 1920–1938, the armed forces were principally concerned with preparing for war outside Europe, either with resistance to rebellion in colonies or with protecting them from attack by other major powers, a tasking that meant, in the 1930s, Japanese challenges to British positions in the Far East. Such tasks required a force structure similar to that of the late nineteenth century, centering on local garrisons and a fleet able to move rapidly in order to secure naval superiority and cover the movement of reinforcements from units based in Britain. As far as land warfare was concerned, the emphasis was not on tanks, which were not well suited to many tasks in imperial protection and were also cumbersome to move. Thus the argument both at the time and subsequently, that the British should have developed a more mechanical army in order better to counter the German *blitzkrieg* they unsuccessfully faced in France in 1940, neglects the circumstances that prevailed in the interwar period. Lieutenant General Sir Philip Chetwode indeed had argued in 1921 that tank specifications and tactics ought to focus on colonial commitments, rather than the possibility of conflict with other regular forces. He pressed for tanks to be armed with a machine gun, not a heavier gun, and for training in the use of tanks against opponents equipped with artillery and machine guns, but not tanks.[1] The Committee of Imperial Defence responded to its critics in 1934 by arguing that "it would not be possible to organize a larger mechanized force than the one we recommend below without upsetting the whole system by which our forces overseas are maintained by the Home Army." The Committee proposed a tank brigade as part of the expeditionary force, but argued that imperial tasks cannot "be met by the creation of a highly specialized 'robot' army at home, even if that were the best system for a Continental war."[2]

However, the rise of Hitler, the collapse of the Disarmament Conference in 1934, and German rearmament, publicly announced in 1935, made the situation in Europe more menacing. German expansionism indeed placed the spotlight on Anglo-French preparedness. In 1938, when, in the Munich crisis, Hitler successfully intimidated Britain and France over the future of Czechoslovakia, the British service chiefs urged caution. Conscious of numerous global commitments, they warned about the dangers of becoming entangled in major military action on the Continent. There was particular concern about the likely impact of the German bombing of civilian targets. The major impact on public morale of German raids on London in World War One seemed a menacing augury. It was believed, in the words of the ex- and future Prime Minister Stanley Baldwin in 1932, that "the bomber will always get through." Air Commodore L.E.O. Charlton developed these themes in *War from the Air: Past-Present-Future* (1935), *War over England* (1936), and *The Menace of the Clouds* (1937). Anglo-French fears of war with Germany may have been excessive, given the weaknesses of the Nazi regime, including a lack of enthusiasm among the German leaders, but there was a fear of causing a second "Great War." Furthermore, the military was poorly configured for war with Germany. As the Deputy Chief of the Imperial General Staff noted in May 1939, "under the plan approved in April 1938, the Field Force was "to be organized primarily with a view to reinforcing the Middle East ...The crisis in September 1938...focused sharply the fact that, even when the programme was complete, our forces would be inadequate for a major Continental war."[3]

Delay in fighting Germany at least permitted investment in improved effectiveness. In response to the threat from German bombers, attention was switched in Britain from building up a bomber force to fighter defense, with the development of the Hawker Hurricane and the Supermarine Spitfire. These planes reflected the transition of fighters from wooden-based biplanes to all-metal cantilever-wing monoplanes with high-performance engines capable of far greater speeds, range, and armament. Alongside early warning radar, they were to be key to resisting the air assault that Germany launched in 1940. There were also improvements in naval readiness in the late 1930s. A large number of carriers, cruisers, and destroyers were laid down, while, after control over the Fleet Air Arm was transferred from the Royal Air Force (RAF) to the Admiralty in 1937, it was greatly expanded. Radar sets were installed in warships from 1938.

In opposing the Munich agreement, Churchill, then a Conservative backbencher, had told the House of Commons on 5 October 1938 that "the maintenance of peace depends upon the accumulation of deterrents against the aggressor, coupled with a sincere effort to redress grievances." The buildup of British forces did not provide a deterrent to further German action, but it was to help strengthen Britain's defenses. However, although Britain was allied to France, the Soviet Union was willing to ally with Germany in 1939, while the United States was not interested in becoming committed to action against appeasement. As the United States was the world's leading industrial power, this gravely weakened the possible response to Fascist aggression. Indeed the lack of Anglo-American cooperation in the 1930s was a major feature in international relations, and one that affected Britain's options.

The eventual German air assault on Britain in 1940 was to be the product of the collapse of Britain's military and diplomatic system that year. Britain and France had declared war on Germany on 3 September 1939, in response to its invasion of Poland, whose security they had guaranteed, but the Anglo-French forces were unable to provide any assistance to Poland, not least by attacking German forces on the French frontier. The British forces sent to France in 1939 were small, short of equipment, particularly tanks, transport, artillery, small arms, and ammunition, and poorly trained for conflict with the Germans. Command and control systems were inadequate, and, due to the fiscal situation, there had been no large-scale army maneuvers for several years. The movement of the British force was too late to have any impact on the war in Poland. Churchill, who had become the First Lord of the Admiralty with the outbreak of war, advocated the dispatch of a fleet to the Baltic specially prepared to resist air attack, but this rash idea, which would have exposed the fleet to air attack in confined waters, was thwarted by his naval advisers.

Despite the rapid fall of Poland in 1939 and Hitler's subsequent call for negotiations, Britain and France were determined to fight on in order to prevent German hegemony. Distrustful of Hitler, skeptical about Germany's ability to sustain a long war, and confident that, as in World War One, the Allied forces in France would be able to resist attack, Neville Chamberlain, the Prime Minister, hoped that it would be possible to intimidate Hitler by a limited war through blockade. The strategy was intended to put such pressure on Germany that either Hitler would be forced to negotiate, or it would lead to his overthrow.

Military activity on the Western Front in what was the particularly bitter winter of 1939–1940 was very limited, leading to its description as the Phoney War. The Anglo-French forces failed to respond to German success in Poland with altered training regimes. Instead training was conventional, and there was little preparation for mobile tank warfare, although more than was subsequently alleged.[4] The British Expeditionary Force and the Allies generally were not lacking equipment compared to the Germans, nor was the equipment itself not really inferior; instead, it was a matter of operational vision, command and control in the mobile battle. Conscription, introduced in 1939, produced a large army, but, once the Germans attacked, neither the troops nor the officers proved able to respond adequately to the pace and character of the German attack. General Claude Auchinleck, who commanded a force sent to Norway in 1940 to respond to the German invasion, in part reflected in his report on the unsuccessful operation the criticism of a traditionalist regular officer of the nature of society, "Generally the morale of our troops was undoubtedly lower than that of the enemy. It is considered that this was due, first, to our inferiority of resources as compared with those of the enemy, particularly in the air. Secondly, it was due to the lack of training of the men as soldiers and a lack of adaptability which induced in them a feeling of inferiority as compared with the enemy. Thirdly their flanks and rear were continually threatened—our men for the most part seemed distressingly young, not so much in years as in self-reliance and manliness generally."[5]

In the Norway campaign, the hastily thrown together British force indeed suffered from inadequate training and equipment, and a lack of air cover and appropriate artillery. Despite terrain that was unsuitable for their attacks, the Germans proved better able to seize and maintain the initiative and to overcome successive defensive positions. The navy was also shown to be unable to cope effectively with German air power, although critical losses were inflicted on the German navy.

Failure in Norway helped discredit the leadership of Chamberlain who had already been affected by disquiet over the energy and style of his war leadership. Churchill's reputation as a resolute opponent of Hitler helped ensure that he became Prime Minister in succession to Chamberlain. He was to remain in this position until after the defeat of Germany in 1945, facing unprecedented challenges for any British war leader.

In the France campaign of 1940, the Allies were outfought by the more mobile Germans, who conquered the Netherlands, Belgium, and France. The British were tied to French strategy and this bears much of the blame for failure, but the British also suffered from particular deficiencies. Army-RAF cooperation was bad, and this ensured a lack of close air support. There was also a shortage of antitank and antiaircraft guns. Much of the army was poorly trained and commanded. It was not adequately prepared for a fighting retreat in the face of a mobile opponent; transport, fuel, and communications all proved insufficient. In the end, getting the army out of France became paramount. Bravery, skill, and luck helped the British save much of their army (but not its equipment), as well as many French troops, in an evacuation from Dunkirk on 27 May–4 June. The navy, which evacuated most of the troops (although private boats also took off an important number), however, took serious punishment from German planes in the process.

The navy's attack on the Germans in Narvik in the Norway campaign, and that by tanks at Arras in the Battle for France, showed that the British could fight effectively as well as bravely, and it would be mistaken to see the defeats of 1940 simply as an indictment of a failed military system. The conflicts were more close run than the results suggested, and the failure in France was one of planning more than fighting,[6] but the consequence was a vulnerability for Britain greater than that when faced by Napoleon because Hitler, now also dominating Western Europe, in addition had both air power and submarines. On 30 June, the Germans occupied the undefended Channel Islands, which were vulnerable to German air attack. Moved forward into France, Belgium, the Netherlands, and

Norway, German air bases were now close to Britain, cutting the journey time of bombers and allowing fighters to escort them.

With his growing interest in an attack on the Soviet Union, Hitler, on 19 July 1940, offered peace, with Britain to retain her empire in return for her acceptance of Germany's dominance of the Continent. Influential politicians, particularly the Foreign Secretary, Lord Halifax, who had come close to succeeding Chamberlain, felt that such negotiations were desirable, while David Lloyd George, Prime Minister in 1916–1922, thought he might be able to succeed Churchill and settle with Hitler. Churchill, however, was determined not to negotiate with Hitler, and his views prevailed.

Moreover, in the Battle of Britain of 1940, the German air assault was defeated. This was a key episode both in British military history and in the history of air power. It was the first major check experienced by the Germans, and one that was critical to the survival of Britain as an independent state, for the air attack was designed to prepare the way for Operation Sealion, the planned invasion, particularly by driving British warships from the Channel. British victory reflected both the deficiencies of the numerically superior German air force, and the capabilities and fighting quality of its numerically inferior British opponents. Radar also played an important role within an integrated air defense system. Initial German attacks on the RAF and its airfields, in what was an air-superiority campaign, designed to force the British to commit their fighters and then to destroy them, inflicted heavy blows on the British, especially on pilot numbers. By early September, Fighter Command, under remorseless pressure by larger forces, seemed close to defeat. However, fighting over Britain, the RAF benefited from the support provided by the ground control organization and could more often recover any pilots who survived being shot down. Furthermore, RAF fighting quality, which had been underestimated by the German planners, was seen in the heavy losses inflicted on the Germans, and the Germans did not appreciate the extent to which the RAF was under pressure.

Once the Germans switched in early September 1940 to bomb London and other cities (the Blitz), a strategy designed to put the German air force center-stage by bombing Britain into submission, the pressure on the RAF diminished. German bombers operating near the edge of fighter escort range provided a vulnerable target, which led the Germans to switch to night attack. There is controversy over losses, but one reasonable assessment is that between 10 July and 31 October, the Germans lost 1,733 aircraft in the Battle of Britain, the British 915. Although German deficiencies played an important role in their failure, British fighting quality, determination, and fortitude were crucial in making these deficiencies manifest, and thus in gaining an important defensive victory.

Nevertheless, the strain on the British people of coping with the Blitz was heavy. The range and repetition of the bombing increased the uncertainty and tension it imposed. For example, the city of Swansea was bombed 44 times in 1940–1943, with 1,238 people killed or wounded, over 7,000 made homeless, and the town center destroyed. In London, my uncle, a teenage fire watcher, was killed in the bombing; and, in 1942, three of the twelve houses on the street in which I live in Exeter were destroyed, as was much of the city center. Nevertheless, on the whole, morale remained high, and fortitude in the face of the attack became a key aspect of national identity. The real and symbolic aspect of the assault on British civil society accentuated the sense of the entire society being under attack, and this had considerable effect both at the time and for postwar Britain. Churchill told the House of Commons on 21 November 1940, "The War Damage (Compensation) Bill...will give effect to the feeling that there must be equality of risk and equality of treatment in respect of the damage done by fire of the enemy."

On 17 September 1940, Operation Sealion had been formally postponed. Irrespective of the serious problems that would have faced any invasion, not least insufficient German naval resources and preparation and the strength of the British navy, it could not be allowed to go ahead without air superiority. Furthermore, the British navy was able to defeat the attack of German surface raiders on British communication links and to limit those by submarines, and the empire provided key assistance, ensuring that, unlike against Napoleon, Britain did not fight alone. Thanks in particular to the support of imperial forces, the British were able to launch a peripheral strategy designed to protect vulnerable interests and to hit at opponents in an indirect fashion. This became more pressing and possible as a result of Italy's entry into the war as an ally of Germany in June 1940. The British strategy entailed the defeat of an Italian invasion of Egypt in December 1940 followed by a successful advance into the Italian colony of Libya; as well as the conquest of the Italian colonies of Somaliland, Eritrea, and Ethiopia (and the recapture of British Somaliland) in February–November 1941, and of Lebanon and Syria, colonies of the pro-German regime of Vichy France, in May–July 1941, and Iraq, whose government had links with Germany, in April–May 1941.

The peripheral strategy had echoes of past British military practice. Churchill's decision to send tanks that were a key part of the strategic reserve to Egypt was important to success against the Italians in North Africa. It reflected his determination to strike at his opponents wherever possible, but also his confidence that an invasion of Britain would not come. The move was prefigured in 1758–1759, when William Pitt the Elder, 1st Earl of Chatham, sent forces to conquer Canada despite the risk of a French invasion of Britain that was, indeed, to be thwarted by the British navy. Operations against far more numerous Italian forces in North and

East Africa in 1940–1941 also reflected the methods the British had employed in colonial warfare, not least the ability to cope with similar problems, such as the difficulty of obtaining supplies in the areas of operation, the extent of territory, the terrain, and the climate. As earlier on the Northwest Frontier of India, artillery proved especially important in attacks on Italian mountainous positions in Ethiopia, while engineering skills in creating and improving routes and bridges were also at a premium. As in many colonial campaigns, the ability of boldly advancing forces to disorientate the opposition was the key to success. Effective doctrine, well implemented by able commanders and impressive troops, brought victory, and could do so with few casualties for the attacker. In Iraq, the British used a mix of the flying columns and employment of native allies seen in earlier imperial operations with the application of more modern weaponry, especially aircraft and armored cars. In Somaliland, once the Italians had been defeated, the British used traditional policing methods. The Somalia Gendarmerie, a force of 3,070 Somalis and other Africans, and 120 British officers in 1943, defeated pro-Italian irregulars, and employed collective punishments to control clan warfare.[7]

This peripheral strategy suffered severe blows in 1941, however, because of greater German commitment in the Mediterranean, first in Libya in support of Italy in March–June 1941, and then with an invasion of Greece in April 1941 that the British failed to stem. The expeditionary force sent to help the Greeks had inadequate air support and was pushed back. The tempo of the German advance, especially its rapid use of airborne troops and armor, brought a decisive advantage, as did the effective use of ground-support aircraft. The dispatch of forces there also gravely weakened the British in North Africa where German forces proved better than the British in mobile warfare and combined land-air operations. British tank-infantry-artillery cooperation was inadequate, British tanks were poor, and the British were driven back into Egypt. Churchill, who had backed the expedition to Greece in order to show that Britain was supporting all opposition to the Axis, swiftly recognized it as an error. The Germans followed up by capturing the Mediterranean island of Crete in May 1941. The British defense there was poorly prepared and not brilliantly commanded. Much of the garrison had hastily retreated from Greece, and was short of equipment, particularly artillery, and lacking in air support. German air superiority also ensured that attempts by the British navy to reinforce, supply, and, eventually, evacuate by Crete proved very costly.

By the early summer of 1941, it was clear that, despite the killing of over 43,000 civilians, the Blitz had failed to shatter civilian morale. It came to an end as the Germans transferred their planes for use against the Soviet Union. Furthermore, as yet, Germany lacked the submarine force necessary to give full effect to their plans for blockading Britain. Moreover, there were important signs of American support for Britain. In September 1940, as an important gesture, the United States provided fifty surplus destroyers (seven of them to the Canadian navy) in return for 99-year leases on bases in Antigua, the Bahamas, Bermuda, British Guiana, Jamaica, Newfoundland, St. Lucia, and Trinidad. In practice, the deal was of limited value, as the ships took time to prepare, but, aside from the psychological value at a time when Britain was vulnerable, no other power was in a position to provide such help. The passage by Congress of the Lend-Lease Act in March 1941, under which U.S. President Franklin D. Roosevelt was granted a total of $7 billion for military *matériel* that he could sell, lend, or trade to any state vital to American security, opened the way for the shipping of American military supplies to Britain. That July, American forces replaced the British in Iceland, keeping it out of German hands: Denmark, the colonial power, had been conquered by Germany in April 1940. Despite American support, the Germans mistakenly hoped that the British people would realize their plight, overthrow Churchill, and make peace. In the event, in the face of British obduracy, Hitler was reduced to trying to link his policies by believing that the defeat of the Soviet Union, which he attacked on 22 June 1941, would make Britain ready to settle and to accept German dominance of Europe. In the meanwhile, the British were unable to mount a serious challenge to the German position in Europe, and were obliged to continue a reliance on the peripheral strategy.

In December 1941, however, the war was transformed when Japan attacked the United States, Britain, and the Dutch. Britain's Asiatic Empire was swiftly revealed as vulnerable. Britain's failures reflected serious weaknesses in preparedness and doctrine, as well as the mishandling of particular operations, notably the land and sea defense of Malaya and Singapore. The British garrison in Hong Kong was attacked by a larger Japanese force on 8 December, forcing surrender on 25 December. The garrison was too weak for the defense, and had only seven outdated aircraft, as well as limited naval support. The Japanese also landed in northern Malaya on 8 December. Two major warships, the *Prince of Wales* and the *Repulse*, were sent without air cover to disrupt the Japanese invasion of Malaya, only to be sunk on 10 December 1941 by air attack. Poorly commanded land forces, unprepared for jungle conflict, were outmaneuvered in both Malaya and Burma by rapidly advancing Japanese troops who displayed greater flexibility in taking advantage of opportunities. In Malaya, the British alternated unsuitable defensive lines with inappropriate withdrawals. They had relied on the jungle to anchor their positions and limit the opportunities for Japanese advance, but this assumption rested on a lack of knowledge of the terrain combined with a failure to appreciate Japanese capability. The speed of the Japanese advance deprived the British of the opportunity to recover their equipoise and make adequate preparations, and also demoralized them.

The surrender of the major British base at Singapore with 62,000 troops on 15 February 1942 was rightly seen as a major humiliation, and was later described by Churchill as the "greatest disaster in British military history." He had informed Roosevelt that Singapore was expected to "stand an attack for at least six months." Its loss was a great blow to British prestige in Asia and thus weakened the respect for the empire. Both strategic misjudgment and military failure were responsible for the failures in Malaya and Singapore, but so also was a more general problem of excessive commitments.[8] As Churchill told the Secret Session of the House of Commons on 23 April 1942, "while we are at war with Germany and Italy we do not possess the naval resources necessary to maintain the command of the Indian Ocean against any heavy detachment from the main Japanese fleet."[9] William Joyce, "Lord Haw Haw," the Nazi propagandist broadcasting from Germany, declared on 28 December 1941 that "the demands on the Royal Navy were such that every single warship had to do the work of at least half a dozen."

The Malaya/Singapore campaign also brought to a head difficulties in Anglo-Australian relations, which had had to respond to serious differences in opinion over the need to respond to Japan or to concentrate on Germany. In large part, this issue focused on the allocation of Australian military resources, and, in particular, British assumptions that they should help protect the Middle East. In Australian eyes, there was a failure to heed the Japanese threat, and to respond to it appropriately; and this has subsequently proved part of a more general discussion of the British failure to defend the empire in the Far East.[10] In the long-term, the dispute over priorities had serious consequences for Anglo-Australian relations, and helped lead Australia to look to the United States. John Curtin, the Australian Prime Minister, writing in the *Melbourne Herald* on 27 December 1941, observed,

> The Australian Government regards the Pacific struggle as primarily one in which the United States and Australia must have the fullest say in the direction of the Democracies' fighting plan. Without any inhibitions of any kind I must make it quite clear that Australia looks to America, free of any pangs as to our traditional links with the United Kingdom.

In the short-term, the consequences were serious before Japan's entry into the war and acute thereafter. Indeed, these disputes with Australia were one of the most important results of the emphasis on the Middle East that followed Britain's defeat in Western Europe and Italy's entry into the war in 1940. The minutes of the Australian War Cabinet made clear anxieties about British priorities in goals and force allocation, and these were shared by the New Zealand government. In July 1942, the Australian

War Cabinet cabled Churchill, "superior seapower and airpower are vital to wrest the initiative from Japan and are essential to assure the defensive position in the Southwest Pacific Area."[11]

In January 1942, the Japanese also invaded Burma. It fell rapidly, with the mismanaged British defense of their colony being exploited by the Japanese, who conquered the country at the cost of fewer than 2,000 dead. As in Malaya, the Japanese proved adroit at outflanking maneuvers and at exploiting the disorientating consequences for the British of their withdrawals; although the garrison was far weaker than that in Malaya. Yet again, British troops were untrained for jungle warfare. Field Marshal Sir William Slim recorded,

> It is no exaggeration to say that we had practically no useful or reliable information of enemy strength, movements, or intentions. Our first intimation of a Japanese move was usually the stream of red tracer bullets and the animal yells that announced their arrival on our flank or rear. We were like a blind boxer trying to strike an unseen opponent and to parry blows we did not know were coming until they hit us....The Japanese were obviously able to move...through jungle that we had regarded as impenetrable....they traveled lighter than we did and lived much more off the country. Nearly all our transport was mechanical, and this stretched our columns for miles along a single road through the jungle, vulnerable everywhere from air and ground. Our British, Indian, and Gurkha troops were a match for the Japanese in a stand-up fight, but, invariably, this being tied to a road proved our undoing. It made us fight on a narrow front, while the enemy, moving wide through the jungle, encircled us and placed a force behind us across the only road. The Japanese had developed the art of the road-block to perfection; we seemed to have no answer to it. If we stood and fought where we were, unless the road were reopened, we starved. So invariably we had turned back to clear the road-block, breaking through it usually at the cost of vehicles, and in any case making another withdrawal...Constant retreats, the bogy of the road-block, the loss of Singapore and Rangoon, and the stories of Japanese supermen in the jungle, combined with the obvious shortages of every kind, could not fail to depress morale.[12]

The Japanese also mounted a naval raid into the Indian Ocean in early April 1942, bombing shore installations on Ceylon (Sri Lanka) and sinking British warships.

By then, Britain's role in the war was very much as part of an (unstable) alliance system, with the Soviet Union, from June 1941, the major opponent of Germany, in terms of German forces engaged, and the United States that of Japan. Relations with the Soviet Union were characterized by mutual suspicion, and Churchill was rightly concerned about Soviet intentions in Eastern Europe. There were also tensions over strategy and goals in the Anglo-American relationship, not least Churchill's opposition to Roosevelt's anti-imperialism. Nevertheless, the relationship was pivotal to the successful prosecution of the war.[13] Hitler's declaration of war on the United States, in support of the attack by his Japanese ally, let Roosevelt off the geopolitical hook, since he agreed with Churchill that Hitler was a greater menace than the Japanese, although not all of American opinion shared this view.

The declaration led to the "Germany First" strategy, which was to see the bulk of American land and air assets allocated to preparing for the invasion of Europe. Such a strategy had already been outlined in the Rainbow 5 war plan and the Anglo-American-Canadian ABC-1 Plan talks in early 1941, which had envisaged a defensive strategy in the Pacific in the event of war with the three Axis powers. Roosevelt had supported this emphasis because of his concern that Britain might otherwise collapse in the face of German pressure. This strategy led the American army maneuvers in 1941 to focus on preparing for European-theatre conflict, and was confirmed, after American entry into the war, by the Washington Conference that began on 22 December 1941, which also led to the creation of an Anglo-American planning mechanism based on the Combined Chiefs of Staff. An emphasis on fighting Germany also greatly (but less than the Americans imagined) helped the Soviet Union by diverting German resources to resist American attacks. The emphasis on Germany also accorded with the need to destroy the stronger adversary first.

After American entry into the war, the British continued to play a key role on certain fronts: against Germany in Egypt and against Japan in Burma; while also being crucial to the air and sea wars against Germany by means of building up forces in Britain in preparation for an invasion of German-held France. The sea war, which focused on antisubmarine operations in the Atlantic, was scarcely a peripheral struggle, as it was central to the eventual ability to apply American power against Germany. Classic peripheral operations included the Anglo-Soviet occupation of Iran in August 1941 in order to create supply routes and ensure strategic depth, and the conquest of Vichy-run Madagascar in May–November 1942 in order to thwart the possibility that it might serve as a Japanese submarine base.

In North Africa, the British were put under serious German pressure in the summer of 1942, but the Germans were checked about 60 miles west of Alexandria. The British then built up their strength in Egypt as part of a more general qualitative improvement in the army. This culminated with victory in the major battle the British (and imperial) forces fought alone on land against Germany: El Alamein in Egypt on 23 October–4 November 1942. Skillful generalship, greater numbers of men and tanks, air support, and the effective use of artillery broke the German-Italian army. General Bernard Montgomery, the British commander, had read the terrain ably and his sequential blows, in which infantry cleared the way for armor, eventually succeeded, not least by forcing Field Marshal Erwin Rommel to commit his forces, thus facilitating the decisive British blow; although initial progress had been slow and Montgomery's ability to read the battlefield should not be exaggerated. Thanks to the victory, Churchill, who announced on 10 November that recent success signified not "the beginning of the end" but "the end of the beginning," was able to survive growing political criticisms of his leadership, while it also provided an important psychological boost in Britain. Victory was exploited to drive the Germans and Italians out of North Africa, the advancing Eighth Army joining the largely American forces that had invaded Northwest Africa in November.[14]

The emphasis on fighting Germany still left strategic preferences unclear, particularly the extent to which it was prudent to mount an invasion of France in 1943, or even 1942. American policy makers were opposed to what they saw as the Mediterranean obsession of British policy, and, in 1943, were reluctant to support an invasion, first, of Sicily and, subsequently, of mainland Italy, because they feared that it would detract resources from the invasion of France and the war with Japan, and also be a strategic irrelevance that did not contribute greatly to the defeat of Germany. British strategic concerns in the Mediterranean, however, were a product not simply of geopolitical interests, but also of the legacy since 1940 of conflict with the Axis in the Mediterranean where the Germans could be engaged as they could not then be in Western Europe.[15] The British had military resources in the region, as well as commitments, and the former could not be readily reallocated. Strategic speculation is apt to overlook this point.

The Mediterranean, the axis of British imperial power, remained a crucial area of British operations, with the British the key protagonists for the invasion of Italy in 1943, a priority deplored by American policy makers who preferred a focus on invading France and engaging the main German force in Western Europe. It has been argued that the British focus on an indirect strategy, designed to attack Germany where it was weakest, led to a mistaken concentration on the Mediterranean that failed to inflict serious damage on Germany, and that culminated, in 1943–1945, in the difficult and costly attempt to fight the way up Italy, against relatively small-scale, but still very effective, German opposition. This issue has been accentuated by suggestions that the British sought a Mediterranean focus because they wished both to protect imperial interests and to fight in an area where they could still wield control, and not be dependent on the United States. Churchill was also worried about Soviet intentions in Eastern Europe, and sought to limit this by Anglo-American moves into the Balkans, a policy the United States resisted. Roosevelt indeed informed Churchill in June 1944 that any setback in the invasion of France would be politically disastrous for him if forces had been diverted by being sent to the Balkans, a view Churchill treated as a major strategic and political error.

The British preference for an indirect approach, weakening the Axis by incremental steps as the preparation for an invasion of France, was important. The difficulties of campaigning in Italy were not appreciated by the British, while it was hoped that a presence there would encourage resistance in Yugoslavia and hold down German forces in the Balkans. The indirect approach was an aspect of long-standing British strategic culture, powerfully fortified by the lessons of World War One, and also a response to the specific military circumstances of 1942–1943.[16] Churchill declared in Washington on 19 May 1943, "[W]e must do everything in our power that is sensible and practicable to take more of the weight off Russia in 1943," but the British were sensibly concerned that a direct attack across the English Channel would expose untested forces to the battle-hardened Germans. Their experience of fighting the Germans in 1940–1941 had made them wary of such a step until the Germans had been weakened, and the bloody failure of the Dieppe Raid on the north French coast on 19 August 1942 underlined the problems of amphibious landings and the need for air superiority.

In contrast, the Americans argued that Italy was a strategic irrelevance that would dissipate military strength, and sought a direct approach, particularly an engagement with the major German forces in Western Europe, and an advance into Germany. German weaknesses in 1943 suggest that this might have been an option that year. Many key German units were allocated to the Kursk offensive on the Eastern Front, the Germans lacked the buildup in munitions production that 1943 was to bring, and their defensive positions in France were incomplete. The Soviets indeed mentioned their suspicion of their allies' failure to open a Second Front to the Germans when probing the possibility of a separate peace. These probings led to a peace offer in September 1943, but Hitler was not interested in pursuing it.

The British, however, were correct to draw attention to deficiencies in Allied preparedness that argued in favor of caution in launching an invasion of France. As yet, there was only limited experience in (and equipment for) amphibious operations, and operations in the Mediterranean brought vital experience in this sphere, as well as in Anglo-American military cooperation.[17] Furthermore, it was still unclear at the beginning of 1943 how far, and how speedily, it would be possible to vanquish the U-boat threat and thus control the Atlantic shipping lanes. Aside from the need to build up forces for an invasion, there was also the requirement of assured air and sea superiority to support both landing and exploitation, and in 1943 the Allies did not yet have sufficient air dominance to seek to isolate an invasion zone, a task that the Anzio (in Italy) and Normandy landings in 1944 indicated was extremely difficult.

In October 1942, *Life* declared, "Of one thing we are sure. Americans are not fighting to protect the British empire." At the Tehran conference the following year, there were differences over the fate of European colonial empires. Roosevelt, who refused to visit Britain during the war, was opposed to colonial rule and, instead, in favor of a system of "trusteeship" as a prelude to independence. He pressed Churchill on the status of both Hong Kong (which he wanted returned to China) and India, and British officials were made aware of a fundamental contradiction in attitudes. Roosevelt told Churchill that Britain had to adjust to a "new period" in global history and to turn its back on "400 years of acquisitive blood in your veins,"[18] although he did not press the point on India. Churchill's determination to save the empire was directed at the United States and the Soviet Union, as well as Germany and Japan. France and Britain indeed had territorial ambitions on the Italian colony of Libya.

There were also serious wartime strategic differences between Britain and the United States over British naval operations in the Pacific in 1943–1945.[19] At the same time, divisions among American policy makers were also evident, with Admiral Ernest King, the Commander-in-Chief of the American fleet, determined to put service interest above Allied cooperation. On the British side, there was similar dissension over how far there should first be a concentration on recapturing Malaya and Singapore. This was seen by Churchill and others as crucial to the prestige of British power, and therefore in resisting Asian nationalism which had been greatly advanced by the politicization following the collapse of British power in 1941–1942.[20] His military advisors, however, argued that Churchill's plan for recapturing the colonies, en route to helping in the attack on the Japanese Home Islands, failed to appreciate operational issues, particularly logistical exigencies. These command disputes focus attention to the difficulties of dealing with Churchill. Roosevelt, in turn, wanted the British to secure routes from Burma into China, in order to help keep the latter in the war, but Churchill correctly regarded operations in northern Burma as an unattractive prospect.

Nevertheless, the general theme was one of cooperation, including in intelligence, with the British and Americans exchanging radio intercepts and American units stationed at the Bletchley Park headquarters of the British Ultra system.[21] This provided vital information on German military moves, for example the location of German submarines. More generally, science and technology was an important sphere of Allied cooperation in which, to a considerable extent, intellectual advances were put to common good. As technology with military applications, such as radar, developed rapidly during this period, this cooperation was particularly important.[22] It was also seen with the development of atomic weaponry. Although there were attempts at Axis cooperation, they neither sought nor attained a comparable level.

Against Japan, geography ensured that the British role was in Burma, and, having done badly in 1942, the Indian Army was remade in 1943–1944, not least with a focus on appropriate training.[23] There was an emphasis on being able to take the fight to the Japanese in the jungle, as well as on all-around defensive positions. A report of 1944 recommended that "each individual infantry soldier must be trained to be a self-reliant big game hunter imbued with a deep desire to seek out and kill his quarry."[24] A Japanese invasion of northeastern India was heavily defeated at Kohima and Imphal in March–July 1944. This provided a basis for the British invasion of Burma from December 1944, which led to a successful drive on the Irrawaddy Valley, and a subsequent advance toward Rangoon (captured on 3 May), supported by an amphibious landing. Slim, the commander, proved one of the best generals of the war, with his ability to outthink the Japanese and then to implement plans in an area where terrain, climate, and disease combined to make operating very difficult.

Meanwhile, in Europe, the British had played a major role in the invasion of Normandy in June 1944 (and supplied most of the naval support), as well as in the battle to break out from Normandy, in which the British took heavy casualties, and in the subsequent advance into Germany. Although there were difficulties in the relationship between the leading British commander in the field, Montgomery (who was also overall Allied field commander in Normandy), and some American generals, on the whole the level of cooperation was high, and considerable mutual support was provided. Other British forces fought alongside the Americans in driving the Germans back in northern Italy in early 1945.

Germany was also heavily bombed by British and American planes (the Americans played a major role once they had built up their air power in Britain), albeit with heavy losses among the bombers. On 19 May 1943, Churchill noted in an address to a joint session of the U.S. Congress that opinion was "divided as to whether the use of air power could, by itself, bring about a collapse of Germany or Italy. The experiment is well worth trying, so long as other measures are not excluded." Despite the limited precision of bombing by high-flying planes dropping free-fall bombs, strategic bombing was crucial to the disruption of German logistics and communications, largely because it was eventually on such a massive scale. An article in the *Times* of 1 May 1945, significantly entitled "Air Power Road to Victory...1939 Policy Vindicated," claimed that reductions in oil output due to air attack had affected German war potential in all spheres, "neither his air force nor his army was mobile." More generally, area (rather than precision) bombing disrupted the German war economy, although it also caused heavy civilian casualties, notably at Hamburg in 1943 and Dresden in 1945,[25] while, by 1943, Anglo-American bombing had wrecked 60 percent of Italy's industrial capacity and badly undermined Italian morale. Air attack on Germany also led to the Germans diverting much of their air force and antiaircraft capacity to home defense, rather than supporting frontline units. Allied air power also helped prepare for the invasion of Normandy.

The casualties inflicted by bombing have become a matter of controversy, but too little attention has been devoted to the expectations, from both domestic opinion and the Soviet Union, that major blows would be struck against Germany prior to the opening of the "Second Front" by means of an invasion of France. The delay of this invasion from first 1942 and then, far more, 1943, led to pressure for action. Furthermore, the Germans had not only begun the bombing of civilian targets, but, with the coming of the VIs in 1944, also launched missiles against British cities. In 1944, the V2s entered the lists. These missiles, which could travel at up to 3,000 miles per hour and could be fired from a considerable distance, could not be intercepted like the slower VIs and inflicted considerable damage.

At sea, the Battle of the Atlantic against German submarines was finally won in 1943. The wartime peak of tonnage sunk by the Germans was reached in November 1942, but, in 1943, success was won with improved resources, tactics, and strategy, including more effective antisubmarine air tactics, and the lessening of the mid-Atlantic air gap. The failure of the U-boat offensive was clarified by Allied, especially American, shipbuilding. In the first quarter of 1943, the Allies built more ships than the U-boats sank, and by the end of the third quarter they had built more than had been sunk since the start of the war. Victory in the Battle of the Atlantic and success in shipbuilding permitted the buildup of forces in Britain that was the preliminary to the invasion of France in June 1944.

The empire continued to play a key role until the war's end. The First Canadian Division was a key unit in the preparations for the defense of Britain against German invasion in 1940. VII Canadian Corps, formed in Britain in July 1940, was crucial to the General Headquarters Reserve south of the Thames. By 1942, 500 Canadian warships were in commission. Canadian troops played a major part in European operations in 1943–1945, and Canada at the close of the conflict had the world's third largest navy and the fourth largest air force. Canada was key to the Commonwealth Air Training Plan. Whereas, in the spring of 1939, there were 10,000 men in the Canadian armed forces, by the summer of 1945 more than 1 million men had served. Canada also provided crucial financial support.[26] Japan's entry into the war massively expanded its scope. Having taken a key role in the Middle East in 1940–1942, Australian forces were involved in arduous campaigning against Japan in New Guinea, and closed the war by invading Borneo. In contrast, the main New Zealand commitment remained the Mediterranean, although a second infantry division was raised in 1942 and deployed against Japan in the Southwest

Pacific. The garrison of Hong Kong which fell to Japanese attack in December 1941, included not only British troops but also two Indian battalions, 2,000 Canadian troops, and Hong Kong defense units.[27] Concern about Japanese attack led New Zealand, like Australia and Canada, to make defensive preparations; in Canada they were made in British Columbia. Indian troops played a key role in operations against Japan, as they had earlier done against Italy. Both roles were shared by troops from British Africa.

The war ended with Britain one of the victorious powers, but with its finances, economy, and society exhausted by the conflict; while there had been 397,800 military fatalities (compared to 292,000 for the United States and about 7.5 million for the Soviet Union). The experience of World War One, and the conviction that this would be a total war, ensured that economic regulation, conscription, and a sense of serious struggle encompassing all of society had both been introduced more rapidly and comprehensively than in the earlier war. Free trade and industrial production were both brought under state control. Concern about the populace led to a social politics that put a greater emphasis than hitherto on welfare.[28] Churchill declared, on 18 December 1940, in a speech at Harrow School, where he had been a pupil, "When this war is won, as it surely will be, it must be one of our aims to work to establish a state of society where the advantages and privileges which hitherto have been enjoyed only by the few shall be more widely shared by the many." However, "The Present Overseas Financial Position of the United Kingdom," a Treasury memorandum by John Maynard Keynes, discussed by the government on 23 August 1945, warned,

> We have not a hope of escaping what might be described, without exaggeration and without implying that we should not eventually recover from it, a financial Dunkirk. Abroad it would require a sudden and humiliating withdrawal from our onerous responsibilities with great loss of prestige and an acceptance for the time being of the position of a second-class power....At home a greater degree of austerity would be necessary than we have experienced at any time during the war.

Nevertheless, there were still hopes of a recovery of imperial power, and authority was reimposed in areas that had been conquered by Japan. Furthermore, British forces reimposed French colonial rule in Saigon.[29] There were even ideas of extending British power, both north from India[30] and into the former Italian Empire. Britain was the occupying power of most of it, and British forces in 1948 suppressed Italian-Somali intercommunal rioting in Mogadishu. The British military also administered the Haud and Ogaden regions of Ethiopia.

In the face of near bankruptcy and political and public attitudes in Britain, these hopes, however, were misplaced, and there was a major retreat from the empire. India and Pakistan were given independence in 1947, Burma, Ceylon (Sri Lanka), and Palestine following in 1948. In 1948, the Ogaden was transferred from British to Ethiopian control (the Haud following in 1954), and in 1949 it was agreed that Italian Somaliland should be restored to Italian trusteeship.

Elsewhere, however, there was an effort to defend the empire. A major attempt was made to maintain control of the economically crucial colony of Malaya, in the face of a Communist insurrection: in the Malayan Emergency of 1948–1960, it took 300,000 men to defeat a Communist force that never exceeded 6,000. The British made effective use of helicopters, improved their intelligence system, carefully controlled the food supply, so that the Communists lost access to food, resettled much of the rural population, and used counterinsurgency forces skilled in jungle craft. Anglo-Australian bombing, however, achieved very little in counterinsurgency operations. The British also ensured a positive political context by not allowing the Emergency to deter them from moving Malaya toward independence in 1957, a process that helped ensure that most of the Malayan public supported Britain. Furthermore, their opponents lacked adequate support from the Communist powers, China, and the Soviet Union. Having largely beaten the insurgents by 1954, pressure was maintained over the following years, in particular by the effective use of the now well-developed intelligence apparatus, further weakening the Communists. This was rewarded with mass surrenders in December 1957.[31] In the 1960s, British success in Malaya was to be contrasted with American failure in Vietnam. The contrast frequently focused on greater British commitment to, and skill in, "hearts and minds'" policies, and on the deficiencies of the American stress on firepower. While this was correct, the situation facing the Americans in Vietnam, in terms both of the political situation there and of the international context, was more difficult.

A different engagement against Communist expansion took place as a result of membership of the North Atlantic Treaty Organization (NATO) from 1949, which guaranteed the security of Western Europe. Britain became a major NATO military base, with American planes joining the RAF in eastern England in providing the key force from which the Soviet Union was to be bombed in the event of war. Britain was also an important base for NATO intelligence surveillance of Soviet activities, which included, in 1956, high-altitude balloons equipped with cameras. Opposition to Communism was also seen with participation in the American-led United Nations coalition that resisted the North Korean invasion of South Korea in the Korean War (1950–1953). In July 1953, the British contingent was the third largest in the coalition forces, although, at 14,198, it was far smaller than the South Korean (509,911) and American (302,483) forces. The Canadians came fourth at 6,146.[32] It was difficult to defend participation in the war in terms of traditional British interests, and the Americans tended to make decisions without much or any consultation, but the Attlee government played a major part in encouraging a firm response in Korea. Under American pressure, Britain also embarked on a costly rearmament program that was to help cause a crisis in public finances in the early 1950s, as Labour was also trying to fund a major expansion in social welfare. This provided another instance of the tensions between welfarism, military expenditure, and financial/taxation considerations also seen with the Liberal government of the late 1900s and early 1910s during the naval race with Germany.

Earlier, Atlee had decided by January 1947 to develop a British nuclear bomb. This policy was regarded as necessary for Britain's independent security and influence and, throughout, the British government sought to play more than a secondary role to the United States. The bomb was ready by 1952. Atomic weaponry was initially entrusted to the RAF, and was to be used in planes based in eastern England, complementing the American planes based in the same areas, before the eventual switch to a submarine-based missile system. The pro-Western policies of Attlee's Labour government were supported by the vast majority of the Labour Party and trade union movement. Communist and Soviet sympathizers within both were isolated and the Communist Party was kept at a distance. This helped prevent the development of a radical Left and was linked to the alliance between labor and capital that was to be important in the postwar mixed economy.

Decolonization and greater Dominion autonomy, however, ensured that Britain could bring less to the strategic table. Indian independence in 1947 was particularly important, as Indian troops had been crucial to Britain's expeditionary capacity in Asia, Africa, and the Middle East. The loss of these troops removed an important mainstay of the military dimension of the British Empire so that, for example, whereas, in 1941, Indian forces had played a major role in the successful invasion of Iraq, a decade later, when Britain was in dispute with the Nationalist government in Iran over its seizure of Britain's oil interests, Plan Y, the plan for a military intervention by the seizure of Abadan, was not pursued, in large part because, without Indian troops, and with British forces committed in Germany and Korea, it no longer seemed militarily viable. There were no Indian troops to help in the attack on Egypt in 1956 during the Suez Crisis, nor to enable Britain to participate in the Vietnam War, had that been a goal. Thanks in part to the fact that Britain could no longer deploy imperial military resources, British intervention in the Middle East in the two Gulf Wars (1991, 2003) was very much as a junior partner of the United States. By then, the idea that Britain might have fought in part by deploying Indian troops was no more than a distant memory.

Assertiveness in the 1950s, particularly in Malaya and Kenya, at Suez and in Cyprus, and in British membership of the Southeast Asia Treaty

Organization and the Baghdad Pact, was intended to protect British interests and to demonstrate that Britain was not weak. However, these commitments put serious pressure on Britain's ability to maintain force levels in Europe as part of NATO, a strategic goal that itself, in turn, seriously compromised Britain's role as a military power outside Europe. At the same time, imperial conflict brought the combat experience and training in "small wars" that NATO membership could not offer. In suppressing the Mau-Mau uprising in Kenya in 1952–1956, the British benefited from linking military to social policies, and from flexibility in both. The move from the initial defensive stage, in which the lessons of Malaya were not learned, to a recapture of the initiative, in which these lessons were applied, was crucial. This move entailed the development of a system of command and control encompassing army, police, and administration, and the introduction of appropriate tactics, including a large-scale attempt to separate the guerrillas from popular support. This entailed fortified villages, a large ditch around the forest, and the detention of possibly over 160,000 Kikuyu, the ethnic group on which the Mau Mau were based. The harshness of this has led to criticism,[33] but at the time it seemed an appropriate response to insurrection.

In 1954, in Operation Anvil, the capital, Nairobi, was isolated and combed, in a move that denied the Mau Mau urban support. The successful use, alongside the regular army and the white settler Kenya Regiment, of loyal Africans, the King's African Rifles, Kenya Police, Kikuyu Home Guards, and former insurgents, was also important; as were (until 1955) larger-scale sweep operations and, later, air-supported forest patrols. Bomber command was particularly active in 1955. From 1955, success led to the withdrawal of troops, and this was accelerated after the capture of Dedan Kimathi, the leading Mau-Mau commander, in October 1956. The following month, the police took over responsibility for operations. A wide-ranging social reform policy, including land reform, in which the government distanced itself from the white colonists and sought to win hearts and minds, was also important.[34] It proved difficult to control events in Cyprus during the Greek Cypriot insurgency of 1954–1959, but, again, by applying the Malayan lessons, it proved possible to contain the crisis, while the use of sympathetic Cypriots was also significant.

The Suez Crisis of 1956, in which Britain (and France) attacked Egypt in response to the latter's nationalization of the Suez Canal, saw a major display of British military power, particularly naval strength and amphibious capability. Much of the Egyptian air force was destroyed as a result of air attack on its bases, and helicopter-borne troops were used by the British in the invasion. American opposition, which underlined the vulnerability of the British economy, was crucial, however, in weakening British resolve, and led to a humiliating withdrawal. The American government felt that the invasion needlessly compromised Western interests in the Third World, particularly the Middle East, and were, more generally, opposed to the retention of colonies and imperial habits by European powers. The British were therefore far more successful when they attacked Egypt in 1882 than in 1956. In 1882, there had been an enormous capability gap at sea, but a far smaller one on land. In 1956, in contrast, British forces could draw on far superior air power (although a lack of practice was held responsible for low bombing standards),[35] while the availability of parachutists greatly expanded the range of possible "landings," and thus enhanced the risk posed to the defenders. Nevertheless, the contrast between 1882 and 1956 indicated a major shift in Western attitudes toward force projection, both by one's own state and by others.

Failure in the Suez Crisis indeed marked the end of Britain's resolve to act independently; and, from then, there was an implicit reliance on American acceptance, as in the Falklands War in 1982. Furthermore, the pace of decolonization dramatically increased after Suez. This was largely due to a shift in attitude within the Conservative governments of 1951–1964, but defense factors did play a role. Colonies now appeared less necessary in defense terms, not only because of alliance with the United States, but also because, in 1957, Britain had added hydrogen to the atomic bomb.

Military deployments, nevertheless, continued in the defense and protection of the formal and the informal empire—particularly in Jordan (1958), Kuwait (1961), Brunei (1962), Malaysia (1963–1966), Aden (1963–1967), East Africa (1964),[36] Anguilla (1969), and Oman (1970–1976)[37]— and this was related to an ambitious sense of British power, one that was in no way restricted to NATO roles. Malaysia, a state composed of former British colonies, was attacked by neighboring Indonesia. The crisis began in 1962 with the Indonesian-supported Brunei revolt, which was suppressed by British forces from the Singapore garrison. President Sukarno of Indonesia then turned on the neighboring, Malaysian, part of Borneo. The Indonesians had good weapons, especially antipersonnel mines and rocket launchers, but the British and Commonwealth forces were well led, had well-trained, versatile troops, and benefited from complete command of air and sea. The British made effective use of helicopters, had a good nearby base at Singapore, and an excellent intelligence network, and were helped by the absence of significant domestic opposition to the commitment. This contrasted with the American position in Vietnam, but the struggle there was longer and more intractable. The British used a flexible response system to counter Indonesian excursions, and, eventually, followed up with cross-border operations of their own, putting the Indonesians on the defensive. Indonesian attempts to exploit tensions within Malaya by landing forces by sea and sending parachutists there failed. Anglo-Malaysian firmness prevented the situation deteriorating, and a change of government in Indonesia in the winter of 1965–1966 led to negotiations.[38]

More generally, Harold Wilson, who became Labour Prime Minister in 1964, and who prefigured Tony Blair in a number of respects, hoped to maintain Britain's role as a major independent power, and sought to act as a leading figure on the international stage. In support of India against China, and reflecting serious concern about the consequences of China's easy victory over India in their brief border war in 1962, Wilson declared that "Britain's frontiers are on the Himalayas." The possibility that China would follow up its victory appeared to threaten the stability of the Indian Ocean rim and, with it, Britain's interests in Southwest and Southeast Asia. British strategic thinking, which owed much to the geopolitical ideas of Halford Mackinder, discerned a tension between the Eurasian heartland and the oceanic rim, and thus saw the stability of South Asia and the Indian Ocean as closely linked. In this conception, Britain could play a key role if it could project its power in that ocean. This strategic assumption looked forward to subsequent British roles, particularly in the Gulf Wars, as the Persian Gulf is an extension of that ocean. The political context was to change, but the geopolitical context remained far more stable.

In 1960, the carrier *Victorious* had joined the Far East station with several nuclear bombs, and planes able to drop them, aboard. Subsequent war planning called for the use of a carrier able to mount nuclear strikes on southern China, and for a second carrier to be deployed in 1964. These carriers were to complement RAF planes based in Singapore. The British presence in the Indian Ocean was anchored with bases in Aden and Singapore. Planning for the new submarines armed with Polaris missiles with nuclear warheads, included firing stations in the Indian Ocean designed both to block Himalayan passes (through which the Chinese could advance on India) and to reach targets in southern Russia.

However, this military capability was out of kilter with Britain's underlying position. The attempt to act as an independent power failed, Britain lacking the necessary diplomatic strength to further its goals. Severe financial problems also hit hard. They led to the major devaluation of sterling in 1967 after a protracted and unsuccessful attempt to defend it. This devaluation was a savage humiliation, and an important symbolic loss of international fiscal power. As a result, under pressure from the Chiefs of Staff, who were concerned about the mismatch between commitments and resources, the government announced in January 1968 that it was abandoning Britain's military position east of Suez, and forces were withdrawn from the Persian Gulf in 1971 and, largely, from Singapore the same year. This was a major shift in British strategic culture, and one that greatly attenuated military links with Australia and New Zealand.

Having been successful in Malaysia, the east of Suez policy had also faced a serious failure in Aden. Nationalist agitation there, which had been increasingly strident from 1956, turned into revolt in 1963. The resulting war, which continued until independence was granted in November 1967, involved hostilities both in the city of Aden and in the mountainous hinterland of what was subsequently South Yemen. The British deployed 19,000 troops, as well as tanks and helicopters (using the latter for example in support of the capture of the rebel stronghold in the inaccessible Wadi Dhubsan in 1964), but their position was undermined by their failure to sustain local support. The British-officered Federal Reserve Army proved unreliable, and, in June 1967, the South Arabian Police and the Aden Armed Police rebelled in the city of Aden. Furthermore, the British were unable to support allied sheikhs in the interior against the guerrilla attacks of the National Liberation Front (NLF). The scorched earth tactics and the resettlement policies seen in Malaya in the 1950s were used, but the NLF's inroads forced an abandonment of the interior in the early summer of 1967. In tactical terms, the NLF made effective use of snipers, while, once the British were clearly on the way out, they found it hard to get accurate intelligence, and this made mounting operations difficult. Reduced to holding on to Aden, a base area that had also to be defended from internal disaffection, and where the garrison itself had to be protected, the only initiative left was to abandon the position, which was done in November 1967, bringing to an end a rule that had begun in 1839.[39]

The changes in British policy and strategic culture in the late 1960s were important aspects of a more general shift in which the United States took over Britain's strategic position in the Indian Ocean and Persian Gulf. Edward Heath, who became Conservative Prime Minister in 1970, succeeding Wilson, maintained the policy of withdrawal from east of Suez. Furthermore, British defenses from the 1960s became more clearly dependent on American weaponry. This was the case with the Polaris missile (and its eventual replacement), Trident, and also with the decision in April 1965 to purchase the F-111A jet in order to fill the gap after the cancellation of the projected British TSR.2 strike reconnaissance plane able to deliver a nuclear weapon, which was overbudget, late, and affected by the Labour government's determination to cut defense costs. The purchase of the F-111A, in turn, was canceled in 1968, as the result of a further British defense review, which, in the terms of the age, meant a retrenchment of forces in light of serious fiscal exigencies.

In December 1962, in what became known as the Nassau Agreement, Prime Minister Harold Macmillan and U.S. President John F. Kennedy had decided that the Americans would provide Polaris for a class of four, British nuclear-powered submarines that were to be built; although

American agreement was dependent on the British force being primarily allocated for NATO duties, an important indicator of the strategic relationship. At the same time, the cooperation underlined the strategic closeness of the two powers, which had been a major theme in world military affairs since 1941. British strategic interests were increasingly focused in the NATO area and on NATO tasks. This can be seen as a military equivalent to membership of the European Economic Community (EEC), which became a governmental priority from the early 1960s, for both Labour and Conservative, finally being achieved in 1973. Yet, the processes were different. The EEC was seen as a way to anchor Western Europe in the anti-Communist camp, but it was also deliberately constructed as a non-military alliance, as it was not intended to challenge NATO and its vital American link. At sea, a focus on the NATO area was a consequence of the buildup of the Soviet fleet from the 1950s, and much of the British fleet was allocated to the standing Naval Force Atlantic, a NATO force established in 1967.

Multilateralism within NATO greatly diminished the independent role of British strategy. This was taken further in February 1966 with the cancellation of the planned CVA-01 carrier, which would have been the first carrier to be built in Britain since World War Two, as well as the first of what the navy hoped would be a class of three large-strike aircraft carriers. This was an important aspect of a major process of defense cuts, seen also for example in the amalgamation of regiments ordered in 1968, that reflected the economic problems, financial stringency, and political priorities of the period. Sir David Luce, the First Sea Lord and Chief of the Naval Staff, resigned in protest at the cancellation, while the Minister of Defence (Navy) resigned over the decision to end an independent British intervention capability.[40]

It was envisaged, that, after the existing aircraft carriers, with their distant strike capability, came to an end of their service, naval air power would amount essentially to helicopters designed to act against Soviet submarines in the Atlantic. An ability to support amphibious operations no longer seemed necessary, a major shift in military tasking. Indeed, the British forces were already in Western Europe, in the former occupation zone within West Germany, as the British Army of the Rhine, so that, in the event of a conflict, there would be no equivalent to the need to move troops to the Continent seen in 1914 and 1939 when troops had been moved to France. British defense priorities were focused on Western Europe and the North Atlantic. Forces were committed to these goals, the British being obliged to maintain 55,000 troops in Germany in order to man the 65 kilometers of the Inner German Border [between West and (Communist) East Germany] that Britain had to defend. If numbers were reduced, for example to help in the situation in Northern Ireland, it was necessary to seek NATO permission and to promise to restore the agreed strength. These obligations were triservice, as part of the RAF was located in West Germany. These priorities were not simply a matter of numbers, but also of capability, for the threat of Soviet attack and the nature of its military obliged the British to upgrade in order to match improvements in the latter. The army as a whole was equipped and trained primarily for this task, with the strategic, operational, and tactical emphasis on resisting heavily armed and more numerous attacking Soviet forces. Thus, there was a stress on defensive fighting, not maneuver. The British military had moved far from its role during the reign of Queen Victoria (r. 1837–1901). It was no longer an imperial force. Nor was its objective, doctrine, structure, and training designed for peripheral conflict against the likely opponent. Instead, the military was now fully committed on the front line of the Cold War.

CHAPTER 8

New Roles, 1968–

An unexpected revival in the commitment to home defense was seen not in the shape of the defense of Britain from invasion, the key issue in 1940, but rather that of dealing with sustained civil unrest in Northern Ireland. Much of the army served there from 1969, and, in terms of manpower and training, Northern Ireland became a major commitment. This underlined the variety of military tasks. In place of the focus on state-to-state conflict with regulars, seen in the North Atlantic Treaty Organization (NATO) training, came the support for the civil power that had proved so important in the defense of the empire. Indeed, the dispatch of reinforcements to Northern Ireland in 1969 followed swiftly on the heels of the withdrawal of forces from the colony of Aden in 1967 after the failure to suppress insurrection there. The need to succeed was more apparent in Northern Ireland, where rioting had broken out in 1968, and the context of domestic political and public scrutiny was much more trying for both military and government. The deployment was intended as a short-term measure, but, instead, the very presence of troops became an issue and led to violence. In 1971, the Provisional Irish Republican Army (IRA), a Catholic nationalist terrorist organization, launched its first major offensive and, amid widespread shooting and bombings the following year, the Catholic population and the army increasingly saw each other as enemies. Despite the difficulties of the situation, the army, which increased its strength in Northern Ireland from 6,000 troops in 1969 to 20,000 in 1972, succeeded, in Operation Motorman, in ending the "no-go" areas in Belfast and Londonderry that the Provisional IRA had created as a standard stage in the Maoist theory of revolutionary warfare. Instead, the Provisional IRA turned to terrorism.

Confronting this proved a more arduous challenge, with the army having to maintain a semblance of order sufficient to demonstrate to the Catholic Nationalist terrorists of the Provisional IRA that they could not win, and also to encourage intransigent Catholic and Protestant politicians eventually to talk with each other. This proved a very long-term commitment, which was accentuated when Protestant "Loyalist" terrorists began armed action against Catholics, providing a new opponent of the army, Northern Ireland placed a major strain on manpower and morale. IRA terrorism made it difficult for the army to fraternize with the population, and ambushes ensured that garrisons had to be supplied and reinforced by helicopters. Furthermore, the IRA found shelter in the Republic of Ireland and it proved impossible to control the border. Nevertheless, the infantry, who bore most of the commitment, proved resilient, training adjusted to the particular challenges of the task, and the army acquired considerable experience in antiterrorist policing. Instead of tanks or bombing, military proficiency was measured in traditional infantry skills, such as patrolling and the use of cover. However, the difficulty of ending terrorism in the absence of widespread civilian support became readily apparent. Policy would probably have been different had there been a conscript army. Conscripts might have been unwilling to serve in Northern Ireland, and the deployment and tactics employed might have placed a greater emphasis on avoiding casualties.

More generally, British strategic options seemed no longer to be those of independence or alliance from a position of strength, but, instead, to be those of centering political interests and defense undertakings on American or European systems. Although lessened by the role of NATO, the tension between American and European alignments was to be the theme of British power politics thereafter. Roles and bases further afield diminished. In 1975–1979, the Simonstown agreements with South Africa were terminated, forces were withdrawn from Singapore and Malta, the Southeast Asia Treaty Organization was dissolved, and there was no pretense that Hong Kong could be defended if China chose to attack. Self-determination for Hong Kong was not an option. Gibraltar could be protected if necessary from Spain, but not Hong Kong from China. The last large, fixed-wing plane, strike carrier, *Ark Royal,* was decommissioned in 1978, the year in which *Eagle* was also broken up. They were designed to be replaced by a new type of carrier equipped with VSTOL (Vertical/Short Takeoff and Landing) planes intended to act against submarines. A marked drawing in had taken place, and there seemed little prospect of anything else. Linked to this was a shift in priorities, with a decline of what had been referred to as a "warfare state" as a result of the growing prioritization of social welfare.[1]

The Falklands War of 1982, however, underlined the unpredictability of military goals and responsibilities. The British military was not configured for such a conflict, nor was it one in accordance with the expectations of government. Indeed, under Margaret Thatcher, who became Conservative Prime Minister in 1979 (serving until 1990), there was a strong focus on the Cold War. East-West tensions had revived markedly with the Soviet intervention in Afghanistan at the close of 1979, and the settlement of the Rhodesia question in 1980 further helped ensure a

British focus on the Cold War. This was seen to mean a concentration on the defense of Western Europe, and not on capability farther afield. This hit hard at the navalist legacy. In 1979, *Blake,* the last active cruiser, was decommissioned, while *Bulwark,* a "commando carrier," was laid up in 1981. That year, the defense review, *The Way Forward,* implied that the navy was not concentrating on what should be its core mission, and, instead, that there was an anachronistic emphasis on the surface fleet. The Defence Secretary, John Nott, argued that obligations to the defense of Western Europe as part of NATO had to come first, and had to determine force structure.

The Falklands War was to suggest otherwise. The archipelago in the South Atlantic had been under British control from 1833 and had a British settler population, but was claimed, as the Malvinas, by the Argentinians. Their navy had long sought to regain the Falklands in order to demonstrate its role in protecting the patrimony, and a desire to propriate naval opinion led the junta who headed the military dictatorship to decide to act. Already in 1976, after a military junta had seized power from the civilian government of Isabelita Peron, the navy had raised the Argentine flag on South Thule in the South Sandwich Islands. However, the following year, threatening Argentinian maneuvers were countered by the British with the response of a task force of two frigates and a submarine. In December 1981, a new junta seized power in Argentina. Under pressure from its naval member, the junta was convinced that the British government, uncertain of the desirability of retaining the colony, would accept its seizure. The decision, in 1981, to withdraw the Antarctic patrol ship *Endurance* was seen as a sign of British lack of interest in the South Atlantic (and was indeed foolish), and, on 2 April 1982, in Operation Rosario, the virtually undefended islands were successfully invaded. Their tiny garrison lacked air and naval support.

The subsequent conflict was important for the politics of both states, and also for the light it shone on British military capability in a particular context. Assured by the First Sea Lord, Admiral Sir Henry Leach, who appeared before the Cabinet in full uniform, that the navy (which was anxious, not least in the face of *The Way Forward,* to assert its indispensability) could fulfill the task, and determined to act firmly in what was correctly seen as a make-or-break moment for the government, Thatcher decided to respond with Operation Corporate: an expeditionary force, dispatched from 5 April, that included most of the navy. Fifty-one ships were to take part in the operation. As another sign of British maritime strength, 68 ships were "taken up from trade," contracted, and requisitioned, including the cruise ships *Queen Elizabeth II* and *Canberra,* which were used to transport troops, and the container ship *Atlantic Conveyor,* which, in the event, was to be sunk by an Exocet missile, taking a large amount of stores to the bottom. The speed with which the operation was mounted contrasted markedly with the time taken for the Suez expedition in 1956. The mismanagement of the latter had given time for hostile domestic and international opinion to be expressed more forcefully.

In 1982, both political and military preparedness were at issue for Britain. Leach argued that if Britain did not act, "in a few months we shall be living in a different country whose word counts for little." Politically, the government, which had not been prepared, benefited from an upsurge of domestic popularity. The Argentinian junta lacked domestic support— despite Nationalist graffiti in Northern Ireland praising the Argentinians, British Catholics did not play a role comparable to that of some Muslims when British forces were committed in Iraq from 2003. Furthermore, the opposition Labour Party leader, Michael Foot, badly misjudged the Conservative response. Thinking that this was another instance of Conservative appeasement, a rerun of 1936–1938, Foot pressed for action against a right-wing dictatorship (he was more tolerant of the left-wing variety), only to find Thatcher provide it. As a result, it was Labour that was split (although only a minority of the Labour Party opposed the war), with, in contrast, very few Conservatives critical of the leadership. The failure before the conflict to provide deterrent signs to Argentina was not brought home to the government at this stage, and critical later enquiries were to lack political weight.

Internationally, the dictatorial nature of the Argentinian junta, and the fact that the Falklanders did not want to be ruled from Buenos Aires, ensured that Britain benefited from a more supportive response than that shown during the Suez Crisis of 1956. American policy, however, proved a particular difficulty. On 29 March 1982, Sir Nicholas Henderson, the envoy in Washington, responded to American pressure for restraint over South Georgia, which the Argentinians seized prior to the attack on the Falkland Islands, by asking how much British neutrality might be appreciated if Puerto Rico was under attack. Lord Carrington, the Foreign Secretary, told an American diplomat that Britain had supported American policy over Sinai and El Salvador without enthusiasm, and against its better judgment, but out of solidarity with its closest ally, and that the government expected an appropriate American response.[2] The Reagan government, nevertheless, supported conservative dictatorial Latin American regimes, such as that in Argentina, and was concerned that a defeated Argentina might go Communist. There was also no wish to see a war between two allies, particularly one that risked dispatching many of NATO's North Atlantic naval assets (in the shape of British warships) to the bottom of the ocean. More generally, the American response was a reminder of the conditional nature of alliances, and of the need, in response, to rely on resolution and to benefit from the divisions among the policy makers of allied states. Indeed, the Falklands War saw the American administration very divided, with the State Department sympathetic to Argentina and the Pentagon pro-British. The United States attempted mediation that would have left the Falklands under Argentinian control, but Thatcher rejected these attempts; sensibly so, as they would have weakened her domestically and left the Falklanders under rule by a military junta. She insisted that any negotiations depended on Argentinian withdrawal. Initially, the British found President François Mitterand of France more ready to offer support, not least information on the Exocet missiles that had been sold to Argentina. The recent claim, by Mitterand's psychoanalyst, that Thatcher threatened the use of nuclear weaponry against Argentina unless France provided such information seems implausible.

There was also the issue of military preparedness. As a result of the shift from large fleet carriers, not least the cancellation of the CVA-01 project in 1966, the expeditionary force lacked a large aircraft carrier, and therefore airborne warning of attacks. It had, however, two smaller carriers. The light fleet carrier *Hermes,* which had been converted to a helicopter carrier in 1971–1973, had, in 1980–1981, been fitted with a ski-jump bow ramp in order to assist the take-off of Sea Harrier fighter-bomber VSTOL planes The 16,000 ton *Invincible,* laid down in 1973 and commissioned in 1980, the largest vessel built for the navy since 1945, was also designed for Sea Harriers.

On 25–26 April, the British recaptured the subsidiary territory of South Georgia and, on 1 May, large-scale hostilities began when the British tried, by bombing, to disable the runway of Port Stanley, the capital of the Falklands. The following day, *Conqueror,* a nuclear-powered submarine, sank the Argentinian cruiser *General Belgrano.* This step was crucial to the struggle for command of the sea, as it led the Argentinian navy to desist from threatening attack and to withdraw to Argentinian territorial waters. There was to be much contention about the sinking of the *Belgrano,* but, as its intention was clearly that of threatening the British task force, a failure to sink the ship would have been a serious neglect of responsibility.

Indeed, as a reminder of the vulnerability of the task force, air-launched Exocet missiles and bombs led to the loss of six British ships. Another eleven were damaged, while thirteen badly fused bombs hit ships but failed to explode, a key instance of the role of chance factors. British losses showed that modern antiaircraft missile systems, in this case Sea Darts and Sea Wolfs, were not necessarily a match for manned aircraft and revealed a lack of adequate preparedness on the part of the navy, which had to rely on missile systems not hitherto tested in war. An Exocet was responsible for the loss of the destroyer *Sheffield* on 4 May, and bombs for the loss of the *Coventry* on 25 May. However, the Argentinians did not sink the two carriers that provided vital air support (but not superiority) for both sea and land operations. Designed for antisubmarine warfare in the North Atlantic, in the event of war with the Soviet Union, the carriers' Sea King helicopters and Harriers demonstrated their versatility. The Harriers did so both in the combat air patrol role, protecting the task force, and in the close air support roles, attacking the Argentinians on the Falklands. The latter outnumbered the British force, and also had both aircraft and helicopters, while the British were short of ammunition because they had underestimated requirements, and were operating at the end of a very long supply line and under pressure to achieve a speedy result. They also lacked sufficient light antiaircraft weaponry. There were also problems in the command structure, not least army-navy co-operation. American logistical and intelligence support, however, aided the British, particularly the supply of 12.5 million gallons of highly refined aviation fuel, as well as Sidewinder missiles and the use of satellite-based communications.

Landing on the Falklands on 21 May, British troops advanced on the capital, Port Stanley, fighting some bitter engagements on the nearby hills, and forcing the 11,400 isolated, demoralized, and beaten Argentinians to surrender on 14 June. In the end, it was a matter of bravely executed attacks, good morale, the careful integration of infantry with artillery support, and the ability to continue without control of the air. By landing, the British had not ensured success, as the Argentinian plan rested on fighting on from fixed positions, in order to wear down British numbers and supplies, and to take advantage of the onset of the bitter South Atlantic winter. Nevertheless, British success in the field, combined with a continued ability to maintain the initiative, destroyed the Argentinian will to fight on, crucially so as they still had plentiful troops, artillery, and supplies when they surrendered, while the British had nearly run out of artillery shells.[3]

It would be easy to chart a course from the Falklands to Gulf War Two, the invasion of Iraq in 2003, arguing that the trajectory of military activity focused on long-range force projection, and that the Falklands War revealed the need for amphibious capability and joint operations that was to become a more constant feature of such activity. Linked to this approach would be a semiautomatic pattern of approbation or criticism of particular investments in weaponry and related policy initiatives. The Falklands War certainly revealed the value of preserving a balanced force structure, so that Britain alone could take action, rather than simply focusing on a number of specialized areas within an alliance division of labor. The latter is key to much current discussion, with an emphasis in particular on a capacity for integration within an American-directed military structure. However, present British plans do include provision for the capability to mount moderate-sized operations alone, or with Britain playing the key role within the coalition. From that perspective, the option of a Falklands-style expedition has been retained, although the risk of defeat if the opponent is strong remains, as does the dependence on

American acceptance. In the Falklands War, the nature of the war, although difficult, played into British hands, as the small local population was friendly and it was possible to isolate the Argentinian occupation force from their base in Argentina. In that respect, the war offered scant guidance to the likely nature and risks of modern expeditionary warfare, seen, for example, in Iraq and Afghanistan.

To chart a course from the Falklands to the invasion of Iraq ignores the indeterminacy of warfare. Furthermore, in the specific case of the 1980s, the Falklands led nowhere. They were developed, after the war, at considerable expense as a military base, ensuring a new triservice commitment; but the key event in the early 1980s was an upsurge in Cold War tension, much of it focused in Europe, an upsurge that encouraged a real growth in the defense budget. Indeed, 1983 was a year in which confrontation came close to conflict. The deployment of Cruise and Pershing missiles by NATO in Western Europe proved particularly sensitive. The shooting down, over Soviet airspace, of a Korean airliner suspected of espionage led to a marked increase in tension, as did Soviet fears of attack during a NATO exercise: the KGB (Russian State Security Committee) provided inaccurate reports of American plans for a surprise nuclear first strike.

Then, and more generally during the Cold War, the risk of war posed major problems for the British military as it would be in the forefront of resisting any Soviet attack. For the navy, there would be the challenge to North Atlantic routes and the need to block Soviet submarines, both in the Denmark Strait between Iceland and Greenland, and between Iceland and Britain. For the Royal Air Force (RAF), there was the problem of protecting Britain and British forces in Continental Europe, in particular of providing a coherent air-defense system capable of intercepting long-range Soviet bombers; as well as the need to take the war to the Soviets.

Although the protection of West Germany from Soviet land attack led to the preparation of fixed defenses, there was a clear need for mobility, and this helped lead the British to emphasize their armor. This was underlined by the lessons drawn from wars abroad. The Israeli victory against Egyptian and Syrian defensive positions in the Six Day War of 1967 and also, eventually, after initial Egyptian and Syrian successes, in the Yom Kippur War of 1973, showed the value of mobility, and, conversely, the vulnerability of forces with a low rate of activity. Greater British engagement with the maneuverist approach, which was called for in Richard Simpkin's *Race to the Swift: Thoughts on Warfare in the Twenth-First Century* (1985), owed much to the role of Sir Nigel Bagnall, successively commander of the 1st British Corps in Germany (1981–1983) and of NATO's Northern Army Group (1983–1985), and Chief of the General Staff from 1985 to 1988. He pushed the maoeuverist approach and the operational level hard.

A requirement for greater mobility and flexibility, combined with the end of conscription, to provide both need and opportunity for an accentuation of the role of training in forwarding the goal for an effective and relatively small regular military. This had been the tendency latent in the century's move toward more advanced military technology, but had been delayed by the requirement for simple mass training provided by fresh cohorts of conscripts. In 1938, the army committee that recommended the merger of the Royal Tank Corps and the newly mechanized cavalry noted that, in the past, troops had been trained within their own regiments, but that "this system is impracticable for a corps equipped with armoured fighting vehicles, and it is clear that in future training will be necessary at a depot equipped with suitable vehicles and staffed by technically qualified instructors."[4] The growing length and specialization of training was important to the professionalism of the military and to the process of differentiation within it.

It is important not to exaggerate the end of the Cold War in 1989–1991 as a break, because many geopolitical issues spanned the divide, while much of the American and the British capability deployed in the 1990s and 2000s stemmed from Cold War procurement policies, tasking, and doctrine. The ability to fight a conventional war in Europe had to be translated to other spheres, which created problems in adaptation, and pressure for transformation, but much of the capability was already in place. In the case of Britain, however, the process of transformation to meet new goals was, particularly initially, very much molded by the drive to restrain costs, that, in part, was a consequence of the serious economic and fiscal downturn of the early 1990s. *Options for Change,* the 1991 defense review, responded to the end of the Cold War by cutting all three services, and most radically the army: its strength was cut from 156,000 men to 104,000. This "peace dividend" was cost-driven, rather than reflecting a clear sense of likely burdens. In particular, there was an underrating of possible future threats, and, specifically, of the needs posed by both peacekeeping and by the problems of retaining a capacity for high intensity warfare. Indeed, the situation was even worse than this, because *Options for Change* was presented not before the lessons of the Gulf War but rather after it had revealed serious deficiencies in the ability of the military, particularly the army, to mount a major operation far from its bases without having to scavenge in order to produce the required resources. In the event, moreover, British military policy from 1990 was to be characterized by force projection.

In the meanwhile, the navy's traditional function of protecting trade had led, in response to the outbreak of the Iran-Iraq War in 1980, to the establishment of the Armilla patrol in the Persian Gulf, which continued until responsibilities broadened in 1990 with the Iraqi attack on Kuwait. The patrol, like the Falklands War, revealed the continued importance of the fleet for the tackling of unexpected tasks. There was a clear response in terms of force structure, with the retention of carrier and amphibious capability and the ordering of new ships. *Invincible* was on the eve of being sold to Australia in early 1982 when the Falklands War broke out. It was retained. Although *Bulwark* was broken up in 1984 and *Hermes* sold to India in 1986, the carrier *Illustrious*, built in 1976–1982, entered service, as did a new *Ark Royal* built in 1978–85. Seventeen frigates were laid down in 1982–1991. However, the major commitment was to the nuclear deterrent. Four 16,000-ton *Vanguard* class submarines, armed with Trident missiles, the replacement to Polaris, were laid down in 1986–1993 and the first, *Vanguard*, was commissioned in 1993.

By then, the strategic landscape had changed. The need to face new tasks was driven home by the Iraqi invasion of oil-rich Kuwait on 2 August 1990. The response defined high-spectrum warfare for the following decade, and was the first major conflict fought against the conventional forces of another state for the British since the Falklands War. The Americans very much took the leading role, but the British made a valuable contribution, at sea, in the air, and on land. Iraq's refusal to meet a UN deadline for withdrawal led, on 17 January 1991, to the start of a major air offensive, in which the British played a prominent role. This offensive worked because of the rapid success in overcoming the sophisticated Iraqi antiaircraft system. Saddam Hussein had used French and Soviet technology to produce an integrated system in which computers linked radars and missiles. The destruction of the air-defense system on the first night was a triumph, not only for weaponry but also for planning, that made full use of the opportunities presented by the weapons, while also outthinking the Iraqis, for example by getting them to bring their radars to full power, and thus exposing them to attack. As a result of the subsequent air assault, Iraqi ground forces were short of supplies, their command and control system was heavily disrupted, so that they could not "understand" the battle, and their morale was low.

In February 1991, Iraq was driven from Kuwait in a swift campaign in which the Iraqis were outgeneralled and outfought by coalition forces that benefited not only from superior technology, but also from their ability to maintain a high-tempo offensive while executing a well-conceived plan that combined air and land forces. Coalition fighting quality, unit cohesion, leadership and planning, and Iraqi deficiencies in each, all played a major role in ensuring victory. For the British, the war raised issues of force projection, logistics, and interoperability, although the last was eased by the experience of cooperation through NATO. The war was short, saw few British casualties, and did not divide the country. It did not lead to any occupation of Iraq, and the ease of the exit from the conflict contrasted markedly with the Gulf War of 2003.

The next Western intervention in which the British played a part was not Somalia or Haiti, in each of which the Americans played a major role, but Yugoslavia. Western intervention to end the conflict there was undermined by a combination of U.S. reluctance, not least from the military leadership, and European weakness, but settlements were eventually imposed in Bosnia in 1995, and in Kosovo in 1999, at the expense of the expansionism and ethnic aggression of a Serbian regime that unsuccessfully looked for Russian sponsorship. In 1998, the *Strategic Defence Review* outlined an expeditionary military strategy, and, the following year, a leading role was taken in the Kosovo Crisis. The Major government (1990–1997) had been reluctant to act over Bosnia, but its Blair successor played a much more active, and moralistic, role over Kosovo and then tried to take the credit for the success. In practice, the eventual Serb withdrawal may have owed more to a conviction, based in part on Russian information, that a NATO land attack was imminent, as well as to the withdrawal of Russian support, than to the air offensive that was launched. However, French, German and, eventually, U.S. rejection of British pressure for a land invasion indicated their doubts of its feasibility. Indeed, a land attack faced a serious logistical challenge, and was dependent on the willingness of neighboring countries to provide access and bases. In this case, Greek opposition to pressure on Serbia was a major hindrance. The Greek government had considerable sympathy for Serbia, in large part due to a pan-Orthodox hostility to the Muslims who lived in Kosovo, but also to concern about revisionism, specifically the fear that an independent Kosovo would contribute to Macedonian expansionism at the expense of Greek control of areas that could be claimed by Macedonia.

George Robertson, the Secretary of State for Defence, publicly scorned commentators who warned about the difficulty of winning the Kosovo conflict by air power alone, and also about the contrast between output (bomb and missile damage) and outcome. The subsequent Serbian withdrawal from Kosovo revealed, however, that NATO estimates of the damage inflicted by air attack, for example to Serb tanks, had been considerably exaggerated. Benefiting from the limitations of Allied intelligence information and its serious consequences for Allied targeting, and from the serious impact of the weather on air operations (a large number canceled or affected), the Serbs, employing simple and inexpensive camouflage techniques that took advantage of terrain and wooded cover, preserved most of their equipment despite 10,000 NATO strike sorties. Furthermore, the air offensive had not prevented the continuing large-scale expulsion of Kosovans from their homes by the Serbs, and this ruthless "ethnic cleansing" badly compromised the success of the operation. Indeed, Operation Horseshoe, the ethnic cleansing campaign, increased as the air attack mounted. Furthermore, the report produced in 2000 by the National Audit Office on British operations the previous year depicted major problems with the RAF. On cloudy days, the planes were unable to identify targets and were grounded which, ironically, prevented an excessive depletion of bombs, to match that suffered by the Americans with cruise missiles. In addition, many bombs mounted on aircraft were unable to survive the shock of take-off, while heat and vibration damage affected missiles, and Tornado jets were reportedly unable to drop precision-guided bombs effectively. A lack of lift capacity led to a reliance on Russian-built Antonovs hired from private contractors, but whose use was dependent on Russian certification. Moreover, the SA80 rifle, the main British infantry weapon, was found to be faulty, while Serbian forces were readily able to monitor British radio communications.

The 1998 *Strategic Defence Review* did not see homeland security as a real issue and made its dispositions accordingly, not least in its attitude to the Army Reserve. Events suggested that this had been overly optimistic. Tony Blair captured the national mood in 2001 when he declared, on the evening of 11 September, that "we in Britain would stand shoulder to shoulder with our friends in the United States against the evil of mass terrorism." The crisis stemming from the terrorist attacks on New York and Washington, D.C., on 11 September 2001 led, however, not to an emphasis on homeland security, but, instead, to a major extension of British military effort, a policy outlined in the 2002 *New Chapter,* which was more explicitly expeditionary in intention than the 1998 *Strategic Defence Review.*

Against Iraq in 2003, Britain played a secondary role, but an important one because of the potential for overstretch created by the relatively small size of the force deployed by the Americans. On the ground 125,000 U.S. combat troops were the crucial element, compared to 45,000 troops from Britain and 2,000 from Australia. The British played a key role in the south, but were too heavily committed there to offer effective assistance farther north. Securing the oil infrastructure rapidly was an important objective in order to prevent a repetition of the destruction wrought by the Iraqis in Kuwait in 1991. Beginning on 20 March 2003, a night helicopter commando assault onto the Al Faw peninsula was the first conventional ground force action of the war, and the first British opposed helicopter assault since Suez in 1956. Naval, air, and ground fire supported the operation. The rapid advance of the 7th Armoured Brigade to the west indicated the range of British capability.

The British ability to act in the Gulf was greater than in the First Gulf War of 1991 as a consequence of the experience of the latter, of preparations for a repetition, and of deployments in the meanwhile. This was true both of operations to deter Iraq, such as the enforcement of the No Fly Zones, and of deployments elsewhere in the region. Exercise SAIF SAREEA in Oman in 2001 was particularly important in building up operational experience in particularly difficult conditions. This was also true of the deployment of troops in Afghanistan. As a result of this background, it became easier to act rapidly in the region.

The response cycle was not simply a matter of operating in the Persian Gulf. There was also a response to the successive operations elsewhere that Britain engaged in. For example, the Kosovo campaign indicated the deficiencies of air warfare, in part because the accuracy of the bombs was limited. In response, the laser-guided bombs were made more accurate by adding Global Positioning System (GPS) guidance with an inertial back-up, an enhancement introduced into operational systems in April 2002. The GPS coordinates could be programmed in the planes while they were airborne, providing enhanced flexibility in Time Sensitivity Targeting. Greater accuracy ensured that the weight of bombs required could be cut. Other weapons were also successfully introduced. Storm Shadow was used in 2003, a weapon that had a considerable standoff range, a high degree of accuracy, aided by en-route navigation systems, and a weapon able to penetrate reinforced concrete. The standoff range reduced vulnerability to ground fire and air interception. The RAF's enhanced capability was not simply a matter of bombing and associated air support. There was also an increase in air-to-air effectiveness, although it did not come into play in 2003 because the Iraqi air force did not contest control of the air. The role of the Tornado F3 was enhanced by improvements in radar, radio links, and armament in the shape of ASRAAM, the Advanced Short Range Air-to-Air Missile. Key army weaponry, particularly the Challenger 2 tank, the Warrior infantry-fighting weapon, and the AS 90 self-propelled artillery, all worked well. Nevertheless, the campaign also revealed problems with providing equipment when required, most conspicuously upgraded flak jackets. In part, this was a matter of the difficulties of a fast-moving campaign. However, there is also the more serious question of a tension between cost-consciousness, with its emphasis on "just sufficient" provision, and the frictions and uncertainties that lead to the more costly "just-in-case" scenario. The Report on Operations in Iraq by the House of Commons Defence Select Committee indicated the need for significant improvements.

More generally, from the 1990s, the individual services saw major shifts in response to changes in goals, with the resulting emphasis on an expeditionary profile. The Permanent Joint Headquarters for the conduct of joint operations, an objective very much pushed by the 1994 White Paper, was established in 1996, the year which saw the publication of a joint British Defence Doctrine. In 1997, the Joint Services Command and Staff College followed. After the 1998 Strategic Defence Review, so did the Joint Doctrine and Concepts Centre. In July 2001, this Centre published a Joint Vision for the U.K. Armed Forces. *Future Navy,* the Navy Board's strategic vision, focuses on littoral warfare and power projection and regards joint requirements and capabilities as crucial.[5]

The 2003 *Defence White Paper* argued that "[p]riority must be given to meeting a wider range of expeditionary tasks, at greater range from the United Kingdom and with ever-increasing strategic, operational and tactical tempo." It stressed the requirement to "maintain a broad spectrum of

...capability elements to conduct limited national operations, or to be the lead or framework nation for coalition operations, at small to medium scale." At the large-scale, it was assumed that the United States would be involved and that, as a result, it would be necessary to be able to operate with the U.S. command and control structures. The 2004 defense review projected cuts including three destroyers, three frigates, three submarines, four infantry battalions, and four aircraft squadrons, but there is also a program of major naval expansion, including two aircraft carriers, a new class of six far more powerful destroyers, the first of which was launched in February 2006, three large amphibious ships, and a new class of submarines.

Power projection was encouraged by the winding down of the Northern Ireland commitment. In 1998, the year of the Good Friday Agreement, the last soldier was killed there, ending a period from 1969 (when troops were deployed) in which 452 military personnel had died there. Although the peace dividend proved slow, by 2005 there were, after much earlier prevarication, positive moves toward IRA disarmament. In response to political failure within Northern Ireland, direct rule by British ministers had been reimposed in 2002, but this occurred without a resumption of civil war, and it proved possible to relocate troops elsewhere. The impact on American opinion of Islamic terrorism limited IRA options by making terrorist attacks on an ally less welcome to American public opinion: alongside Libya and criminal activity in Northern Ireland, Irish-Americans had proved the major financial support to the IRA.

Although security concerns in Northern Ireland have declined, in the early 2000s, there was a more direct reliance on the army in Britain. Whereas troops were not deployed against strikes by coal miners in 1972, 1974, and 1984–1985 that posed a serious challenge to the power and authority of the government, in the face of the blockades of petrol depots by tax protesters in 2000, the government considered using force to reopen supply routes. Blair argued that "[n]o government can act on the basis of people threatening to bring the country to a halt." In fact, shocked by the crisis and uncertain of the police, the government abandoned the policy of raising fuel duties by more than inflation, a concession that helped make a mockery of its energy and environmental policies. However, in late 2000, the government responded to the possibility of a resumption of the blockades by training 1,000 soldiers to drive oil tankers so that picket lines could be breached. The following year, the military provided a key command and control role during the serious outbreak of foot-and-mouth disease, offering a capability that looks toward future challenges in the shape of human pandemics. The military indeed has capabilities that the civil authorities lack. The Civil Contingencies Act of 2004 and the creation of the Civil Contingencies Secretariat in the Cabinet Office understandably emphasize the nonmilitary dimension but a capacity to provide military assistance is necessary for government.

The ability of the government to turn to the army to provide coverage during the firemen's strike of 2002 was important in enabling it to resist the challenge to pay restraint. Indeed, at a time when the invasion of Iraq was being planned, this was an instructive guide to the range of tasks, and therefore capabilities, demanded from the military. This range was taken further when terrorism became a key element in the threat to Britain. The deployment of troops, most obviously to Heathrow Airport in 2003, was a very public demonstration of concern about this threat. The troops were sent to provide help to the police at a time of an intelligence report about an Al Qa'ida plan to hijack a plane in Eastern Europe, where security is lower than in Britain, and then to fly it into a passenger terminal in Heathrow. Concern about such plans led also to instructions to the RAF to shoot down passenger jets that had been hijacked, a total change to earlier policy. In the event, so far action against Islamic terrorism in Britain has been left to the police and the security services.

Defense policy unites key problems facing Britain. It stands at the juncture of foreign and fiscal policy, external goals and domestic security, and extends to include issues such as the import of illegal drugs and problems created by poorly controlled mass immigration, which has helped build up the corpus of Islamic terrorists in the country. Defense policy has to respond to rapidly changing circumstances, at the same time that an able execution of its unpredictable tasks requires adequate preparation in the shape of appropriate doctrine, training, and weaponry. These problems are amply demonstrated at the present day, and confront defense professionals, politicians, both in government and in opposition, seeking to define policy, and external commentators. The range of unpredictability has increased greatly over the last decade due to a marked rise in power projection and the beginnings, in 2005, of Islamic terrorism in Britain. There is no sign that this situation will change.

CHAPTER **9**

Conclusion

History as story and analysis depends not only on the perception of the scholar but also on the context in which this is formed. Writing in 1975 or 1985, it would have been appropriate to focus on big power confrontation and this would have led to a story line, culminating in the Cold War, in which the Napoleonic War and the two World Wars would be the key episodes. Transoceanic power projection, the characteristic in particular of British military activity in 1816–1913, would have seemed an imperial interlude and one that was no longer valid. In 2006, this seems a less sure perspective. Instead, there are calls for a revival of "small wars" doctrine and even tactics, and for a force profile that permits such power projection. Possibly this may, in turn, be a stage that ends rapidly if state-to-state confrontation becomes more pronounced. The currently central narrative of conflict with irregulars may then seem less pertinent. Whatever happens, this serves as a reminder that several narratives of British military power are possible. This is also the case if attention is devoted to domestic control. A major strand until, and including, the eighteenth century, this was only a minor theme in the nineteenth and twentieth centuries. It may recur as a major strand, not least if the domestic strand for the British military is understood as the European Union.

Whatever the prioritization, it is the variety of military environments that is striking. It posed, and continues to pose, a major challenge to the British military system. Insofar as military roles were/are primarily fulfilled by regular forces, these forces and their commanders had/have to adapt to very different tasks. Varied challenges and requirements obliged the British military to have a multiple capability and to have a positive synergy between different services. These could be at least as important as the crude resource level available. Military capability developed in response to challenges and threats, and were thus part of the general history of the country. The emphasis on challenges prevents any simple reading from structural strengths to inevitable victory. It serves as a reminder that success was a finely balanced situation that was open to extension, challenge, and redefinition. Further, the contentious nature of political requirements made it difficult to establish a widely accepted level of military preparedness.

Resources were important but have to be considered within a number of contexts. First, political, specifically the nature and number of external and internal commitments, and the dynamics of the international system, not least the exigencies of alliance relationships. Secondly, the conversion of resources—men, *matériel*, and money—into military units is, and was, not an automatic or uncomplicated process, but rather one that reflects and reflected different conventions and administrative practices and possibilities. This also had a political dimension, with often bitter debates about the most appropriate form of force structure. If in the eighteenth century, this meant a controversy (also picked up in North America) about the merits of militia as opposed to regulars, in the early twentieth century the debate included the merits of conscription as opposed to emphasizing regulars and, in particular, the navy. Thirdly, the effectiveness and use and weaponry were, and are, not simply the product of the quantity of resources, but of tactics, strategy, morale, and social-military characteristics, such as discipline and leadership.

Both strategy and socio-political context invite the question whether there was a "British way of warfare," a distinctive military situation, response, and culture; indeed an exceptionalism in which Britain was different to the position elsewhere, particularly in Continental Europe. Clearly, in comparison to the last, the island nature of Britain was crucial in encouraging navalist needs and opportunities. This was compromised for much of British history, particularly in 1066–1558, 1714–1837, and 1949–, by commitments to the Continent, but, despite this, island status and naval strength provided particular opportunities for the formulation and pursuit of transoceanic goals. Naval strength was matched for much of Britain's military history by a relatively small home army (the large army in India was a very different matter). This small size arose from the absence of conscription and the economic opportunities available to those who might have volunteered for service, as well as the need to provide sufficient sailors. In his *Discourse on the Establishment of a National and Constitutional Force in England* (1757, reprinted 1794), Charles Jenkinson, who was to serve as Secretary at War in 1778–1782, pressed for a militia on the grounds that a strong army threatened national liberties, a repeated claim in British history,

> we are in this dilemma, either to keep our army so low as to be inadequate to the purposes for which it was intended; or to raise it so high as to make it one time or other dangerous to our constitution; for certain it is that any number of troops which will be sufficient to repel the strength of France, will have the power, if they should have the inclination, to enslave us.[1]

As a result of the relatively small size of the army, there might seem to be pragmatic reasons to avoid direct engagement with the main field army of Britain's opponents (and this was the basis of what was seen as the strategy of the "indirect approach"); and, instead, to use the mobility offered by the amphibious capability offered by naval power. Such a strategy was seen at work in the Peninsular War in 1808–1813, with the British not committed against Napoleon's main force, which was just as well. This strategy was also seen in the pressure for an invasion of Italy in 1943, which was presented by American critics as a diversion from the task of invading France in order to fight the principal German forces not engaged against the Soviets. Britain then had conscription, but there was concern among British policy makers about the fighting ability of the citizen army, and a sense that if the main field army was destroyed it would be impossible to replace. The stress on the indirect approach also led to criticism of the "Westerners" who, in World War One, supported a focus on the Western Front, rather than probing the opposing Central Powers for weaker points where Britain could employ its forces more effectively.

The applicability of the general argument is limited by the extent to which each war posed particular strategic issues, not least in response to different goals and the dynamics of alliance politics, a point that is also pertinent for the future. As far as the idea of the indirect approach as crucial is concerned, in the Nine Years' War and the Wars of the Spanish and Austrian Successions, the British engaged the main French field army. Insofar as there was a distinctive approach in British strategy, it related to the role of naval power in defensive and offensive capability, ranging, in the latter case, from commerce raiding to blockade, lift, and amphibious operations. Britain's island identity ensured distinctive naval tasks as well as accentuated responsibilities.

To a considerable extent, this was an aspect of the joint operational capability that was a key feature of the British military experience going back to medieval roots. This capability had long attracted commentators, for example Thomas More Molyneux in his *Conjunct Expeditions; or Expeditions that have been carried on jointly by the Fleet and Army* (1759) and C.E. Callwell's *Military Operations and Maritime Preponderance: Their Relations and Interdependence* (1905). Looking back on the war with Germany, a *Times* editorial of 7 March 1945 wrote of

> the outstanding lesson of the past five years: that in spite of the natural tendency of accomplished specialists to self-reliance and self-sufficiency, each of the three services exercises its peculiar powers with the most decisive effects upon the enemy only when the efforts of all three are intimately coordinated by men who have learnt to plan and execute a strategy embracing land, sea, and air, which has been conceived as an indivisible whole.

Indeed, as an instance of air-sea cooperation in 1943, Admiral Sir Dudley Pound, the First Sea Lord, noted,

> At the moment we are doing all we can to produce super long-range aircraft so that we can cover the whole of the Atlantic from one side to the other, as there is no question but that if you can put aircraft over the U-boats during the day, it prevents them getting into position for their night attacks. I am hoping very much that we shall be able to blast them out of their operational bases in the Bay of Biscay [in France] by air attack.[2]

Alongside the emphasis on jointness, came competition between the services, which indeed remains the case today. In 1936, when he resigned the post of Chief of the Imperial General Staff, Sir Archibald Montgomery-Massingberd wrote,

> I feel that the biggest battle that I have had to fight in the last three years is against the idea that on account of the arrival of air forces as a new arm, the Low Countries are of little value to us and that, therefore, we need not maintain a military force to assist in holding them...the elimination of any army commitment on the [European] Continent sounds such a comfortable and cheap policy...especially amongst the air mad...If there are any lessons to be drawn from the present war in Abyssinia [Italian conquest of Ethiopia], it seems to be that even against savages with no air force and no anti-aircraft weapons of any value, a strong airforce is unable to bring about an early decision.

Indeed, he claimed that a war on the Continent would still be decided on land.[3]

Domestically, the crucial politico-cultural context from the late-seventeenth century was of a military that was clearly and consistently subordinated to a representational political system and the rule of law. The ability of the military to support government was an aspect of politics, but usually an implicit one, and a "hidden hand" held very much in reserve. Partly as a result, Britain has had a more benign military history than most countries. There have been defeats and setbacks as well as victories in war outside the country, but, within it, there have been relatively few occasions in which the military has been expected to act against compatriots. This is crucial to the country's military history and also to the public perception of the military, particularly over the last 150 years. This perception is very different in Ireland and in other former colonies where the experience of British rule is, at best, controversial, but the extent to which colonial methods were not applied in Britain was important to its history and helped make it very different to those of France and Spain.

Success in war was part of the experience of national identity and the recovered memory of this was important to the way in which this identity was expressed and disseminated. The arts were important to this process.

Thus, Benjamin West (1738–1820), an American Loyalist who was Histori-cal Painter to George III from 1772, exhibited *The Battle of Boyne* and the *Destruction of the Battle of La Hogue* in 1780. Produced in a period of nation-al challenge and defeat during the War of American Independence, this depiction of crucial victories in 1690 and 1692 greatly increased West's popularity. His *Edward III Crossing the Somme* (1788) was part of a series on fourteenth-century victories. Next century, parliamentarians were reminded that liberty had had to be defended: Daniel Maclise received £7,000 for painting *Wellington and Blücher at Waterloo* (1861) and *The Death of Nelson* (1864) for Parliament. His oeuvre, for example *Alfred the Great in the Tent of Guthruyn* (1852), reflected the demand for an exemplary nation-al history on canvas, especially a history of monarchs and war. Alfred shared with Arthur the happy role of providing distinguished ancestry for notions of valiant liberty, and in 1873 the carving of a white horse in a hillside near Westbury that was held to commemorate Alfred's victory over the Danes at Ethandune in 878 was restored. Novels made similar points. Charles Kingsley (1819–1875), a clergyman who was Regius Pro-fessor of Modern History at Cambridge from 1860 to 1869, wrote a num-ber of historical novels glorifying heroes from the past, including *Westward Ho!* (1855), an account of the Elizabethan struggle with Philip II of Spain, and *Hereward the Wake* (1866) about resistance to the Norman Conquest. The historical accounts that the war correspondent George Alfred Henty (1832–1902) provided in his popular adventure sto-ries for boys continued to enjoy substantial sales until after World War Two, and were read by the author as a schoolboy. His novels included *Under Drake's Flag* (1883), *With Clive in India: or the Beginnings of an Empire* (1884), *St. George for England: A Tale of Cressy [Crécy] and Poitiers* (1885), *With Wolfe in Canada: The Winning of a Continent* (1887), and *Held Fast for England: A Tale of the Siege of Gibraltar* (1892): all accounts of past victories. A. E. W. Mason's novel *The Four Feathers* (1902) presented imperial endeavor in Sudan as a definition of manliness and heroism.

The cultural location of British military activity was greatly challenged by the presentation of World War One from the 1930s, and, more, persist-ently, the 1960s. Then, the antiwar beliefs of the 1930s were revived in a potent context that owed much to the culture of the 1960s, the end of national service, opposition to the Vietnam War, and the impact of the Campaign for Nuclear Disarmament. Antiwar culture became more insistent and two dimensional. This focused on World War One. The lost generation and the futility of the war are myths so deeply imbedded in popular consciousness that they have become irrefutable facts, as well as folk memory passed down through families, and any attempt to disabuse believers is treated with hostility. Belief in the wrongness of killing has made it difficult to understand the values of the combatants.[4] In many respects, this response to World War One continues to mold the more general perception of war held by a society that is singularly lacking in bellicosity. This is linked to the need to adopt a moralistic attitude to foreign military commitments in order to seek to win support for them, a marked characteristic of the politics of the 1990s and 2000s. If this provides an important element of contemporary strategic culture, it is far from clear how this situation may change in the future. The implications of terrorism, growing European Union direction, and resource crises, on military activity are all unclear, and underline the need when looking at the past, present, and future to avoid the pitfalls of clear-cut accounts of change and of determinism.

Notes

Chapter 1

1. R.P. Abets, *Alfred the Great: War, Kingship, and Culture in Anglo-Saxon England* (London, 1998).

2. R.A. Brown, *English Medieval Castles* (London, 1954); N.J.G. Pounds, *The Medieval Castle in England and Wales: A Social and Political History* (Cambridge, 1990); C. Coulson, "Cultural Realities and Reappraisals in English Castle-study," *Journal of Medieval History,* 22 (1996), pp. 171–207; R. Higham and P. Barker, *Timber Castles,* 2nd ed. (Exeter, 2004).

3. D.S. Bachrach, "The Military Administration of England: The Royal Artillery 1216–1272," *Journal of Military History,* 68 (2004), pp. 1083–1104.

4. A. Ayton and P. Preston (eds.), *The Battle of Crécy* (Woodbridge, 2005).

5. A. Curry, *The Hundred Years War* (Basingstoke, 1993).

6. M. Prestwich, *Armies and Warfare in the Middle Ages. The English Experience* (New Haven, 1996), pp. 260–1.

7. O. Creighton and R. Higham, *Medieval Town Walls: An Archaeology and Social History of Urban Defence* (Stroud, 2005).

8. With a focus on 1387–1388, A.R. Bell, *War and the Soldier in the Fourteenth Century* (Woodbridge, 2004).

9. R. Higham, "Public and Private Defence in the Medieval South West: Town, Castle and Fort," in Higham (ed.), *Security and Defence in South-West England before 1800* (Exeter, 1987), pp. 40–42.

10. J. Gillingham, *The Wars of the Roses* (London, 1981); A Goodman, *The Wars of the Roses: Military Activity and English Society, 1452–1497* (London, 1981); A.W. Boardman, *The Battle of Towton* (Stroud, 1994) and *The Medieval Soldier: The Men Who Fought the Wars of the Roses* (Stroud, 1998); P.A. Haigh, *The Military Campaigns of the Wars of the Roses* (Stroud, 1995) and *The Battle of Wakefield* (Stroud, 1996); A.J. Pollard, *The Wars of the Roses* (Basingstoke, 1998).

11. N. Barr, *Flodden 1515* (Stroud, 2001).

12. M. Merriman, *The Rough Wooings* (Edinburgh, 2000).

13. C.G. Cruickshank, *Army Royal: Henry VIII's Invasion of France, 1513* (Oxford, 1969); C.S.L. Davies, "Provisions for Armies, 1509–60: A Study in the Effectiveness of Early Tudor Government," *Economic History Review,* 17 (1964–1965), pp. 234–48; S.J. Gunn, "The Duke of Suffolk's March on Paris in 1523," *English Historical Review,* 101 (1986), pp. 596–634; M.C. Fissel, *English Warfare 1511–1642* (London, 2001).

14. G.J. Miller, *Tudor Mercenaries and Auxiliaries, 1485–1547* (Charlottesville, 1980).

15. H.A. Lloyd, *The Rouen Campaign, 1590–1592: Politics, Warfare and the Early-Modern State* (Oxford, 1973); R.B. Wernham, *After the Armada: Elizabethan England and the Struggle for Western Europe, 1588–1595* (Oxford, 1984) and *The Return of the Armadas: The Last Years of the Elizabethan War Against Spain, 1595–1603* (Oxford, 1994).

16. C. Martin and G. Parker, *The Spanish Armada* (London, 1988).

17. C. Falls, *Elizabeth's Irish Wars* (London, 1950); J. McGurk, *Elizabethan Conquest of Ireland* (1997); C. Brady and J. Ohlmeyer (eds.), *British Interventions in Early Modern Ireland* (Cambridge, 2005).

18. A.J. King (ed.), *Muster Books for North and East Hertfordshire 1580–1605* (Hertford, 1996); G. Phillips, "Longbow and Hackbutt. Weapons Technology and Technology Transfer in Early Modern England," *Technology and Culture*, 40 (1999), pp. 576–93.

19. H. Morgan (ed.), *The Battle of Kinsale* (Bray, 2004).

20. A. Grosjean, *An Unofficial Alliance: Scotland and Sweden, 1569–1654* (Leiden, 2003).

21. M.C. Fissel, *The Bishops' Wars: Charles I's Campaigns Against Scotland, 1638–1640* (Cambridge, 1994).

22. J. Morrill, *Revolt in the Provinces: The People of England and the Tragedies of War 1630–1648*, 2nd ed. (Harlow, 1999).

23. M. Wanklyn and F. Jones, *A Military History of the English Civil War* (London, 2005), pp. 92–94.

24. A. Marshall, *Oliver Cromwell-Soldier: The Military Life of a Revolutionary at War* (London, 2004).

25. I. Gentles, *The New Model Army in England, Ireland and Scotland, 1645–1653* (Oxford, 1992).

26. J.R. Jones, *The Anglo-Dutch Wars of the Seventeenth Century* (London, 1996).

27. B. Capp, *Cromwell's Navy, the Fleet and the English Revolution, 1648–1660* (Oxford, 1989).

28. R. Hutton, *The British Republic 1648–1660*, 2nd ed. (Basingstoke, 2000).

29. L.G. Schwoerer, *No Standing Armies: The Anti-army Ideology in Seventeenth-century England* (Baltimore, 1984); P. Seaward, *The Restoration 1660–1688* (Basingstoke, 1991).

30. J. Childs, *The Army of Charles II* (London, 1976).

31. J. Childs, *The Army, James II, and the Glorious Revolution* (Manchester, 1980); E. Cruickshanks, *The Glorious Revolution* (Basingstoke, 1999).

Chapter 2

1. Jenkinson to Amherst, 24 Oct. 1780, NA. WO. 34/127 fol. 155.

2. P. Lenihan, *1690. Battle of the Boyne* (Stroud, 2003).

3. J. Childs, *The British Army of William III, 1689–1702* (Manchester, 1987).

4. J.B. Hattendorf, *England in the War of the Spanish Succession: A Study of the English View and Conduct of Grand Strategy, 1702–1712* (New York, 1987).

5. J.R. Jones, *Marlborough* (Cambridge, 1993), p. 183.

6. Richards Diary, BL. Stowe papers vol. 467 fols. 21–23.

7. J.A. Houlding, *Fit for Service: The Training of the British Army, 1715–1795* (Oxford, 1981).

8. A. Guy, *Economy and Discipline: Ownership and Administration in the British Army, 1714–63* (Manchester, 1985).

9. Richmond to Grey, 27 Ap. 1782, Durham, University Department of Palaeography, papers of 1st Earl Grey, no. 61.

10. R. Harding, *Amphibious Warfare in the Eighteenth Century: The British Expedition to the West Indies, 1740–1742* (Woodbridge, 1991).

11. A.W. Massie, "Great Britain and the Defence of the Low Countries, 1744–1748," Ph.D. (London, 1988).

12. C. Duffy, *The '45* (London, 2003).

13. Stewart to John, 2nd Earl of Stair, 10 Sept. 1741, New Haven, Connecticut, Beinecke Library, Osborn Shelves, Stair Letters, no. 70.

14. C.M. Hand, *The Siege of Fort Beauséjour, 1755* (Fredericton, 2004).

15. Conway to Duke of Devonshire, 7 Oct. 1756, Derby Library, Catton Collection, WH 3450.

16. M. Ward, *Breaking the Backcountry. The Seven Years' War in Virginia and Pennsylvania, 1754–1765* (Pittsburgh, 2003).

17. Journal, possibly by Henry Fletcher, Providence, Rhode Island, John Carter Brown Library, Codex Eng. 41.

18. P. Mackesy, *The Coward of Minden: The Affair of Lord George Sackville* (London, 1979).

19. S. Brumwell, *Redcoats: The British Soldier and War in the Americas, 1755–1763* (Cambridge, 2002).

20. C. Wilkinson, *The British Navy and the State in the Eighteenth Century* (Woodbridge, 2004).

21. Bull to General Amherst, 15 Ap. 1761, NA. CO. 5/61 fol. 277.

22. M. McConnell, *Army and Empire. British Soldiers on the American Frontier, 1758–1775* (Lincoln, 2004).

23. G. Cornwallis-West, *The Life and Letters of Admiral Cornwallis* (London, 1927), pp. 50–51.

24. N.A.M. Rodger, *The Safeguard of the Sea: A Naval History of Britain, I, 660–1649* (London, 1997), pp. 430–34.

Chapter 3

1. George to Viscount Melville, 12 July 1804, BL. Add. 40100 fol. 319.

2. Oliver to John Parsons, 30 Dec. 1789, Gloucester, County Record Office D214 F1/93.

3. J. Gwyn, *Frigates and Foremasts: The North American Squadron in Nova Scotia Waters, 1745–1815* (Vancouver, 2003).

4. J.D. Grainger, *The Battle of Yorktown, 1781. A Reassessment* (Woodbridge, 2005).

5. S.R. Taaffe, *The Philadelphia Campaign, 1777–1778* (Lawrence, 2003).

6. G.J. Bryant, "Asymmetric Warfare: The British Experience in Eighteenth-Century India," *Journal of Military History*, 68 (2004), p. 469.

7. Fawcett to George, 22 Feb. 1786, A. Aspinall (ed.), *The Later Correspondence of George III, 1783–1810,* 5 vols. (Cambridge, 1962–1970) I, 211.

8. Memorandum, BL. Add. 33120 fol. 162.

9. Pelham to Henry Addington, First Lord of the Treasury, 23 Sept. 1801, BL. Add. 33120 fol. 59.

10. A. Burne, *The Noble Duke of York* (1949); R. Glover, *Peninsular Preparation: The Reform of the British Army, 1795–1809* (Cambridge, 1963); R.H. Thoumine, *Scientific Soldiers: A Life of General Le Marchant, 1766–1812* (London, 1968); J.L. Pimlott, "The Administration of the British Army, 1783–1793," Ph.D. (Leicester, 1975); D. Gates, *The British Light Infantry Arm c. 1790–1815: Its Creation, Training and Operational Role* (London, 1987); K. Bartlett, "The Development of the British Army during the Wars with France, 1793–1815," Ph.D. (Durham, 1998).

11. J. Cookson, *The British Armed Nation, 1793–1815* (Cambridge, 1997).

12. R.G. Glover, *Britain at Bay: Defence Against Bonaparte, 1803–14* (London, 1973).

13. Dundas, memorandum, Oct. 1796, BL. Add. 59280 fols. 189-90.

14. R. Hopton, *The Battle of Maida 1806: Fifteen Minutes of Glory* (Barnsley, 2002).

15. C. Hall, *British Strategy in the Napoleonic War, 1803–1815* (Manchester, 1992); D. Gates, *The Spanish Ulcer: A History of the Peninsular War* (London, 1986); R. Muir, *Britain and the Defeat of Napoleon, 1807–1815* (New Haven, 1996).

16. P. Griffith (ed.), *Wellington Commander* (Chichester, 1985); R. Muir, *"So Brilliant a Victory": Wellington at Salamanca* (New Haven, 2001).

17. BL. 56088 fol. 5.

18. Gordon to General Craig, 7 May 1808, BL. Add. 49512 fol. 17.

19. *Atlas of Portsmouth* (Portsmouth, 1975), section 3/6(d).

20. L. Brockliss, J. Cardwell, and M. Moss, *William Beatty, Naval Medicine and the Battle of Trafalgar* (Oxford, 2005).

21. Hely-Hutchinson memorandum, 22 Nov. 1806, BL. Add. 59282 fols. 76–81.

22. R.G.S. Cooper, *The Anglo-Maratha Campaigns and the Contest for India: The Struggle for Control of the South Asian Military Economy* (Cambridge, 2003).

23. R.N. Buckley, *Slaves in Red Coats: The British West India Regiments, 1793–1815* (New Haven, 1979).

24. Silhouette to Amelot, French foreign minister, 7 September 1741, NA. SP. 107/49.

25. C.J. Bartlett and G.A. Smith, "A 'Species of Milito-Nautico-Guerilla-Plundering Warfare'. Admiral Alexander Cochrane's Naval Campaign against the United States, 1814–1815," in J. Flavell and S. Conway (eds.), *Britain and America Go to War. The Impact of War and Warfare in Anglo-America, 1754–1815* (Gainesville, 2004), pp. 187–90.

26. P. Taylor, *Indentured to Liberty: Peasant Life and the Hessian Military State, 1688–1815* (Ithaca, 1994).

27. I. Gordon, *Soldier of the Raj* (Barnsley, 2001), pp. 92–93.

Chapter 4

1. K. Bourne, *Palmerston: The Early Years, 1784–1841* (London, 1982).

2. S.H. Myerly, *British Military Spectacle from the Napoleonic Wars through the Crimea* (Cambridge, MA, 1996).

3. J. Beckett, "The Nottingham Reform Bill Riots of 1831," in C. Jones, P. Salmon, and R.W. Davis (eds.), *Partisan Politics, Principle and Reformation in Parliament and the Constituencies, 1689–1880* (Edinburgh, 2005), pp. 121–9.

4. P. Hofschröer, *Wellington's Smallest Victory: The Duke, the Model Maker, and the Secret of Waterloo* (London, 2004).

5. H. Strachan, *Wellington's Legacy: The Reform of the British Army 1815–1854* (Manchester, 1984).

6. P. Burroughs, "An Unreformed Army? 1815–1868," in D. Chandler and I. Beckett (eds.), *The Oxford Illustrated History of the British Army* (Oxford, 1994), p. 164.

7. J.F. McMahon, "The British Army: Its Role in Counter-Insurgency in the Black War in Van Diemen's Land," *Tasmanian Historical Studies*, 5 (1995–1996), pp. 56–63.

8. D.M. Peers, *Between Mars and Mammon: Colonial Armies and the Garrison State in India, 1819–1835* (London, 1995).

9. M. Turner, *Slaves and Missionaries: The Disintegration of Jamaican Slave Society, 1787–1834* (Urbana, 1982); E.V. d'Costa, *Crowns of Glory, Tears of Blood: The Demerara Slave Rebellion of 1823* (New York, 1994).

10. J.A. Norris, *The First Afghan War, 1838–42* (Cambridge, 1967); L. Dupree, "The Retreat of the British Army from Kabul to Jalalabad in 1842: History and Folklore," *Journal of the Folklore Institute*, 6 (1967), pp. 25–45; T. Heathcote, *The Afghan Wars, 1839–1919* (London, 1980).

11. B.S. Nijjar, *Anglo-Sikh Wars, 1845–1849* (New Delhi, 1976).

12. Pierce's journal, 27 January 1846, BL. IO. MSS. Eur. A 108 fol. 14.

13. Letter by an unidentified officer of Bengal 30th Native Infantry, 26 January 1849, BL. IO. MSS. Eur. C 605 fols. 1–2.

14. BL. Add. 54483 fol. 22.

15. A.D. Lambert, *The Crimean War: British Grand Strategy, 1853–56* (Manchester, 1990).

16. H. and A. Gernsheim (eds.), *Roger Fenton, Photographer of the Crimean War: His Photographs and his Letters from the Crimea* (London, 1954); N. Bentley (ed.), *Russell's Despatches from the Crimea, 1854–1856* (London, 1966).

17. J. Sweetman, *War and Administration: The Significance of the Crimean War for the British Army* (Edinburgh, 1984); O. Anderson, *A Liberal State at War: English Politics and Economics during the Crimean War* (London, 1967).

18. J.A.B. Palmer, *The Mutiny Outbreak at Meerut in 1857* (Cambridge, 1966); S.N. Sen, *Eighteen Fifty-Seven* (New Delhi, 1957); R. Mukherjee, "'Satan Let Loose upon Earth': The Kanpur Massacres in India in the Revolt of 1857," *Past and Present*, 128 (1990), pp. 92–116; B. English, "Debate: The Kanpur Massacres in India in the Revolt of 1857," *Past and Present*, 142 (1994), pp. 169–89.

19. J. Belich, *The New Zealand Wars and the Victorian Interpretation of Racial Conflict* (London, 1988).

20. Lister to Secretary to Governor of Bengal, 2 Feb. 1850, BL. Add. 49016 fol. 88.

21. E.K. Senior, *Redcoats and Patriotes: The Rebellions in Lower Canada, 1837–38* (Stittsville, Ontario, 1985).

22. D.A. Campbell, *English Public Opinion and the American Civil War* (Woodbridge, 2003).

23. J.M. Hitsman, *Safeguarding Canada, 1763–1871* (Toronto, 1968).

24. A.V. Tucker, "Army and Society in England 1870–1900: A Reassessment of the Cardwell Reforms," *Journal of British Studies*, 2 (1962), pp. 110–41; E.M. Spiers, *The Army and Society, 1815–1914* (London, 1980).

25. C.J. Bartlett, *Great Britain and Sea Power 1815–1853* (Oxford, 1963).

26. M.J. Salevouris, *"Riflemen Form": The War Scare of 1859–1860 in England* (New York, 1982).

27. N.A.M. Rodger, "The Dark Age of the Admiralty, 1869–85," *Mariner's Mirror*, 61 (1975), pp. 331–44, 62 (1976), pp. 33–46 and 121–8.

Chapter 5

1. A.R. Skelley, *The Victorian Army at Home: The Recruitment and Terms and Conditions of the British Regular, 1859–1899* (London, 1977).

2. W.S. Hamer, *The British Army: Civil-Military Relations, 1885–1905* (Oxford, 1970); H. Kochanski, *Sir Garnet Wolseley: Victorian Hero* (London, 1999); I.F.W. Beckett, *The Victorians at War* (London, 2003).

3. R. Lock and P. Quantrill, *Zulu Victory: The Epic of Isandlwana and the Cover-Up* (Mechanicsburg, 2005).

4. A. Greaves, *Crossing the Buffalo—The Zulu War of 1879* (London, 2005), p. 225.

5. B. Robson (ed.), "The Kandahar Letters of the Reverend Alfred Cane," *Journal of the Society for Army Historical Research*, 69 (1991), p. 215.

6. M.E. Chamberlain, "The Alexandria Massacre of 11 June 1882 and the British Occupation of Egypt," *Middle Eastern Studies*, 13 (1977), pp. 14–39.

7. A. Preston, "Wolseley, the Khartoum Relief Expedition and the Defence of India, 1885–1900," *Journal of Imperial and Commonwealth History*, 6 (1978), pp. 254–80.

8. E.M. Spiers, *The Victorian Soldier in Africa* (Manchester, 2004).

9. P.S. Thompson, *The Natal Native Contingent in the Anglo-Zulu War* (Scottsville, 2003).

10. B. Beal and R. Macleod, *Prairie Fire: The North-West Rebellion of 1885* (Edmonton, 1984).

11. BL. Add. 49357.

12. BL. Add. 50300 fol. 177.

13. J.W.M. Hichberger, *Images of the Army: The Military in British Art, 1815–1914* (Manchester, 1988); J.M. Mackenzie (ed.), *Popular Imperialism and the Military, 1850–1950* (Manchester, 1992).

14. L.H. Hamilton 1/2/7/2.

15. K.T. Surridge, *Managing the South African War, 1889–1902* (Woodbridge, 1998); S.M. Miller, *Lord Methuen and the British Army: Failure and Redemption in South Africa* (London, 1991).

16. H.C.B. Cook (ed.), "Letters from South Africa 1899-1902," *Journal of the Society for Army Historical Research*, 69 (1991), pp. 240–1.

17. S.M. Miller, "In support of the 'Imperial Mission'? Volunteering for the South African War, 1899–1902," *Journal of Military History*, 69 (2005), pp. 691–712.

18. N. Riall (ed.), *Boer War: The Letters, Diaries and Photographs of Malcolm Riall from the War in South Africa 1899–1902* (London, 2000), p. 152.

19. D. Lowry (ed.), *The South African War Reappraised* (Manchester, 2000).

20. J.T. Sumida, *In Defence of Naval Supremacy: Finance, Technology, and British Naval Policy, 1889–1914* (Boston, 1989); N.A. Lambert, *Sir John Fisher's Naval Revolution* (Columbia, 1999).

Chapter 6

1. Chetwode to Montgomery-Massingberd, 1 July 1921, L.H. MM. 8/22.

2. Report of the Committee on the Mechanized Cavalry and Royal Tank Corps, 1938, NA. WO. 33/1512, pp. 7–8.

3. G.R. Wilkinson, *Depictions and Images of War in Edwardian Newspapers, 1899–1914* (Basingstoke, 2003).

4. G. Phillips, "Douglas Haig and the Development of Twentieth-Century Cavalry," *Archives*, 28 (2003), p. 155.

5. N.A. Lambert, *Sir John Fisher's Naval Revolution* (Columbia, SC, 1999) and "Strategic Command and Control for Maneuver Warfare: Creation of the Royal Navy's 'War Room' System, 1905–1915", *Journal of Military History*, 69 (2005), pp. 361–410.

6. A. Gollin, *No Longer an Island: Britain and the Wright Brothers, 1902–1909* (London, 1984) and *The Impact of Air Power on the British People and their Government, 1909–1914* (London, 1989); H. Driver, *The Birth of Military Aviation: Britain, 1903–1914* (Woodbridge, 1997).

7. Hamilton to Sir William Nicholson, 2 January 1909, L.H. Hamilton papers 4/2/7.

8. M.S. Seligmann, *Spies in Uniform. British Military and Naval Intelligence on the Eve of the First World War* (Oxford, 2006).

9. I.F.W. Beckett, *Ypres: The First Battle, 1914* (Harlow, 2004).

10. C. Messenger, *Call to Arms: The British Army, 1914–18* (London, 2005).

11. BL. Add. 49703 fols. 137–8.

12. R. Anderson, *The Forgotten Front: The East African Campaign, 1914–1918* (Stroud, 2004).

13. B.C. Busch (ed.), *Canada and the Great War* (Montreal, 2003).

14. M. Cooper, *The Birth of Independent Air Power* (London, 1986).

15. BL. Add. 49703 fols. 184–9.

16. G.K. Williams, *Biplanes and Bombsights: British Bombing in World War I* (Maxwell Air Force Base, AL, 1999).

17. M. Paris, *Over the Top: The Great War and Juvenile Literature in Britain* (Westport, 2004); J.S.K. Watson, *Fighting Different Wars: Experience, Memory and the First World War in Britain* (Cambridge, 2004).

18. M. Hardy, "'Be Cheerful in Adversity': Views from the Trenches, 1917–1918," Buckinghamshire Record Office, *Annual Report and List of Accessions*, 1995. See, more generally, R. Holmes, *Tommy: The British Soldier on the Western Front, 1914–1918* London, 2004).

19. L.H. Ismay 3/1/1-83, quotes pp. 55, 58.

20. Chetwode to General Sir Archibald Montgomery-Massingberd, 1 July 1921, L.H. MM. 8/22.

21. Montgomery-Massingberd to Chetwode, 18 January. 1929, L.H. MM. 10/2.

22. Rawlinson to Montgomery-Massingberd, 16 July 1923, L.H. MM. 8/28.

23. B. Bond, *British Military Policy Between the Two World Wars* (Oxford, 1980); H. Winton, *To Change an Army: General Sir John Burnett-Stuart and British Armoured Doctrine, 1927–1938* (Lawrence, 1988); J.P. Harris, *Men, Ideas, and Tanks: British Military Thought and Armoured Forces, 1908–1939* (Manchester, 1995).

24. T. Travers, *How The War Was Won. Command and Technology in the British Army on the Western Front, 1917–1918* (London, 1992), pp. 179–82.

25. Montgomery-Massingberd to Chetwode, 3 December 1928, L.H. MM. 10/1.

26. M. Smith, *British Air Strategy Between the Wars* (Oxford, 1984).

27. I.M. Philpott, *The Royal Air Force...the Inter-war Years. I. The Trenchard Years, 1918 to 1929* (Barnsley, 2005), pp. 194–208.

28. Field-Marshal Sir George Milne, "The Role of the Air Force in Relation to the Army," undated. Catalog says [1925–6], but the document contains a reference to a document of March 1930, L.H. Milne Box 3.

29. Military Report on Mesopotamia (Iraq), Area 1 (Northern Jazirah), 1922, NA. WO. 33/2758, p. 39.

Chapter 7

1. Chetwode to Montgomery-Massingberd, 6 September 1921, L.H. MM. 8/22.

2. NA. CAB. 16/109 fol. 15.

3. L.H. Adam 2/3, pp. 2–3.

4. N. Smart, *British Strategy and Politics During the Phony War: Before the Balloon Went Up* (Westport, 2003).

5. NA. PREM 3/328/5, pp. 24–26.

6. N. Jordan, "Strategy and Scapegoatism: Reflections on the French National Catastrophe, 1940," in J. Blatt (ed.), *The French Defeat of 1940: Reassessments* (Oxford, 1998), pp. 13–38; W. Murray, "May 1940: Contingency and Fragility of the German RMA," in M. Knox and W. Murray (eds.), *The Dynamics of Military Revolution, 1300–2050* (Cambridge, 2001), pp. 154–74; B. Bond and M.D. Taylor (eds.), *The Battle for France and Flanders: Sixty Years On* (London, 2001).

7. I.M. Lewis, *A Modern History of the Somali*, 4th ed. (Oxford, 2002), pp. 119–20.

8. Churchill to Roosevelt, 18 December 1941, W. Kimball (ed.), *Churchill and Roosevelt: The Complete Correspondence* I (Princeton, 1984), p. 299; A. Warren, *Singapore 1942: Britain's Greatest Defeat* (London, 202); B.P. Farrell, *The Defence and Fall of Singapore 1940–1942* (Stroud, 2005).

9. C. Eade (ed.), *Secret Session Speeches* (London, 1946), p. 47.

10. J. Gooch, "The Politics of Strategy: Great Britain, Australia, and the War against Japan, 1939–1945," *War in History*, 10 (2003), pp. 424–47.

11. War Cabinet Minutes, 29 July 1942, Canberra, National Archives of Australia, p. 1404. See also, e.g., 30 June 1942, pp. 1378–79.

12. William Joseph Slim, *Defeat Into Victory* (London, 1956), pp. 28–30.

13. M.A. Stoler, *Allies in War. Britain and America Against the Axis Powers, 1940–1945* (London, 2005).

14. N. Barr, *Pendulum of War: The Three Battles of El Alamein* (London, 2004).

15. M. Howard, *The Mediterranean Strategy in the Second World War* (London, 1968).

16. P. Danchev, "Great Britain: The Indirect Strategy," in D. Reynolds et al. (eds), *Allies at War* (New York, 1994), pp. 1–26; B.P. Farrell, *The Basis and Making of British Grand Strategy 1940–1943: Was There a Plan?* (New York, 1998).

17. D. Porch, *The Path to Victory: The Mediterranean Theater in World War II* (New York, 2004).

18. N. Smith, *American Empire: Roosevelt's Geographer and the Prelude to Globalisation* (Berkeley, 2003), p. 360. See also W.R. Louis, *Imperialism at Bay: The United States and the Decolonisation of the British Empire, 1941–1945* (New York, 1978); A.J. Whitfield, *Hong Kong, Empire, and the Anglo-American Alliance at War 1941–45* (Basingstoke, 2001).

19. M. Coles, "Ernest King and the British Pacific Fleet: The Conference at Quebec, 1944," *Journal of Military History*, 65 (2001), pp. 105–29; N. Sarantakes, "One Last Crusade. The US-British Alliance and the End of the War in the Pacific," *RUSI Journal*, 149, 4 (August 2004), pp. 62–67; J. Charmley, "Churchill and the American Alliance," *Transactions of the Royal Historical Society*, 6th series, vol. 11 (2001), pp. 353–71; M.A. Stoler, *Allies in War. Britain and America Against the Axis Powers 1940–1945* (London, 2005).

20. C. Bayly and T. Harper, *Forgotten Armies: The Fall of British Asia, 1941–1945* (London, 2005).

21. T. Holt, *The Deceivers: Allied Military Deception in the Second World War* (London, 2004); P.L. Soybel, *A Necessary Relationship: The Development of Anglo-American Cooperation in Naval Intelligence* (Westport, 2005).

22. R. MacLeod, "'All for Each and Each for All': Reflections on Anglo-American and Commonwealth Scientific Cooperation, 1940–1945," *Albion*, 26, 1 (Spring, 1994), pp. 79–112; R. Buderi, *The Invention That Changed the World* (New York, 1996), on radar; D. Zimmerman, *Top Secret Exchange: The Tizard Mission and the Scientific War* (Montreal, 1996); D.H. Avery, *The Science of War: Canadian Scientists and Allied Military Technology during the Second World War* (Toronto, 1998).

23. D. Marston, *Phoenix from the Ashes: The Indian Army in the Burma Campaign* (Westport, 2004); T.R. Moreman, *The Jungle, the Japanese and the British Commonwealth Armies at War 1941–1945. Fighting Methods, Doctrine and Training for Jungle Warfare* (London, 2005).

24. Military Mission report on how best to fight the Japanese, Ap. 1944, NA. WO. 33/1819, p. 50.

25. F. Taylor, *Dresden, Tuesday, 13 February 1945* (London, 2004).

26. C.P. Stacey, *Arms, Men and Government: The War Policies of Canada, 1939–1945* (Ottawa, 1970); F.J. Hatch, *The Aerodrome of Democracy: Canada and the British Commonwealth Air Training Plan 1939–1945* (Ottawa, 1983).

27. T. Banham, *Not the Slightest Chance: The Defence of Hong Kong, 1941* (Vancouver, 2003).

28. S. Rose, *Which People's War? National Identity and Citizenship in Wartime Britain, 1939–1945* (Oxford, 2003); J. Gardiner, *Wartime: Britain, 1939–1945* (London, 2004).

29. M.A. Lawrence, *Assuming the Burden. Europe and the American Commitment to War in Vietnam* (Berkeley, 2005), pp. 104–5.

30. P.J. Brobst, *The Future of the Great Game: Sir Olaf Caroe, India's Independence, and the Defense of Asia* (Akron, 2005).

31. R. Stubbs, *Hearts and Minds in Guerrilla Warfare: The Malayan Emergency, 1948–60* (Singapore, 1989).

32. A. Farrar-Hockley, *The British Part in the Korean War* (London, 1990).

33. C. Elkins, *Imperial Reckoning: The Untold Story of Britain's Gulag in Kenya* (London, 2005).

34. A. Clayton, *Counter-insurgency in Kenya* (Nairobi, 1976).

35. K. Delve, *RAF Bomber Command 1936–1968. An Operational and Historical Record* (Barnsley, 2005), p. 146.

36. T.H. Parsons, *The 1964 Army Mutinies and the Making of Modern East Africa* (Westport, 2003).

37. J. Akehurst, *We Won a War: The Campaign in Oman, 1965–75* (Salisbury, 1982).

38. H.D. James and D. Sheil-Small, *The Undeclared War: The Story of the Indonesian Confrontation, 1962–66* (London, 1971).

39. J. Paget, *Last Post: Aden, 1964–67* (London, 1969).

40. A. Gorst, "CVA-01," in R. Harding (ed.), *The Royal Navy, 1930–2000. Innovation and Defence* (Abingdon, 2005), pp. 170–92.

Chapter 8

1. D. Edgerton, *Warfare State. Britain, 1920–1970* (Cambridge, 2006).

2. L. Freedman, *The Official History of the Falklands Campaign*, 2 vols. (London, 2005), I, 191.

3. S. Badsey, R. Havers, and M. Grove (eds.), *The Falklands Conflict Twenty Years On: Lessons for the Future* (London, 2005).

4. NA. WO. 33/1512, p. 3.

5. M. Mäder, *In Pursuit of Conceptual Excellence: The Evolution of British Military-Strategic Doctrine in the Post-Cold War Era, 1989–2002* (New York, 2004).

Chapter 9

1. Jenkinson, *Discourse*, 2nd ed. (London, 1757), p. 66.

2. Pound to Admiral Layton, 9 February 1943, BL. Add. 74796.

3. L.H. MM. 10/6.

4. J. Terraine, *The Smoke and the Fire: Myths and Anti-Myths of War 1861–1945* (London, 1980); I.F.W. Beckett, *The Great War 1914–1918* (Harlow, 2001); B. Bond, *The Unquiet Western Front. Britain's Role in Literature and History* (Cambridge, 2002).

Selected Further Reading

All books are published in London unless otherwise stated.

C. Barnett, *Britain and Her Army, 1509–1970* (1970).

T. Bartlett and K. Jeffery (eds), *A Military History of Ireland* (Cambridge, 1996).

J.M. Black, *The British Seaborne Empire* (New Haven, 2004).

J.M. Black, *Britain as a Military Power, 1688–1815* (1999).

D. Chandler and I. Beckett (eds), *The Oxford History of the British Army* (Oxford, 1996).

C. Duffy, *The '45* (2003).

D. French, *The British Way in Warfare, 1688–2000* (1990).

D. French, *Military Identities: The Regimental System, the British Army, and the British People c. 1870–2000* (Oxford, 2005).

A.J. Guy (ed.), *The Road to Waterloo: The British Army and the Struggle against Revolutionary and Napoleonic France, 1793–1815* (Stroud, 1992).

C. Hall, *British Strategy in the Napoleonic War 1803–1815* (Manchester, 1992).

R. Harding (ed.), *The Royal Navy, 1930–2000. Innovation and Defence* (Abingdon, 2005).

K. Jeffery, *Field Marshal Sir Henry Wilson: A Political Soldier* (Oxford, 2006).

P.M. Kennedy, *The Rise and Fall of British Naval Mastery*, 2nd ed. (1983).

J. Luvaas, *The Education of an Army: British Military Thought, 1815–1940* (Chicago, 1964).

R. Muir, *Britain and the Defeat of Napoleon 1807–1815* (New Haven, 1996).

D. Omissi, *Air Power and Colonial Control: The Royal Air Force, 1919–1939* (Manchester, 1990).

N.A.M. Rodger, *The Safeguard of the Sea: A Naval History of Britain, I, 660–1649* (1997).

N.A.M. Rodger, *The Command of the Ocean: A Naval History of Britain, II, 1649–1815* (2004).

E.M. Spiers, *The Army and Society, 1815–1914* (1980).

H. Strachan, *The Politics of the British Army* (Oxford, 1997).

H. Strachan, *From Waterloo to Balaclava: Tactics, Technology, and the British Army, 1815–1854* (Cambridge, 1985).

H. Strachan, *Wellington's Legacy: The Reform of the British Army 1830–54* (Manchester, 1984).

Index

About the Author

JEREMY BLACK is Professor of History at Exeter University in the United Kingdom. His books include *The British Seaborne Empire, War and the World 1450–2000, War since 1945,* and *Altered States: America since the Sixties.* He is a Fellow of the editorial board of the Royal United Services Institute and a Fellow of the Royal Society for the Encouragement of Arts, Manufactures and Commerce.